THE INDIAN
VILLAGE

Books by Surinder S. Jodhka

Caste (Oxford India Short Introductions) (2012)
Caste in Contemporary India (2015)
The Indian Middle Class (with Aseem Prakash) *(2016)*

Books edited by Surinder S. Jodhka

Village Society (2012)
A Handbook of Rural India (2018)
Contested Hierarchies, Persisting Influence: Caste and Power in 21st Century India (with James Manor) (2018)
India's Villages in the 21st Century: Revisits and Revisions (with Edward Simpson) (2019)
Mapping the Elite: Power, Privilege and Inequality (with Jules Naudet) (2019)
Agrarian Change in India (2022)

THE INDIAN VILLAGE

Rural Lives in the 21st Century

SURINDER S. JODHKA

ALEPH

ALEPH

ALEPH BOOK COMPANY
An independent publishing firm
promoted by *Rupa Publications India*

First published in India in 2023
by Aleph Book Company
7/16 Ansari Road, Daryaganj
New Delhi 110 002

ISBN: 978-93-91047-19-1

1 3 5 7 9 10 8 6 4 2

Printed in India.

For Anhad

The 'country way of life' has included the very different practices of hunters, pastoralists, farmers and factory farmers, and its organisation has varied from the tribe and manor to the feudal estate, from the small peasantry and tenant farmer to the rural commune, from the *latifundia* and the plantation to the large capitalist enterprise and the state farm.... Even the idea of the village, which seems simple, shows in actual history a wide variation as to size and character, and internally in its variation between dispersed and nuclear settlements, in Britain as clearly anywhere.

—Raymond Williams, *The Country and the City*, p. 1.

CONTENTS

INTRODUCTION

The binary of village and city has come to be one of the core constructs of modern times. Identification of 'modern' with the 'urban' also superimposes a preordained order and pattern of change over the diverse forms of human settlements. It is a well-known fact that in most places, cities or urban settlements co-evolved with rural settlements, the villages. The 'evolution' of settled agriculture made it possible not only for villages to emerge, but also produced a surplus, which made it possible for the elite to live-off such a surplus without doing physical labour. They could also afford to live away from the site of food production, in urban settlements, and thus evolve a state-system or a power centre.

Interestingly enough, even though agriculture has seen a relative decline over the past two centuries, rural settlements persist. During the second decade of the twenty-first century, agriculture contributed only 4 per cent to the global GDP. However, the absolute number of people living in rural settlements is the highest ever in human history. It was only in 2007 that globally the absolute size of the urban population surpassed those living in rural settlements. In 2021, as many as 3.42 billion people lived in rural settlements, nearly twice their number in 1900 when their population stood at 1.38 billion.[1]

In the most obvious sense, the 'village' is a type of human settlement, different from 'town' and 'city'. Calling it so implies that it has certain attributes that distinguish it from the latter two. However, doing so also evokes a sense of difference. Naming is a cultural process, whereby the object in question acquires an identity, a socially shared meaning. In other words, identities are cultural constructs. They invoke certain attributes, a set of assumptions about the quality and form of the object in question which thereby also distinguishes it from others; the village from the town or the city, in this instance.

'Constructs' are described to be so because they do not simply reflect the realities of the objects they represent. They frame them in specific ways, which may highlight certain facets, imagined or real, over other attributes of the same reality. They are also narratives, as they invoke images and stories and thereby also suggest what they ought to be, framed through a given perspective. As cultural constructs, they are embedded with power and judgement, just like all language and narratives. Categories of villages, towns, and cities, for example, tend to also suggest a frame of hierarchy. In other words, they are not merely different, they are also judged differently.

To say this is not to imply that the 'village' does not exist as a reality. Villages, towns, and cities have been aspects of human civilization for a very long time. They have been shaped by human history and they, in turn, shape the social and cultural universe of humans—their livelihoods, their ways of organizing personal and private lives, and even their modes of doing politics. While their forms and properties have changed over time, villages, towns, and cities have, in most places and in most times, always paralleled each other, integrated through a wide range of processes: material, sociocultural, and political.

Within the larger universe of narratives on human settlements, the idea of the Indian village occupies a special and distinct place. Like elsewhere, cities evolved in the South Asian region alongside the village. Yet, the idea of India as a land of villages caught on and has persisted for a rather long time. As we know from a wide range of rich historical literature, such a narrative about the region commenced during the British colonial rule, when they began to produce knowledge about the region for themselves.

Following the colonial representations of villages in India as autonomous 'republics', it came to be widely seen as a reality that encompassed almost everything about the region. In the colonial constructs of the social life of an average Indian, the village was the world. It was here that India as a society and culture presumably reproduced itself, untouched by politics and the happenings beyond its boundaries. This included the apparently rigid nature of its social organization (the caste system), its history (supposedly frozen in time by its social structure and belief system), and its presumed autonomy (from the political process).

In the early twentieth century, a section of Indian nationalists turned the colonial view around and invoked the idea of village to make claims about the cultural unity and perseverance of India as a society and a nation. Freedom, for them, was thus to recover the lost village, where a true swaraj, an alternative collective or community, morally 'uncorrupted' by the influence of the Western ways of living, could be built.

Thanks to the widespread influence of colonial narratives and its nationalist appropriations, the Indian village emerged as an obvious signifier of the 'native life', a methodological entry point into the nature and dynamics of the Indian society, its social institutions, its values and belief systems. Village, for the early generation of Indian social scientists and journalists, was the 'real' India, where a diverse range of processes could be observed: agriculture, craft, folk cultures, the working of electoral democracy, poverty, health, education, consumption patterns, and almost everything else that mattered to the nation-in-making. A wide range of empirical studies were, therefore, carried out to assess what was changing on the ground as the new nation attempted to develop its economy and modernize its social life and value frames. The proof of India's developmental change had to be verified from the village.

Around the 1990s, India stopped thinking and worrying about its villages. In the globalizing world and liberalizing economy, the site of the nation's self-realization shifted to its cities where software engineers worked for global companies and generated wealth at a heretofore unprecedented pace. The expanding middle classes in the urban corporate economy no longer worried about the rural masses and their concerns. They also no longer found the state sector jobs tempting enough. Though the best among them had been educated in state subsidized institutions like the IITs (Indian Institutes of Technology) and IIMs (Indian Institutes of Management), they saw themselves as self-made; their only obligation was unapologetic self-gratification, as consumers in the new world of mediatized relationships. They also moved away to the ghettos of prosperity, living in gated communities, where they could access cosmopolitan lifestyles that were comparable to the best anywhere in the world.

The village, however, has not gone away. Neither has it receded in size nor has it given up on itself. It has indeed seen a significant decline in its influence and a persistent neglect. Yet, even when ignored by policymakers or the middle-class elite of India, it has continued to survive and change. In terms of absolute numbers more Indians live in rural settlements today than ever before. It is integrated, as it has always been, in the larger economic process. The corporate economy and urban real estate flourish partly because of the availability of cheap labour, at their beck and call, from the villages. The village enables the city to prosper, and the city keeps the village going.

This book provides a glimpse of how the village in India has been changing. However, it must be emphasized that rural realities are not singular processes; they have been historically diverse and their trajectories of change are different across regions. The Indian village has also been internally differentiated, and 'change' is experienced differently across caste, class, and communities. Besides looking at the patterns and processes of change across different 'variables', this book also offers a critical entry point into the making of the *idea* of the Indian village and the possible alternatives to the orientalist view on the subject. How did we come to see India as a land of village republics? Why did the nationalist leadership of India uncritically accept the colonial views on Indian culture and the nature of its past? How and why do such notions survive and continue to inform the popular media, state policy, and even social sciences?

This book aims to critically examine the popular notions of the village. It goes on to explore the changing dynamics of rural life, without presuming that the only destiny of the rural residents is to become urban, either through migration or through a non-agrarian expansion of its economy or the sources of livelihoods. It does not assume a hierarchy of settlements as a 'natural' or obvious fact of life. Such an exercise would necessarily require a conceptual and historical journey that makes it easier to situate the trajectories of the contemporary common sense. The opening chapter thus explores the popular imaginaries of the 'rural' as a site of deficit.

In the next chapter, I specifically provide a critical examination of the popular and persisting view of the 'rural' and 'urban' in social sciences and state policy. I do so by showing their close proximity to the colonial narratives that, to begin with, informed the early generation of Western social science theorists and their conceptions of the non-Western world. In the subsequent chapter, I provide a brief overview of the nationalist appropriations of colonial ideas and ideals. I attempt to show how an uncritical acceptance of the colonial classificatory categories by the nationalist leaders of India ended up producing an imagination of the village which tended to legitimize and normalize the hegemonic power of the new middle-class elite that replaced the colonial rulers after Independence.

The next chapter, entitled 'The Actually Existing Villages', attempts to provide an exposition of the empirical realities of the so-called traditional village life in the subcontinent, as they have been researched and written about by professional historians and social scientists. These writings clearly point to the diversities and ever-changing nature of rural and agrarian lives in the subcontinent.

The next three chapters focus on the subject of 'development and change', which became a preoccupation with the independent Indian state and a wide range of global actors. These chapters include discussions of the policies and programmes of rural development and changing nature of rural livelihoods. Since agriculture is the presumed mainstay of rural economy, the book includes two chapters on this—the first on the nature of agrarian change with a focus on the early decades after India's Independence; second on the relative decline of agriculture during the post-1980s period and the steady growth of rural non-farm economy.

This is followed by chapters on the emergent nature of social life in rural India and the changing modes of rural power structure. These chapters critically examine the prevailing popular notions of caste, class, gender, and rural power, and go on to provide a broad overview of the realities on ground, as they have been documented by social scientists through extensive on-ground scholarly work. The chapters also show that despite its growing marginalization, it is hard to ignore the rural realities for long. Given its demographic weight, a democratic political regime cannot wish it away.

The final chapter of the book attempts to speculate on a possible alternative approach to the realities of rural life in contemporary times, which could also enable us to visualize its possible futures beyond the teleological imperatives of its inevitable disappearance.

chapter 1

'VILLAGE'
THE LOST HOME?

'The village is not what it used to be.' A man who was perhaps in his late sixties or early seventies said this to me during a casual conversation over a cup of tea at the India International Centre (IIC) in New Delhi after a panel discussion where I had spoken on a related subject. This was sometime in November 2019. Everything changes all the time; our cities are also not what they were two or three decades ago, I wanted to respond. Our ways of cooking, dressing, housing, obtaining news have all changed over time. India is also not the country it used to be a few decades ago. However, that is not what he was expecting from me and, so, I kept mum. In fact, he had said it not to enter into an argument with me, but as an icebreaker to start a conversation. This, for him, was a safe starting point, an obvious fact of common wisdom, a point that no one would have any disagreements over.

But he also spoke with a sense of authority, which normally comes with having had long personal experience in one's field of work. As it turned out, my assessment was not far-off. He had worked as a senior bureaucrat with the Government of Madhya Pradesh for nearly three decades and had moved to Pune after his retirement. During his long and eventful career, he had travelled extensively across the country and abroad. He told me that he belonged to a landed agrarian community, a Hindu 'upper' caste family, in the Konkan region of Western India. He was born in a village and a part of his extended family still lived there. His immediate family had left the village a few years after he was born. His father worked for the Indian Railways in its Southern Zone and he completed his schooling in different towns of South India owing to his father's transferable job. However, they kept going back to visit the extended family, and his father decided to return to the village after his retirement to spend his old age there, surrounded by his kin.

Over the years, despite his hectic job schedule, he too kept returning to the village along with his wife and children to visit his old parents. 'It felt good to be away from the hustle and bustle of city life.' However, with his parents' passing, the frequency of his visits began to decline. His children had no interest in land or agriculture. He too began to find the village less welcoming and more alien than before. Those who knew him were either people of his generation or older, and several of them had died. It no longer gave him the feeling of community, or a sense of belonging, that he always felt during his childhood and through much of his adulthood. The younger residents of the village neither recognized him nor had any memory or respect for him and his family.

'The village is not what it used to be.' In this single sentence lay hidden a sense of nostalgia, of personal loss, and even concern, about the village. Many of his 'type' or 'class' would identify with this sentiment, and see in his story very familiar trajectories of their own. Their parents too may have voluntarily left the village, just as many continue to do so even today, perhaps with greater fervour, aspiring for a better life, for education and mobility. The retired bureaucrat was one among those who had done very well in life, for himself and for the future of his family. His son was working with a multinational company based in Germany and lived in Heidelberg with his family. His daughter was a bureaucrat. Besides having a house in Pune, he also owned a decent apartment in South Delhi where he often came and stayed. It allowed him a change of scene and to catch up with old friends in the evenings at the IIC and attend events or discussions of interest to him. There was really no reason to look back at the village, yet it never quite left him.

The bureaucrat is not alone in thinking about the village with a sense of longing and loss. Most human beings relate to the place of their birth and origin emotionally and feel nostalgic about it. Many do go back and choose to spend their old age at the place where they were born, after spending their working life away from 'home'. However, there is something far more special about the Indian village. It is not simply a place or even a category for the demographic classification of the population. It is an idea. It has been a signifier of India's national identity, of its past tradition, and its distinctive culture. 'India lives in its villages'—the dictum popularized by Gandhi is often referred to by a wide variety of individuals, and in different contexts, while speaking about the country, its pasts, and its possible futures.

I have done a good amount of fieldwork in the villages of Haryana and Punjab. I have also done some work in the rural settlements of Himachal Pradesh, Bihar, and Gujarat. I have lived and travelled extensively in some of the South Indian states. The nature of village life, the processes and patterns of its change have been among the most popular areas of social science research in India. As we know from a wide range of ethnographic accounts, other empirical studies and surveys, the realities of rural life in India have always been very diverse. The nature and dynamics of their change are also very complex and varied. However, across these diverse regions, I noticed significant similarities in the perceptions about the nature of change taking place on the ground. Almost every time I go to a village for fieldwork, I ask the inhabitants about their perception of change in the village, particularly in their own lives, and their social and economic well-being.

The patterns are surprisingly similar. Those belonging to the non-dominant communities of the village, most of whom are officially listed as Scheduled Castes (SCs) or the Other Backward Classes (OBCs), tend to always say that life is certainly better than what it used to be in the past. They also make for a majority of the village population, almost everywhere. When they invoke the term 'better', they refer to their ability to now eat two or three meals a day as against the starvation in their previous generations, their improved position in rural power relations, their social status in the larger society, and their ability to speak up. Those from the dominant communities, on the other hand, tend to provide a wider range of negative responses. They often express a sense of loss of their position and influence in the village.

The available social science literature confirms many of these perceptions. Rural poverty has declined almost everywhere. A much larger proportion of villagers live in pukka houses. Almost every child goes to school, and many go to private 'English-medium' schools. Nevertheless, the story is not that of a linear progress and development on a predestined path, as my comments here may suggest. The nature and processes of change are marked by significant diversity across regions and complexities of detail and are discussed at length in the different chapters of this book. The point I wish to underline here is that the popular urban middle-class view of the village may have very little to do with what is happening on the ground, and perhaps much to do with where we are located on the ladder of social and caste hierarchy. Further, sources of the commonly held view among the Indian middle classes on the village are generally derived from elsewhere.

The idea of the 'Indian village' has been widely written about and analysed by the social scientists and historians of modern

India. However, the popular idea of a single homogenous construct has been and continues to be a useful way of framing the subject for the actors who matter. As I discuss in detail in the following two chapters, the popular idea of the Indian village was first put together, or constructed, by the British colonial rulers and a section of European orientalists. The Indian nationalists found some of these ideas politically useful and invoked them in their politics against the colonial rulers. Thus, the colonial knowledge production about Indian society and the nationalist appropriation of these colonial categories and conceptions together constructed an image and idea of India, which was largely mythical but served the new elite of India—the emerging urban middle classes—who came to decide what was good for the rest of the country.

The retired bureaucrat I spoke to at the IIC is perhaps a good example of this narrative being kept alive even today. The story of the declining village he narrated was not simply about his native village having lost its presumed cohesiveness, its imagined community culture. Underlying it was also a much wider narrative of supposed loss, popular among sections of the 'traditionally' dominant groups, their imagination of Indian-ness and its 'authentic version'. The villager in actuality seemed to be speaking for herself and himself, in many different and diverse voices. This book is an exploration of these complex and diverse trajectories of change in the rural life of India.

Exploring the Idea

The idea of the 'village' has a distinctive place in the life of the Indian nation. As Gandhi had popularized, the village was the site of the real and authentic India. For genuine independence of the country, the village needed to be recovered and uplifted. From popular Hindi cinema and folk stories on native life to narratives of development around the challenges of India's poverty and 'backwardness', the village was at the centre of national self-imaginations. It understandably became an obvious site for a wide range of social science research and explorations of what was changing in the lives of ordinary people and what was not. Political scientists and journalists documenting the problems and perils of local democracy or the social churning taking place on the ground invariably invoke 'rural realities' to sound authentic. The emblematic frail-looking peasant who perpetually lived in scarcity and worked under the hot sun, or a tractor-driving Sardar with his flowing beard in the post-Green Revolution fields of Punjab, were not merely images of rural life. They represented the new nation, signifying its challenges and achievements; its pasts and present. This remained an influential way of envisioning the country until around the 1980s, when its weight and value began to see a steady erosion.

The village and the city, or the rural and the urban, have been popular and convenient ways of classifying human settlements across the world, and over a long period of time. The beginning of human civilization is often traced to the growth of agriculture when *Homo sapiens* were believed to have learnt the art of cultivating land. This enabled them to live together, in stable communities. The settlements we call villages would have emerged around that time. The ancient city too arose a little while after that. Settled agriculture implied that human beings had invented tools with which they could produce more than what they required for their subsistence. They were no longer hunter-gatherers. Spared from the constant challenge of finding food, they could not only put up shelters for themselves, but also invest in leisure.

As their lives stabilized, they would have developed more complex notions of kinship, power, and a normative social order with a system of institutions, beliefs, and rituals. The surplus produced by agriculture made it possible for some to be able to live off others, without having to work. These could have been the older members of the kinship or lactating mothers, or simply those who could not work due to some disability. However, as we know from the history of human inequalities, the surplus also made it possible for the emergence of a 'class' that could subjugate others into working for them.

With expanding capabilities, human beings would have also diversified into other activities and services. The ability to work with metal and the use of copper and, later, iron, for example, would have helped them to develop more sophisticated tools to better deal with nature and the vagaries of chance. These specialists would have tended to live in larger settlements, serving those living in smaller settlements in their proximity. It is around this time that the idea of politics would have taken shape, where some managed to emerge as a kind of ruling elite. They would have expanded their strength and spheres of influence by recruiting soldiers who could provide protection to everyone, fight on the behalf of rulers and collect taxes from the common cultivators and other working people.

As the sphere of their influence expanded, they would have also moved to, or set up, even larger settlements—towns and cities. Latter-day historians would describe them as the ruling aristocracy. The ruling aristocracy would have also brought others to inhabit the larger settlements, the service providers such as the artisan, mason, entertainer, medic, priest, etc. Early human history seems to have evolved along roughly similar lines in many regions of the world as we know them today.

The South Asian region too saw the rise of vibrant cities from very early on, such as Harappa and Mohenjo-daro. Some continued to grow over time, some declined with the waning fortunes of the region. Overall, as we know from the available historical literature on the region, the number of cities continued to grow and expand, in the South Asian region through ancient and medieval times, mostly supported by the agrarian economies and rural settlements surrounding them. Agra, Dilli,

Varanasi, Lahore, Amritsar, Darbhanga, Bhopal, Gwalior, Patna, Ahmedabad, Udaipur, Mysore, Pune, Aurangabad, Hyderabad, Kozhikode, Vijayanagar, Trichy, and many more cities emerged. Their size and influence exhibited the growing prosperity of different regions, of their agriculture and artisan economy. In other words, their prosperity was also a reflection of vibrant rural economies of those regions. No doubt, as the ruler and regimes changed, specific cities and their prominence also changed.

When the British began to write about India, after they established their rule in the subcontinent during the eighteenth century, they rarely highlighted the native urban culture, the architecture, art, and music that flourished here. Nor did they speak of the urban economic riches, social diversities, the flourishing religious shrines of a wide range of faiths visited by followers from across the subcontinent, including from its far-flung interiors. For example, the city of Varanasi, or Kashi, was known to a section of Hindus no matter where they lived: Malabar, Kashmir, Punjab, or Bengal. Visiting scholars and travellers from other lands have written about these flourishing cities and trade much before the European visitors came to the Indian subcontinent and very active social, cultural, and economic networks already existed between this region and the rest of the world. Traders from Arabia regularly visited Malabar and other regions of India. Christianity and Islam had therefore come to the region soon after they emerged in the Arab lands. Buddhism, Jainism, and Sikhism were born here too. Zoroastrianism and Judaism had arrived in the region, courtesy fleeing refugees, much before British colonization occurred. In other words, in religious terms too, the region had witnessed a very rich set of varied interactions and cross-talk, not all of which was peaceful or non-violent.

But the British entry into the region was markedly different in one aspect. They had arrived as traders, seeking the riches of India, the source of which mostly lay in its diverse agrarian crops, spices, and indigo. But they soon became colonizers who sought to exploit the wealth and resources of its colonies to fund its race for supremacy among the European nations that were being in turn propelled by the overwhelming success of the Industrial Revolution. But the military conquests and exploitation needed to be justified to its own people. So, the British chose to tell their fellow citizens in Britain that India was a land of villages, undifferentiated and similar in size and composition all across the subcontinent, and its conquest would in no way perturb these independent microcosms. In the view that they popularized, the rural settlements were homogenous 'republics', with no notion of private property and conflict, a social order that was marked by harmony and interdependence among different caste groups that had continued in perpetuity irrespective of ruler or conqueror. This was, of course, a lie, a deliberate misrepresentation.

It is true that very large proportions of the Indian population have always lived in rural settlements and nearly two-thirds of it continues to do so even today, in the third decade of the twenty-first century. However, as mentioned above, from the days of the Harappan civilization, and well into the eighteenth century when British colonial rule was being established over much of the subcontinent, cities had been an important part of native cultures. Flourishing urban settlements were an integral part of each sub-region's social and cultural formations, political economies, and regimes of power. Their economy and prosperity were closely tied to the rural and agrarian economies of their regions. It was primarily through the land revenue collected from the cultivating classes, and their labour, that monuments like the Qutb Minar and the Taj Mahal, or the palaces and forts of the subcontinent, and the visibly prosperous Hindu temples of present-day South India, such as those in Tirupati, Trivandrum, and Madurai, were constructed.

Villages were not isolated in a sociocultural sense either.

Inhabitants of one village frequently interacted with residents of other villages in their everyday lives. Most regions of the subcontinent practised village exogamy and marriages were rarely arranged among families living within the same village. Thus, the structure of kinship ties would have also required them to visualize their social life within a given region or sub-region, across forms of zaats and biradaris (castes and fraternities), as the circles of kinship are known in northwest India.

Yet, the idea of the idyllic village republic has survived. What explains such a fixation with the idea of the autonomous village among middle-class Indians, the political elite, and even academics, while thinking about the pasts of social life in India? Why does the village alone carry the burden of being traditional and authentic? Why have the narratives of rural life come to be largely framed in metaphors of 'negatives' and 'declines', when the rural in India has, in fact, continued to grow and expand? How do we explain its persistence in some regions of the world and its near disappearance from other regions?

I provide possible elaborate answers to some of these questions in different chapters of the book. For example, as I discuss further in Chapter 3, the British used the concept of the village republic to justify and rationalize their rule over India to the British tax-paying citizen. But the construct of India as a land of village republics had many takers among sections of the Indian educated elite as well, including a wide range of Indian nationalists, most prominent among them being Gandhi. The nationalists found this concept politically useful, and used it to define India as unique and different from the rest of the world. It helped them make a counterpoint in support of India's qualification of being 'a nation' despite its enormous diversities of language and culture. Whenever the colonial rulers tried to dismiss the nationalist claim for independence on grounds of the country's immense diversity, the nationalists could juxtapose the colonial view of the Indian village in their response. After all, colonial representations of India themselves suggested that the region was marked by unique foundational unity, despite its apparent diversities of language, region, and faith, they could argue. This is not to suggest that the Indian nationalist elite used the construct merely as a manipulative strategy. Educated, as they were, about India's history and culture in colonial schools, colleges, and universities, they had bought into these narratives readily and took the colonial representations of India as obvious facts of history. Through their writings and political invocations, they turned the dictum, India as a land of villages, into a common sense imagination of the country.

Such a view of India fit well into the emerging social science theories of social change, development, and economic growth during the post-World War II period. The idea of development, for example, also had an implicit demographic narrative woven into it, a point I elaborate in Chapter 2. Countries of the developing world were presumably poor because they were 'backward', as a large majority of their population lived in villages. In contrast, the developed countries were 'advanced' because nearly everyone lived in cities.

India's Rural–Urban Demographics

As mentioned above, for a long time, the categories of 'rural' and 'urban' have been popular and convenient modes of classifying settlements and populations across the world. India's demographic establishment distinguishes 'rural' and 'urban' by using a range of criteria, including the given political contingencies. However, Indian census officials may identify a settlement as urban, even when it is not yet classified as such for administrative or governance reasons. For the census enumerator, a settlement becomes a 'Census Town' when it meets the following three criteria: a population of 5,000 or more, population density of 400 per square kilometre or more, and

75 per cent or more of the male workforce engaged in non-farm/
non-agricultural activities.

Historically speaking, the available estimates suggest that
a large majority of Indians indeed lived in the countryside
during the early nineteenth century when the British and other
European orientalists began to comment on the exceptional
features of India. However, this does not imply that India did not
have urban centres or that those who lived in a rural settlement
lived in complete isolation. As indicated above, the growth of
cities and towns in the South Asian regions was comparable
with that in other 'civilized' regions of the world. Not only were
there a good number of urban centres in the region, it also had a
large number of people living in these settlements, much higher
than in any European country at the time.

According to one estimate, at the beginning of the
nineteenth century, India had as many as 17.6 million people
living in its towns and cities.[1] This was much larger than the total
population of Great Britain in 1801, which was at 10.5 million.
In proportional terms, the South Asian region was not any
less urbanized than any other region of the world at that time,
although during the nineteenth century, after the establishment
of the British colonial rule in the region, India did undergo a
process of de-urbanization.

Patterns of settlement formation are also shaped by a
wide range of factors: ecology, economy, culture, and political
expediencies. Their strict classification into the binary of
rural–urban is a relatively recent practice. It was only with
the emergence of modern-day nation states that demographic
data began to be collected systematically for reasons of policy
and statecraft. Nation states, as we know them today, became
globally institutionalized only during the middle of the twentieth
century. However, despite a nearly common language of
classifying settlements into rural and urban for administrative
purposes today, their diversities persist, across regions of the

world as well as within a given region or country. And, like the urban settlements which have a wide range of diversities, villages too vary, both in size and quality.

Bernard Cohn, an anthropologist at the University of Chicago, who studied Indian society all his life, identified three broad types of villages or rural settlements found across the regions of India. First of these are 'the nucleated' villages. These are the villages that the popular media, social scientists, and even the policymakers/administrators tend to typically invoke when they talk about rural India. These villages tend to be multi-caste settlements with houses and streets close to each other. They are mostly present in the plains of northern and northwest India. They are also found in some parts of other regions in India. Second are those that are formed by a number of small settlements. He describes them as the 'hamleted' villages. They tend to have one central settlement with 'several hamlets, and satellite settlements scattered over the fields of the village'. These are 'more typical of middle and lower Gangetic plains and parts of Tamil Nadu and Andhra Pradesh'. The third type of villages of the subcontinent are even more dispersed where there is no 'obvious village, because homesteads are dispersed, generally on or near the fields owned or worked on by the agriculturists. This form of settlements is found in wide range of regions, from the Kerala coast to the hill regions of the northern and central highlands.'[2]

Accompanying differences of ecology, form, and social composition, these rural settlements of India also vary in terms of their demographic size. In terms of their population, a rural settlement could vary from a mere 50 or 100 persons or 10 to 20 households to a highly dense settlement of 500 or more households, with the population going up to 30,000 persons or even more. This is also reflected in the demographic spread of the rural population. For example, at the turn of the century, in 2001, India had nearly 600,000 settlements classified as rural.

However, more than half of the total rural population of India (over 54 per cent) lived in and around 3 per cent of the relatively large villages with a population size of 2,000 and above. They made for 18,768 settlements. Nearly 220,000 rural settlements had a population size of less than 500 persons.[3] Thus, even demographically the Indian village is a fluid category with a significant diversity of size and form. More importantly, despite many social and economic changes, diversities remain, and their relevance for policy and otherwise continues to be critical.

Europe's urbanization is a late twentieth century phenomenon. It was only by the 1970s that Europe had more people living in urban areas than in its villages. Even in 1960, all of Europe (except for the USSR) had only 44 per cent of its population living in urban centres.[4] Notably, India's trajectory of urbanization appears to be very different from that of Europe. Even the urban in India is not expanding at the cost of the rural. Though the urban has grown at a faster pace over the past century, India's rural population in its absolute size has also been consistently growing. This is clearly borne out by empirical data collected by the decadal census. For example, the proportion of India's urban population grew by nearly three folds over the past century, from 10.29 per cent in 1911 to 31.16 per cent in 2011. The absolute numbers are even more impressive. While only 26 million Indians lived in its urban settlements in 1901, their numbers had gone up to 377 million by 2011. While some of this increase would indeed be due to the natural growth of the urban population, a larger share in the rising numbers would be due to migrations of rural residents to urban centres and the additions to the numbers of urban settlements with reclassification of the expanding villages.

Table 1.1: India's population and rural/urban
settlements over decades

Census years	% Urban population and (settlements)	% Rural population and (settlements)	Total urban population (millions)	Total rural population (millions)
1901	10.84 (1827)	89.15 (567,000)	25.8	212.5
1921	11.18	88.82	28.1	223.2
1941	13.86	86.14	44.1	274.5
1951	17.29 (2,853)	82.71	62.4	298.6
1961	17.97	82.03	78.9	360.2
1971	18.24	81.76	109.1	489.0
1981	23.33	76.66	159.5	523.8
1991	25.72	74.28	217.2	627.1
2001	27.78 (5,161)	72.22 (638,588)	285.4	741.6
2011	31.16 (7,935)	68.84 (640,867)	377.0	833.0

Sources: Pranati Datta, 'Urbanisation in India', pp. 1–16, available at casi.sas.upenn. edu/sites/default/files/iit/Urbanisation%20in%20India.pdf, accessed 10 December 2021. Also see relevant table at censusindia.gov.in/census.website, accessed 10 December 2021.

These numbers also tell us another story. Just the urban population of India is significantly larger than the total population of any other country of the world except for China. The total population of the third largest country of the world, the USA, in 2011 was nearly 300 million. This is significant not merely as a demographic number, it also has implications for policy and indicates the potential of middle-class consumption that a country could possess. Of the ten largest cities of the world, two are in India: Delhi and Mumbai. India has also seen a consistent increase in the number of its urban settlements, from 1,827 in 1901 to 5,161 by 2001 and further to 7,935 in 2011 (see Table 1.1).

However, the rural population in India has also been growing consistently over the past century. In other words, the pace of the growth of rural population has been significantly larger than the rates of their outmigrations to urban centres. It grew from 212.5 million in 1901 to 480 million in 1971, and further to 742 million in 2001. According to the census of 2011,[5] a total of around 833 million Indians lived in rural areas, nearly four times their size in 1901. Interestingly enough, despite the reclassification of a large number of villages into towns, the number of rural settlements has not gone down. They too have been growing over the decades, from 5,67,000 in 1901 to 6,38,588 in 2001 and further to 6,40,867 in 2011. This could obviously be due to a mushrooming of new rural settlements during this period.

Marginalizing the Village

The 1990s were an important turning point in the history of the modern world. It marked the end of an era in global politics, which had begun in the second half of the 1940s, soon after World War II. The collapse of the Soviet Union in December 1991 marked the end of the Cold War between the two superpowers of the time, USA and USSR, and established the victory of one kind of politico-economic philosophy over another. Neoliberalism triumphed over state-led socialism. Its immediate impact was political, and felt mostly in the eastern parts of Europe. The Berlin Wall had already been brought down a couple of years earlier. Besides Germany, several other countries of Eastern Europe saw a restructuring of their geographical boundaries and several new nations emerged through divisions of the older countries around this time. All of these events also had wider implications for the larger world, including India, in political as well as economic terms.

With economic liberalization and the growing visibility of urban middle classes in the decade of the 1990s, the village began to recede from the national imagination. A 'new' India was on the anvil, a nation on the way to becoming a global power. The rising new cities, Bengaluru, Gurgaon, Hyderabad, and many other metropolitan centres began to be seen as the sites of India's self-realization in the emerging world. Led by the 'new economy' and the service sector, India grew at a much faster pace than ever before for the next two decades. This new prosperity, largely confined to its emerging urban centres and their expanding middle classes, also changed cultural values that the common people grew up with. Even though its numbers were still nearly one-fourth of the total population, middle-class status emerged as the new normative for everyone. The marginalization of the agrarian economy accompanied the rise of the Indian middle-class. Even when agriculture continued to witness positive growth, its share in the national economy began to see a steady fall. The value of village life also saw an erosion. Educated rural youth from farming families began to increasingly aspire to move out of the village, into urban occupations, to join the ranks of the middle classes.

Such processes also took the attention of the policymakers away from the village. It is no accident that India began to witness a neglect of agriculture and rural residents. From commercial print and electronic media, to the social science researcher, almost everyone who mattered began to turn away from reporting on the dynamics of the rural and agrarian realities. The only narrative through which the village began to be spoken about was that of crises, of agrarian economy, of agriculture as an occupation, of progressively shrinking land holdings of cultivators, of water and pollution created by indiscriminate use of chemicals in agriculture, of rural unemployment and the state of hopelessness among the rural youth, its poverty and its deprivations.

While many of these may indeed be true depictions of what is happening on the ground, they do not apply uniformly to the rural realities of the entire subcontinent. Not to put too fine a point on it, the realities of India's villages are diverse and they emerge from the fact that there is no simple homogenous entity called 'the Indian village'. For example, the state of Bihar has consistently been one of the poorest regions in the country with less than 12 per cent[6] of its population living in urban centres. Yet, the region has hardly reported any incidence of farmers committing suicides because of unmanageable debts, as is frequently reported from some other, more prosperous, regions. Incomes from agriculture and the size of average holdings also vary significantly across regions, and so do the cropping cultures and social profiles of cultivating caste groups and communities.

Beyond the Imperatives of Decline and Disappearance

The rural is no longer a relevant demographic category in many countries of the Western world. Even though farming survives as an occupation in many parts of Europe and elsewhere, and agriculture remains an important economic activity in the so-called developed countries of the Global North, the idea of a distinct universe of rural life has nearly disappeared. According to the early social science imagination, what happened in the West should eventually happen everywhere in the world. Urbanization, in such an understanding, is a function of economic growth and development. Such an assumption emanates from a Eurocentric mode of thinking and must be abandoned. Rural and urban, or village and city, are social constructs. The meanings and values that are attributed to them stem from a kind of politics, the purpose of which is to normalize inequalities of power, and a hegemony of the urban middle classes and elite over the rest of society. While villages undergo changes over time, they do not need to disappear. The urban and rural are simply types of settlement, and neither needs to be necessarily superior to the other. I discuss this idea in greater detail in Chapter 2.

While such terms of classification enable us to identify differences they often also simplify and obscure the diversities and complexities involved. The range and variety of human settlements cannot be encapsulated in the simple rural–urban binary. Perhaps, we require a more nuanced classification of settlements that does not reduce them merely to the differences in certain demographic attributes. Just as there are many rurals, shaped by their geography, ecology, history, and sociocultural evolutions, so also there are many urbans. The quality of life in a small mofussil town of Jharkhand or Karnataka is not comparable, in any meaningful way, with the social and cultural realities of the cities of Bengaluru or Mumbai. Further, villages and cities are also internally differentiated and diverse. While internal differentiation of cities is a widely accepted fact, even villages have historically been differentiated in the caste divided society of the subcontinent.

chapter 2

HOW THE VILLAGE COMES TO BE SEEN AS A SITE OF DEFICIT

'Village' could signify a range of things: a type of settlement; an economy dominated by agriculture; or a kind of lifestyle closer to 'tradition' and 'nature' where residents presumably lead a simple and uncomplicated life with a strong sense of community. The term has also come to be used as a signifier of a life marked by proximity and smallness of size—the sense in which the expression 'global village' is invoked for an increasingly connected world, made possible by the advances in information technology. Revolutions in information technology and artificial intelligence have transformed human life, as we knew it until the 1980s, into a kind of accessible neighbourhood, compressing separations of space and time across the globe and even making the boundaries of nation state less relevant.

However, in much of its prevalent usage, and in popular media images, 'village' is primarily seen as a negative signifier: a collective of conservative mindsets, deeply patriarchal and rigidly hierarchical. It is a place to be left behind, a site of poverty, ignorance, and backwardness. This negative invocation of the term has become particularly frequent in the post-World War II framings of rural lives in countries of the Global South, where 'village' has come to be commonly viewed through the narratives of development. The idea of 'development' that shaped the state policy after India's independence from colonial rule foregrounded the village as a site and source of many of the country's 'problems' that desperately needed to be solved from 'above', by the centralized state through centralized planning and a range of economic and political reforms. The twentieth century social science writings and the so-called mainstream theories of development and change have also played their roles in popularizing, and even institutionalizing, such a notion of the 'village'.

How Do the Framings of 'Development' Construct Village Life?

'Development' emerged as a powerful and hegemonic idea during the 1940s when global politics was being reconfigured following World War II. The post-War period saw independent nation states emerging in regions of Asia, Africa, and Latin America that had been colonized by European powers for centuries. Long experience of colonial plunder had left nearly all of them economically poor, socially restive, and politically porous. The native elite, who had themselves mostly emerged under the colonial patronage, mobilized the 'poor masses' of their lands with the promise of a better life after their independence from foreign rule. These new nation states that emerged on the world scene in the middle of the twentieth century came to be known collectively as the Third World.

Some of the native political elite in these newly carved out nation states were attracted to the idea of socialism, and turned to the emerging global powers, the Soviet Union and other countries of the Socialist Bloc, also known as the Second World, for patronage and help. However, the influence of the Western power block, or the First World, remained very significant even after decolonization. With the war substantially reducing the influence of erstwhile European powers, the United States of America (USA) emerged as the new leader of the 'free world'. The Western powers under the leadership of the USA aggressively advocated an alternative path to development for the Third World states to overcome their poverty and economic deprivations. They produced a wide range of theories that provided explanations for the persistent poverty of the new nation states. They also provided policy advice for getting out of the prevailing scenario and gloomy state of affairs. Using the newly set-up institution of the United Nations, they put in place a wide range of organizations such as the World Bank, United Nations Development Programme (UNDP), and International Monetary Fund (IMF), among others, to help developing countries with financial aid and policy prescriptions.

Avoiding any reference to their colonial past and economic plunder by the European powers, the newly worked out theories of development emerging from the Western academy tended to put the burden of their 'underdevelopment' on their 'backward-looking', traditional cultures and 'outdated' social institutions that presumably characterized all the newly independent countries of Asia, Africa, and Latin America. A way out of their 'underdevelopment' was possible only if their newly crowned political elite were willing to work as per the prescriptions received from these Western advisers who advocated a dire need to modernize 'old' ways of thinking and living, radically altering their values and institutions.

The newly evolved discipline of 'development studies' thus proposed that it was only through such moves that a ground for progressive change could be created, paving the way for economic growth and prosperity. The elite and middle classes of the 'new nations', who had themselves emerged directly under the colonial patronage, were very willing to look up to the 'developed' Western world as a model for their own future, since it comprised countries that were the lands of their dreams, where a good number of them had themselves been educated, and had been socialized into the ways of modern-day democratic politics. It was in this context that 'the village' came to be seen as a source and site of economic underdevelopment as well as social and cultural backwardness.

Village through the Prism of Development

The native elite, who had mostly been all urban, hardly showed any hesitation in accepting the 'developmentalist view' or such descriptions of village life in their own societies.

What they witnessed empirically, the realities on the ground, did appear to affirm many of the claims made by the Western theorists. Villages were indeed sites of chronic poverty and hunger in many of these countries. A large majority of their populations lived in rural settlements. At the time of Independence, India, for example, had nearly 85 per cent of its population living in rural areas and their national incomes in most regions were very low. Even though nearly 75 per cent of the Indian population was directly or indirectly employed in cultivating agricultural lands, India could not even produce enough food to feed its entire population.

However, while describing the prevailing situations on the ground, the development theorists rarely made any reference to the centuries of colonial mismanagement and plunder that had badly hurt the agrarian economy in the first place and which, to a large extent, had been responsible for the decline of agriculture and the local craft. The colonial policies had also resulted in the rise of a new kind of landlordism and tyranny of the local moneylenders over the cultivating 'peasants'.

The Western development theories looked at the rural realities of countries like India as being a 'natural' state of affairs, a pre-development stage, which was attributable to their inability to evolve out of a stasis of hopelessness and low levels of technology. Most of their arguments and propositions were drawn almost entirely from the historical experience of West European countries, which had presumably been more dynamic and driven to change, although continuing to overlook the advantages possessed by these countries as colonizers ruling over large parts of the world.

From Enlightenment to Modernization

Some of the core ideas and assumptions that Western theorists claimed as universal facts had largely been European in origin, especially those that emerged during the period of 'Enlightenment' which had advocated the values of reason and the method of science for organizing human life. It was also around this time that some of the European thinkers developed the notion of 'evolution' with the underlying claim that the developed countries of the Western world were not only materially prosperous but also at a higher stage of the evolutionary process. Correspondingly, countries of the developing world appeared lower down on such a scale simply because they were economically poorer at that moment in time.

The idea of evolution was mostly operationalized through a set of binaries: the old and the new; the underdeveloped and the developed; and, most importantly, the East and the West, the Orient and the Occident. The foundational binary that informed development studies, and the emerging 'common-sense' view of social change, was that of 'traditional' and 'modern'. Modernity and modernization thus emerged as the mantras for the new world of developing nations, their new political elite and their emerging urban middle classes.

Everything in the developing world was seen as affirming the ideas of tradition, while everything in countries of the Western world came to be viewed as modern. The presumed differences between 'rural' and 'urban' or 'village' and 'city' seemed to fit very easily and neatly into this framework. Much like the presumed distinction between 'traditional' and 'modern', the ideas of 'village' and 'city', as indicated in the previous chapter, are also invoked as contrasting or binary categories, as if they are mutually exclusive with completely different attributes and ways of life.

In the emerging narrative of the rural–urban binary, the site of 'modernity' was the industrial city of nineteenth century

Europe, where everything was fluid, diverse, and changing. The Indian village was constructed as a spatial and social category and presented as a contrast to the European city, where everything had presumably been stable and stagnant for centuries and millennia. While the 'city', in this framing, signified individualism, anonymity, and instrumentality, the village was where life was lived collectively and informally, with no sense of anonymity or instrumentality.

The idea of evolution was invoked in relation to the rural–urban binary as well. A larger share and size of the rural population relative to the urban population of a region or a country served as an indicator of its 'low' level of development and evolution. In other words, the process of social change and development would inevitably be accompanied by a process of urbanization of a region's population. Urbanization was thus assumed to be both desirable and inevitable during the process of economic growth and social development. It signified that a society was moving ahead. By implication, according to the underlying assumptions of mainstream developmental thought, the village would and should die in due course, if the society and economy have to move forward on the path of progress and become modern.

Institutionalizing the Binaries

The above-mentioned ideas have come to frame the textbook view of the 'rural' and 'urban' as two types of spatial domains of social life, which are fundamentally distinct from each other, mutually exclusive, and frozen in time. These presumed differences have also come to be accepted by social science practitioners and by those framing state policies and shaping popular imaginations: officials, politicians, public intellectuals, journalists, and those working with civil society organizations across the contemporary world. They take this binary view of 'rural' and 'urban' for granted and use it, not only in the assessment of demographic distributions or for the classification of populations, but also in their analyses of cultural differences, political trends, and economic processes.

Much of the mainstream Western sociology has been a study of urban life, as being different from rural communities. This presumed difference in the spatiality of the rural and the urban has been very central to the imagination of the difference between sociology and social anthropology. While sociologists studied 'society', anthropologists studied 'community'. The terms, 'society' and 'community', were also visualized in an evolutionary schema by the nineteenth century founders of the two disciplines. 'Urban' or 'city life' for them symbolized a complexity of life, where a diverse variety of populations belonging to different ethnic groups and cultures lived together but without a strong sense of bonding or identification with one another, a feature presumed to be found in smaller communities.

The city was not only demographically larger in size, but it also had a fundamentally different type of economy, culture, and normative order, when compared to its counterpart, the village, it had a distinct 'way of life'.[1] Rural economy was presumed to be structured around agriculture, while industry, commerce, and services were seen as the main sources of livelihood in the city. Urban residents practised a much larger range of occupations. This also implied that, compared to the village, the urban economy and its collective social life was far more diverse, differentiated, and unequal.

Underlying these assumptions about the differences between the city and the village is the Eurocentric view of history. According to this view, it was in the Western city that modernity and individuality were born. This was a radical shift in the grammar of social life. The ties of community life became significantly weaker, or simply non-existent, and were replaced by the self-oriented and agential or choice-making individual. Urban identities thus began to be presumably formed around education, occupation, social class, individual taste and consumption, without any influence of religion, ethnicity, and other markers of ascription, which were all assumed to be features of community life in rural settlements.

Such a binary view was not only presented in the descriptive accounts of the changing times but also shaped the classical social science theories of human society developed by a range of Western scholars during the nineteenth and twentieth centuries. Nearly all of them approached the 'rural' and the 'urban' as what Émile Durkheim would have described as distinctive realities, sui generis—they were out there, objectively and normatively.

This imagination of differences between the rural and urban as articulated by social scientists was also widely accepted by the elite and the emerging middle classes in the Western world and came to be part and parcel of the emerging common sense among them. By implication, thus, a 'modern man' lived in the city. As Teodor Shanin, a scholar who has extensively written on peasant life, argues, in terms of its self-image, the post-nineteenth century Western world saw itself as a 'world without peasants'. The division of societies into 'modern' and 'traditional' in the evolutionist schema of early social theory also meant that conceptually, the rural populations were reduced to an unspecified part of the mixed bag of 'remainders of the past'.[2]

Persistent Rural

However, such a shift in their self-imagination or the declining share and value of rural economy in the national life did not imply a complete disappearance of the 'rural', socially or demographically, from the landscape of all Western societies. Even when their numbers declined, farming and rural identities did not go away. In some cases, they continue to exercise a degree of political influence over the national life in countries of the Western world even today. Despite the growing hegemony of the urban bourgeoisie and other sections of the emerging middle classes in the social life of Western countries during the nineteenth and early decades of the twentieth century, the rural realities were hard to forget.

The growing power and prosperity of cities attracted a large number of people living in the smaller settlements. Cities emerged as sites of mobility and aspirations. The prospects of large-scale migration of the rural populations to urban centres alarmed the policymakers and political elite of the time. The political establishments had to thus also engage with the 'rural' and comprehend what was happening there.

It was in this context that a specialized discipline of rural sociology was born in the United States. The long Civil War during the late nineteenth century had also created a serious 'farm crisis' in its countryside. Farmers' organizations also expected help from the federal state to solve the compelling problems of rural areas, afflicted by severe depression. Rural sociology, as an applied discipline, came into existence as a response to this crisis.[3] The appointment of the Country Life Commission by President Theodore Roosevelt in 1908 gave a big boost to this field of study.

As an applied area of study, the main concern of 'rural sociology' was understanding and diagnosing the social and economic problems of American farmers, with a greater focus on questions relating to the internal structure of 'community life' and the changing composition of rural populations.[4] A little later, the idea of a separate discipline of rural sociology also found purchase in Western Europe when its rural areas confronted a similar state of crisis following the devastations caused by World War II. Though the idea and practice of rural sociology emerged in the context of wider social and political crises and the challenges they posed to lives and livelihoods of the farming classes of the US, and later of Western Europe, its practitioners remained caught in the binary modes of thinking and classifying human society.

'Rural sociology' saw itself as a science of 'rural society', which continued to view the 'rural' like mainstream sociology did, as a sui-generis reality with its distinctive form and character, different from its oppositional counterpart, the urban society. In other words, it did not recognize the obvious fact: that the context of its emergence was itself shaped by the larger social and political processes that rural US or Europe encountered due to the challenges and changes encountered by the Western world post World War I. The 'rural' was clearly an integrated part of the larger political and economic life and shaped by it, not an insulated segment with its own internal modes of social organization functioning independently of the rest.

However, textbooks of 'rural sociology' on the subject sought to define and characterize the 'rural' by contrasting it with the 'urban'. They argued that while social relationships in the village were governed by values of status, city life was fractionated along class lines. The village had been an eternally 'stable' and 'static' society because of its cyclical view of time. The city dwellers, in contrast, had a progressive outlook, which made them aspirational and mobile, compatible with the values of modernity. This list of contrasting features or attributes of the two could be easily expanded further.

The 'distinctive characteristics of rural life', as the American sociologist Lowry Nelson writes in his book on the subject, could be 'easily discerned by comparing them with those of the city life'. 'The culture of city is one thing, the culture of the country is quite another. Cities are by comparison large, impersonal, and complex in social structure; country communities are small, intimate, and simple in organization.'[5]

The influence of such an approach was also felt in India. The early Indian sociologist A. R. Desai, for example, summarized the classical Western view as follows:

All rural sociologists recognize that the social life of the community is divided into two distinct segments, rural and urban. Though these segments interact among themselves, each is sufficiently distinct from the other. All of them hold the view that social life in rural setting exhibits characteristics and tendencies which are peculiar to it... and...therefore sharply distinguish it from life in urban setting. ...[T]he prime objective of rural sociology should be to make a scientific, systematic and comprehensive study of the rural social organization, of its structure, functions and objective tendencies of development, and, on the basis of such a study, to discover the law of its development.[6]

There have been many criticisms of such an approach that divided society into 'rural' and 'urban' as if they were two distinct types of societies, or that they represented two different stages in the process of human evolution. The American anthropologist Robert Redfield (1947) and some others pointed to the obvious empirical flaws with such a binary view and showed through their work the degree of continuities and overlaps that social life in the two types of settlements exhibited. However, the idea of 'rural–urban continuum' too assumes an underlying difference of quality and two ends of a spectrum.

The issue here is not simply that of empirical confusion or flaw in recognizing the elements of continuum between rural and urban. This was actually a theoretical, or even a political, question because such a binary construct invoked a hierarchy in settlements with urban being more advanced and superior to the rural. Articulated through a language of development or as stages in a theory of social change, the rural would inherently imply infantile and the urban its mature and 'grown-up' future.

Also, it is simply impossible to assume and study the two sets of settlements as independent domains of social life, as if they could exist without influencing and being influenced by the other. Alessandro Bonanno, for example, argues, 'the two could not be conceptualised as autonomous or sui-generis realities, which could be understood and analysed in isolation from the larger social, historical and political context in which they were located at a given point in time.'[7]

Scholars have also pointed to other problems. Human civilizations have had a large variety of settlements. As there are big, medium, and small-sized cities, there are similarly a wide range of 'rural' settlements. This sociological distinction between 'rural' and 'urban' has become even more difficult to sustain in a rapidly globalizing world, where telecommunication and mass media have nearly erased the old differences between the city and the countryside.

From West to India: Colonial Imagination of the Indian Village

The ideas of village and city, or classification of settlements based on their demographics and quality of life, were not alien to the cultures and languages of the subcontinent. There are specific words for them in many Indian languages. For example, words like gaon, gram, dehaat, basti (in Hindi), pind, vasson (in Punjabi) for rural settlements and likewise, sheher, nagar, pur, bad, or kasba for urban settlements used by speakers of different languages across the subcontinent, not only denote difference of rural and urban, but also point to a classification suggesting a wider variety of settlements.

As indicated in the previous chapter, cities have indeed been a part of the social and cultural landscape of the South Asian region for a very long time. Their origin in the region paralleled their emergence in other parts of the world during 'ancient times'. Their numbers and sizes also grew over time, though not always in a linear fashion. For example, the disappearance of the ancient civilization of Harappa and Mohenjo-daro also implied a decline of cities in the region; but they re-emerged a few centuries later with the rise of new empires and the growth of agrarian economies in different pockets of the region.

Around the time when traders from Europe began to arrive on the western coast of Goa and Malabar, or even later when the East India Company established its rule over parts of the region, the Indian subcontinent had a good proportion of its population living in settlements that could be described as urban—comparable to, if not higher than, regions of medieval Europe. It is a well-known fact that the establishment of the British colonial rule led to a process of 'de-urbanization' of the region when a large proportion of those employed in the local craft economy were rendered unemployed with the decline of many urban centres in the region thanks to the policies of the British colonial rulers. This process was also described as the 'de-industrialization' of the region by some scholars, most famously by D. R. Gadgil.[8]

However, when the British colonizers began to write about India, for themselves and for those at home in Britain, they presented a simple and singular view of the region as being a land of small rural settlements, 'village republics', which they insisted had been a fact of life since time immemorial. Beginning with the early nineteenth century, writing about the Indian village almost became a fashion among colonial administrators. Thomas Munro was perhaps the first to invoke the idea of the village republic. In a report he prepared on India in 1809, called the *Fifth Report from the Select Committee on the Affairs of the East Indian Company*, he underlined the indifference of rural residents to what happened outside its boundaries. 'The inhabitants gave themselves no trouble about the breaking up and division of kingdoms; while the village remains entire, they care not what power it is transferred or to what sovereign it devolves, its internal economy remains unchanged'.[9] However, the most popular and influential representation of this view, which also affirmed Munro's claim, was presented by Sir Charles Metcalfe in the early 1830s through the following passage:

> The village communities are little republics, having nearly everything that they want within themselves, and almost independent of any foreign relations. They seem to last where nothing else lasts. Dynasty after dynasty tumbles down; revolution succeeds to revolution...but the village communities remain the same. In times of trouble, they arm and fortify themselves: a hostile army passes through the country: the village communities collect their cattle within their walls and let the enemy pass unprovoked.
>
> If plunder and devastation...be irresistible, they flee to friendly villages at a distance; but when the storm has passed over, they return and resume their occupations.[10]

He goes on to provide a judgement about the Indian societies, its presumed inability to change and progress, through his description of the nature or qualities of its village life.

> This union of village communities, each one forming a separate state in itself, has, I conceive, contributed more than any other cause to the preservation of the people of India.[11]

These writings were widely circulated in the English-speaking world and the view that India was a land of ever-present and never-changing villages became so influential in Western Europe that almost everyone accepted it as an empirically true depiction of the social and economic realities of the region. Even someone like Karl Marx, who laid stress on empirical history and facts, echoed Metcalfe's depiction of the Indian village when he wrote: 'The simplicity of the organisation for production in these self-sufficing communities that constantly reproduce themselves in the same form and, when accidentally destroyed, spring up again on the spot and with the same name....'[12]

This was in no way an accurate depiction of the prevailing situation. Why did they, almost unanimously, present such a view? Bernard Cohn provides a very compelling argument to explain this. The British colonizers, he argues, did not simply occupy territories by defeating the existing rulers in the region, they also produced arguments and 'theories' to justify their colonization of India to themselves and to their fellow citizens back home. The idea of the Indian village, as they framed it, was also useful for confirming the evolutionary view of the world. The Indian village was what Europe or Britain would have been in the past time. While Britain had moved on, along the path of modernity, India was still stuck in its past and the typical Indian village represented a pre-modern traditional society with a set of attributes that should undergo a near complete change with the onset of modernization.

Such a view not only worked well for the traditional–modern binary, which was to be later invoked in the above discussed theories of social change (modernization) and economic growth (development), but also presented British colonization as desirable.[13] These theories were also used to 'educate' the 'native' Indians who studied in the schools and colleges opened by the colonial rulers to train the babus who would assist British rule in India. Many among the English-educated middle classes that emerged under British patronage more or less agreed with the colonial masters about the presumed positive values of India's colonization, of it being good for the welfare and progress of a region which on its own would not have been able to come out of its pre-modern state of irrationality and ignorance. India-born English journalist Joseph Rudyard Kipling had famously popularized this idea through his poem 'The White Man's Burden' (1899).

The idea of 'India being a land of village republics' was thus a construct, produced for a purpose that was more political than empirical or academic. It helped the British rulers to create a ground for their hegemony, implying an acceptance of their rule by those being ruled. Such was the power of this construct that, despite lack of any supportive evidence from the ground, it came to be accepted not only in Britain and much of the Western world but also by educated Indians, including a large section of the Indian nationalists irrespective of their political moorings.

The image of the idyllic Indian village persists even today. The nostalgia of its loss is also a construct which presumes India had a set of qualities in its past which, to begin with, were derived from a construct located in the traditional–modern binary. Such an understanding could perhaps also help us decode 'the loss of the village' narrative. The idealized version of the village that many in the middle class continue to carry in their minds has very little to do with the realities of life on the ground, or the diverse variety of settlements and their ever-changing nature. The wistfulness associated with its loss is as much about the alienation that modern urban life produces, as it is about the village. It is the story of the making of the 'self' of an average urban middle-class Indian, informed and constituted by the colonial hegemonic view of India and its cultures, and which acquired a greater salience during the nationalist struggle. Sections of the Indian middle class and its elite that came to rule over the country after independence have continued to carry the colonial condescension towards the rural.

To a significant degree then the educated middle-class elite, who succeeded the British rulers in 1947, must carry the burden for the persistence of the idea of the idyllic Indian village in independent India. Their uncritical acceptance of the colonial constructs meant that the idea acquired legitimacy and became part of the 'common sense' on India. In the following chapter, I will try to show how these constructs of the village found space in the nationalist discourse through a reading of the prominent ideologues of the movement for India's freedom and social change.

chapter 3

THE VILLAGE AS THE NATION
MAKING OF THE INDIAN COMMON SENSE

The colonial writings on India were not simply a matter of mistaken assumptions or a set of 'fake news', as we understand the notion of misrepresentation in the present-day context. The colonial view evolved over a period of time. It had started to take shape even before the British administrators began to write on the nature of social life in the subcontinent. Its origin lay in the classical orientalist and Indological scholarship on the region. The Indologists and orientalists were a group of scholars spread across the countries of Europe who specialized in the study of classical languages, literatures, and traditions of the non-Western regions and cultures. India had been a source of fascination for Western scholars for a long time. However, their interest in India was not born merely out of a scholarly curiosity.

They began with the assumption that everything about India was different from their own society and culture, as it was unfolding during the nineteenth century. As Ronald Inden has very rightly pointed out, they saw the 'essence' of this difference, and of India, in the institution of caste which, in their view, was founded on a purely religious belief and was practised collectively.[1] It had no grounding in reason or individual choice, which were presumably features of Western cultures. Thus, unlike the West, where rationality was the founding norm, Indian culture was characterized by its opposite, where neither rationality nor politics played any role. According to this view, in the absence of individual agency and political conflict, the caste system and the social life of the Hindu in general had remained unchanged since ancient times. The colonial constructs of India in many ways extended and reinforced the self-aggrandizing view of the Western intellectual of the nineteenth century.

At another level, the emerging ideas of the Enlightenment and modernity also supported a binary view of the world. The world, as per this view, had evolved out of tradition into modernity; from myth to reason; from collective will to individual agency. Modernity, as sociologist Gurminder Bhambra argues, invoked the ideas of rupture and difference. Its advocates underlined that the societies of the modern West had gone through a process of a temporal rupture, a complete break from the agrarian ways of life in the past. The modernist conception of the world simultaneously also equated the agrarian societies of the non-Western world as being similar to the pasts of Western Europe. The difference between the West and the non-West was thus constructed in a manner that the two were viewed as being at different stages of their evolutionary process.[2]

The colonial formulations of India as being a land of village republics that had remained aloof from any kind of politics and outside influence, unchanged for centuries and millennia, were clearly born out of the emerging thinking in the West about non-Western societies and cultures. This paradigm for understanding the past, present, and future of human life also shaped social science theories of society, economy, and politics. They influenced the academia of the times and the emerging political elite, everywhere in the world. These formulations or constructs of the Indian society continue to be influential ways of thinking about social change even today. The Indian nationalist elite was no exception to this. Their views on the differences between 'rural' and 'urban' were clearly drawn from the colonial and modernist imaginations of India and the world. However, as I have mentioned in the earlier chapters, the Indian nationalists also turned these formulations around and made use of them in their own politics and political imaginations of the possible futures of India.

This chapter provides a brief glimpse into the writings of three of the most prominent political thinkers, who shaped the idea of India—Gandhi, Nehru, and Ambedkar—whose views on the village also reflect their visions for the 'free' nation. Their views of the Indian village were not mere political rhetoric invoked to counter the colonial power. They continued to shape state policy and political visions during the post-Independence period as well. In some senses, they are still invoked as sources of authority in popular deliberations on the nature of Indian tradition and its 'essential' qualities. The most influential of them has been Gandhi, whose ideas and ideological views on the 'village' are very widely known. However, as I show below, his views of the village evolved over time and underwent some important shifts.

Gandhi on Village and Village-ism

In a letter written to Jawaharlal Nehru in 1944, Gandhi had emphatically stated, 'For me, India begins and ends in the villages.'[3] This was not the first time that he had made such a pronouncement. Nor was it the last. This had been a line he held for much of his political life. However, he was also not alone in making such an assertion. A large majority of the Indian nationalists, his contemporaries, such as Tagore, Nehru, and even Ambedkar, or those who came later, continued to make such claims. A closer reading of such a preoccupation with the village would also suggest that Gandhi, and others, did not deny the presence of cities or urban settlements, but saw them as being culturally alien to the native life of India. This is strange because this had never been the case. As we have discussed in the previous chapters, towns and cities had been a part of cultures and economies of the region for a very long time. As a matter of fact, Gandhi was himself born in a town, as were Nehru and Tagore. The coastal town of Porbandar, where Gandhi was born and where his ancestors had lived for many generations, was not a colonial city. It has a long history and finds reference even in popular Hindu mythology. Sudama, the poor Brahmin friend of Lord Krishna, is also believed to have hailed from the town of Porbandar.

However, Gandhi continued to underline the value of village in his writings all his life. His advocacy of such a view played an important role in converting the colonial idea of India as a land of villages into a common-sense and popular belief that pre-colonial India was indeed what the British had suggested. As is well known, he was the most ardent and persuasive advocate of the idea of 'the village being the soul of India'. However, his ideas and ideals evolved over time. Even though the village remained at the core of his vision of a free India, as well as in his social and political philosophy, his perception of it also underwent many changes as his engagement with the political process and the nationalist freedom struggle increased. An overview of his writings provides us a useful starting point for this chapter. This chapter will also provide a discussion of other contending views of the village that Gandhi's contemporaries articulated. Their views on the village also reflect their differing perspectives on the nature of India's past and visions for its future.

Early Preoccupations

Gandhi's preoccupation with the village begins with his growing involvement with public life. His invocation of the idea of the Indian village appears to have begun during his days in South Africa. There are at least three different stages in his engagement with the idea of the Indian village. In the first, he invoked it to distinguish Indians from the native black population of South Africa and thereby to establish an equivalence of the Indians living there with those from the 'civilized West', the whites.

In the second phase, he counterposed the social and

cultural universe of the village against 'urban culture' in a binary construct. He identified urban with the colonizing spirit of the modernist West. In doing so, he proposed a critique of Western culture and civilization, which, in his view, had been a source of moral corruption for Indians. Thus, for him, true 'freedom' from British colonialism would require not just 'self-rule' but also a recovery of the 'lost self', the village.

The third phase of his engagement began with his visits to the actually existing villages of India, which proved to be a source of much disappointment. He thus, emphasized on the ways and means of reforming the village. However, this did not imply a shift away from the idea of the village. He continued to see it as an alternative way of living, a utopia, even when he found faults with the actual realities of rural life in the Indian countryside. As we know from historical writings on his evolution as a leader and a thinker, his views on possible alternatives to the western materialist modernity were also shaped by the writings of philosophers like Leo Tolstoy, H. D. Thoreau, and John Ruskin.[4] His views on village as a utopia, as he articulates them during this third phase, seem to also reflect those influences on him.

In the Racial Context of South Africa

It was perhaps in 1894 that Gandhi for the first time invoked the idea of the Indian village in quite a controversial political context. This was in a petition to the white government of South Africa, an 'open letter' written to the members of Legislative Assembly in Durban to demand voting rights for the people of Indian origin at par with the ruling English people. In a petition demanding racial separation of the Indians in South Africa from the native population of the blacks, he had argued that:

> In spite of the Premier's opinion to the contrary...I venture to point out that both the English and the Indians spring from a common stock, called the 'Indo-Aryan'.[5]

The idea of the village, as the British had framed it, was very important to his argument and he invoked it to further corroborate his point and establish equivalence between the Indians in South Africa and those belonging to the ruling white race. This is quite evident in his 'petition to the Natal Assembly', submitted in the same year, where he made reference to Sir Henry Maine's writings on the 'Indian village communities'. He argued that Maine had:

> ...most clearly pointed out that the Indian races have been familiar with representative institutions almost from the time immemorial.... The word *panchayat* is a household word throughout the length and breadth of India, and it means...a council of five elected by the class of the people whom the five belong, for the purpose of managing and controlling the social affairs of the particular caste.[6]

While demanding representation for Indians, Gandhi did not invoke any universal value of human equality. Nor did he refer to any of the popular thinkers of European Enlightenment and their ideas of freedom, fraternity, or equality. Instead, he invoked a kind of view that compared populations belonging to different 'racial stocks' and their differential levels of evolution. The Indians deserved the right to vote not because the idea of representation required universal franchise, but because of their being more evolved than the native black population, a certification of which was provided by a white man from Britain, and thus their eligibility for self-representation. By invoking the notion of the village panchayat and the five elected members as a representative institution, he also affirmed his approval of the hierarchical order of caste, which in his view, had been functioning as a representational channel in the Indian village for a long time.

The Village as 'Swaraj'

Gandhi's move from South Africa to India changed his political context and concerns. Though in some crucial sense his notion of the Indian village remained the same, his engagement with the idea of village became more critical and far more extensive. He also puts this idea to use very differently. An increasing involvement with the movement for independence had changed his political perspective towards the British colonizers. The question of securing voting rights for the Indian people and establishing equivalence with the whites was no longer his agenda. As he began assuming a leadership role in the struggle for independence, he saw himself in a greater oppositional role. The project was now to drive the colonial rulers out of India. The British had used the idea of India as a land of 'village republics' to legitimize their presence in the region. Waging a struggle for independence required the delegitimization of the British rule over India.

Gandhi did not give up on the 'village'. Instead, he turned the politics around it upside down. Gandhi built his narrative using the binary of village and city to produce an anti-colonial ideology. The village, he argued, represented the authentic self of India, its essence. It was simple and pure, self-reliant and self-governing. The modern cities, in contrast, were a colonial imposition. They symbolized domination and colonial plunder. His invocation of the village–city binary also extended to his vision of freedom or independence. Overthrowing of the colonial rule would bring self-rule, but only politically. Real self-rule or *swaraj* could only be achieved by restoring the civilizational strength of India, by a revival of its village communities. 'The uplift of India depended solely on the uplift of the villages'. The growth of big cities, particularly those established by the British, was no sign of progress. They were signs of degeneration, 'the real plague spots of India'.[7] Elsewhere, in a letter addressed to

Lord Ampthill in 1909, he wrote:

> To me the rise of cities like Calcutta and Bombay is a
> matter for sorrow rather than congratulation. India has lost
> in having broken up a part of her village system.[8]

He elaborated it further in *Young India*, the newspaper he edited,
in 1921:

> Our cities are not India. India lives in her seven and a
> half lakhs of villages, and the cities live upon the villages.
> They do not bring their wealth from other countries. The
> city people are brokers and commission agents for the
> big houses of Europe, America and Japan. The cities have
> cooperated with the latter in the bleeding process that has
> gone on for the past two hundred years.[9]

He reiterated this twenty-five years later, in 1946, speaking to
industrial workers on how cities are exploitative settlements,
and a part and parcel of the colonial rule:

> When the British first established themselves firmly in India
> their idea was to build cities where all rich people would
> gravitate and help them in exploiting the countryside.
> These cities were made partially beautiful; services of all
> kind were made available to their inhabitants while the
> millions of villagers were left rotting in hopeless ignorance
> and misery.[10]

He underlined the village–city binary and its significance:

> The village civilisation and the city civilisation are
> totally different things. One depends on machinery and
> industrialisation, the other rests on handicrafts. We have
> given preference to the latter. After all, this industrialisation
> and large-scale production are only of comparatively recent
> growth. We do not know how far it has contributed to our

development and happiness, but we know this much that it has brought in its wake the recent world wars....

Our country was never so unhappy and miserable as it is at present. In the cities people may be getting big profits and good wages, but all that has become possible by sucking the blood of villagers.[11]

The city, for him, was also an immoral place from where rural folk picked up vices. Writing in another article he published in *Young India* in 1927, he pontificated:

Some of the villages are deserted for six or eight months during the year. Villagers go to Bombay, work under unhealthy and often immoral conditions, then return to their villages during the rainy season bringing with them corruption, drunkenness and disease.[12]

Celebration of village life was perhaps also a strategic move for him, to shift the self-imagination of the nascent Indian nation away from the site of its birth, the urban middle class and elite preoccupation, to the common people, the peasants and artisans living in the hinterlands. Ainslie Embree is perhaps right when he argues that such a move by Gandhi was also meant to give the masses of India 'a sense of involvement in the nation's destiny'.[13]

Until Gandhi arrived on the scene, the nationalist movement had largely been an urban phenomenon. 'For the early nationalist generations, independence meant being free to emulate colonial city life.'[14] By foregrounding the village as India, Gandhi managed to turn this view upside down. The nationalist leaders, who had nearly all been urban elite and who had acquired their political imagination either while studying in England or while working in the cities of Bombay, Calcutta, or Madras were no longer the sole torchbearers of the fight for independence. By arguing for the village as the site of 'India's soul', Gandhi was perhaps also asking for empathy for the poor masses and creating a space for them that was built on their legitimate claim and not simply born out of elite patronage.

As is evident from the discussion above, for Gandhi, the Indian village was not simply a place or a type of settlement; it also had a moral value, a design, a view of human life, which had the potential of providing an alternative to the technology-driven view of life of the Western city. He continued to invoke the text of the colonial scholar, Sir Henry Maine, while speaking for the village. Even as late as 1939, he wrote in *Harijan* that:

> ...Indian society was at one time unknowingly constituted on a non-violent basis. The home life, i.e., the village, was undisturbed by the periodical visitations from barbarous hordes. Maine has shown that India's villages were a congeries of republics.[15]

Reforming and Recovering the Self

Gandhi blamed the colonial rule and its policies for impairing the rural settlements, making them less creative and more dependent on the outside world. As he writes, 'the villager of today is not even half so intelligent or resourceful as the villager of fifty years ago.'[16] However, everything had not been lost. The spirit of the village could still be seen on ground, in the interior. He, for example, told a group of foreign visitors that if they truly wanted to 'see the heart of India', they ought to 'ignore big cities' as they were but poor editions of their big cities and

> Go thirty miles from the railway line, and you will see that the people show a kind of culture which you miss in the West...you will find culture which is unmistakable but far different from that of the West. Then you will take away something that may be worth taking.[17]

Gandhi's advocacy of the village was not to celebrate traditionalism; his was a plea for a kind of equality whereby the village is not treated as an inferior place. The village deserved a kind of autonomy, if India was to claim to be an independent nation:

> The cry of 'back to the village', some critics say, is putting back the hands of the clock of progress. But is it so? Is it going back to the village, or rendering back to it what belongs to it? I am not asking the city-dwellers to go to and live in the villages. But I am asking them to render unto the villagers what is due to them.[18]

He found many flaws in the actually existing villages and did not see all of their ills being a result of colonial rule or urban influence. The two things that he vehemently campaigned against, and saw as stemming from native culture, were the practice of untouchability and a near absence of a general sense of cleanliness. Compared to the cities, where people were 'educated and broad-minded to a little extent at least', untouchability was a more serious problem in the villages, which were 'the centres of orthodoxy'.[19]

Not only did he ask the dominant communities of the village to give up the practice of untouchability, he also called upon those from the so-called untouchable castes to keep themselves clean, 'refrain from eating meat of dead animals and from drinking, send their children to schools, remove untouchability among themselves and generally carry on such reforms from within as is possible'.[20]

The problem of lack of hygiene was not confined to the untouchable castes. He was often disappointed by the disregard for cleanliness among the villagers in general:

> If we approach any village, the first thing we encounter is the dunghill and this is usually placed on raised ground. On entering the village, we find little difference between the approach and what is within the village. Here too

there is dirt on the roads.... If a traveller who is unfamiliar with these parts comes across this state of affairs, he will not be able to differentiate between the dunghill and the residential parts. As a matter of fact, there is not much of a difference between the two.[21]

In another piece, he praised the Europeans in Africa as being worthy of imitation:

There is no gainsaying the fact that our villager betrays a woeful ignorance of even the rudiments of village sanitation. One could deplore the race prejudice amongst the South African Europeans, but their attempts to keep their towns healthy and sanitary were heroic and worthy of imitation.[22]

Gandhi was keen on reviving aspects of traditional rural economy, particularly its 'defunct handicrafts', which could save the peasant from the ills of industrialization and the inevitability of moving to the cities.[23] However, he was also a reformist and asked for its 're-construction':

My idea of village swaraj is that it is completely republic, independent of its neighbours for its own vital wants, and yet interdependent for many others in which dependence is a necessity. Thus, every villager's first concern will be to grow its own food crops and cotton for its cloth.... Then if there is more land available, it will grow useful money crops, thus excluding ganja, tobacco, opium and the like.... Education will be compulsory up to the final basic course. As far as possible every activity will be conducted on the cooperative basis. There will be no castes such as we have today with their graded untouchability.... The government of the village will be conducted by a panchayat of five persons annually elected by the adult villagers, male and female, possessing minimum prescribed qualifications....[24]

For him, it was only in 'the simplicity of village' that a non-violent society could be imagined and realized. Given the size of India's population, Western-style urbanization would simply not be viable. 'Crores of people would never be able to live in peace with each other in towns'. However, 'simplicity' did not mean a complete disregard of modern science and modern means of communication. He also did not ask for a destruction of the existing urban centres. What he asked for was 'considerable revision' in their lifestyles, if the living standard of those living in the villages had to be improved.[25] Village, thus, becomes a utopia, an imaginary community, possessing all those qualities that are desirable for a nearly perfect living, collectively.

Though India's ruling elite have hardly taken his prescription seriously, Gandhi's ideas survive across a range of people. As the rural–urban inequalities grow, with the urban middle-class elite becoming increasingly hegemonic, and rural/agrarian India experiences further marginalization, Gandhi's views provide a useful intellectual resource for those who demand a more equitable growth.

His writings on the village offer a vision on the impending crises of ecology and environment and suggest alternative possibilities of development. India's growing urban mess, with increasing numbers of migrants arriving from rural areas as the sources of livelihood shrink in India's agrarian economy, make his suggestions all the more pertinent. However, his ideas have also been widely criticized. Many of his contemporaries, including those who worked with him, disagreed with him. The two most influential of these individuals are Jawaharlal Nehru and B. R. Ambedkar, whose views I present below.

Nehru the Modernist

Jawaharlal Nehru has perhaps been the most important and influential leader of India's nationalist movement after Gandhi.

While he was one of Gandhi's loyal lieutenants until the latter's death in 1948 and agreed with him on most issues of national importance, Nehru's views and visions for the village, its past and future, significantly differed from those of Gandhi.

Most importantly perhaps, Nehru did not believe that in the 'village' lay the future of India, and he rarely ever identified himself with village life, or saw it as being morally superior to the city. This fact is important to emphasize because he was independent India's first prime minister. He was the catalyst of development planning and played a critical role in shaping its policies, including those of rural development and agrarian change. As with Gandhi, Nehru's writings too can be classified into distinct categories. Firstly, for him too, the idea of village is quite central to his notion of pre-colonial or traditional India, most of which draws from his readings of Western and colonial writings on the region. Secondly, his view of the Indian village also undergoes a change as he encounters 'the actually existing villages'. However, his prognosis of the ills caused by colonial rule differ significantly from those of Gandhi.

The Bourgeois Nehru

Nehru had little hesitation in admitting that until around 1920, his 'political outlook' had been that of his class, 'entirely bourgeois'.[26] It was only when he started his political career and came in direct contact with the common rural masses that he began to think differently. It was 'a new picture of India...naked, starving, crushed, and utterly miserable'.[27] Over the years he articulated his own understanding of history and specificities of Indian society and culture. They are perhaps best spelt out in his most famous book, *The Discovery of India* (first published in 1946).

Having been educated in Britain, he took the Eurocentric ideas of evolution and modernity as facts of life or modes of scientific thinking. The village was easily placed with other things that had presumably been features of traditional social arrangement in pre-modern societies everywhere. 'The autonomous village community, caste and the joint family', that he identified as the three basic concepts of the 'old Indian social structure', had something in common with traditional societies in general as the organizing principles were the same everywhere:

> In all these three it is the group that counts; the individual has a secondary place. There is nothing very unique about all this separately, and it is easy to find something equivalent to any of these three in other countries, especially in medieval times.[28]

He further elaborates his 'functionalist' and Eurocentric view of an integrated social order of the traditionalist village society:

> ...The functions of each group or caste were related to functions of the other castes, and the idea was that if each group functioned successfully within its own framework, then society as a whole worked harmoniously. Over and above this, a strong and fairly successful attempt was made to create a common national bond which would hold all these groups together—the sense of a common culture, common traditions, common heroes and saints, and common land to the four corners of which people went on pilgrimage. This national bond was of course very different from present-day nationalism; it was weak politically, but socially and culturally it was strong.[29]

Though Nehru did not celebrate the old 'village republics' of India as Gandhi did, the sources of their understanding of the pasts of the region were largely common—writings of colonial administrators and the Western scholars on India's past—and both accepted them uncritically.

> Originally the agrarian system was based on a cooperative or collective village. Individuals and families had certain

rights as well as certain obligations, both of which were determined and protected by customary law.[30]

He quotes, almost verbatim, what Metcalfe and later Marx said about the stability and autonomy of village life:

> Foreign conquests brought war and destruction, revolts and their ruthless suppression, and new ruling classes relying chiefly on armed force.... The self-governing community, however, continued. Its break up began only under the British rule.[31]

He continues to argue that the traditional values emphasized 'the duties of the individual and the group' and not 'their rights'.

> The aim was social security: stability and continuance of the group; that is of society. Progress was not the aim, and progress therefore had to suffer. Within each group, whether it was the village community, the particular caste, or the large joint family, there was a communal life shared together, a sense of equality, and democratic methods.[32]

Quite like Gandhi, he believed that the idealized village had degenerated, with various ills becoming common practice; rigid hierarchies of caste was one of them.

> ...the ultimate weakness and failing of the caste system and the Indian social structure were that they degraded a mass of human beings and gave them no opportunities to get out of that condition—educationally, culturally, or economically.... In the context of society today, the caste system and much that goes with it are wholly incompatible, reactionary, restrictive, and barriers to progress. There can be no equality in status and opportunity within its framework, nor can there be political democracy, and much less, economic democracy.[33]

Beyond the Harmony of Caste and Community, the Kisans and Landlords

Unlike Gandhi, Nehru saw no virtues in reviving the traditional social structure, as the colonial and orientalist writings had presumably visualized or constructed it. The solution to the problem of caste, for him, lay in moving forward, towards a democratic and modern social order. As he travelled through the rural hinterlands, he was pained by the existing class disparities and the exploitative social order they produced. He often referred to the poverty and misery of peasants/kisans and the exploitative character of landlords. He described the landlords as a 'physically and intellectually degenerate' class, which had 'outlived their day'[34] and to 'the kisans, in the villages'[35] as constituting the real masses of India. Describing his first-hand experience of working with kisans, he writes:

> I listened to their innumerable tales of sorrow, their crushing and ever-growing burden of rent, illegal extraction, ejectments from land and mud hut, beatings; surrounded on all sides by vultures who preyed on them—zamindar's agents, moneylenders, police; toiling all day to find that what they produced was not theirs and their reward was kicks and curses and a hungry stomach.[36]

Landlordism had close ties with the colonial rule. The British rule had disturbed the old economic equilibrium of the village and implanted in its place the landlord system 'with disastrous results'.[37] It destroyed the local industry, the non-agricultural sources of employment:

> The Indian farmer who used to supplement his income by plying the *charkha* in his spare time was also suddenly deprived of his extra income. Weavers, carders and dyers became unemployed. They were forced to fall back on the land for livelihood, by cultivating the land or by working

as labourers, but there was already enough pressure on the land. The result was that the majority of the people were compelled to act as farm labourers, and somehow keep alive.... And this poverty began from the time the British came here because they started their own trade while destroying ours.[38]

He also felt dismayed at the politically docile and fatalistic nature of the Indian peasant, who, he believed:

...has an amazing capacity to bear famine, flood, disease, and continuous grinding poverty—and when he could endure it no longer; he would quietly and almost uncomplainingly lie down in his thousands or millions and die. That was his way of escape.[39]

Development Planning and India's Rural Futures

Nehru seemed to agree with Gandhi on the nature of traditional Indian village society and that the British colonial rule was responsible for disturbing its 'equilibrium'. However, his critique of the actually existing village lives was very different from that of Gandhi. He had no love for caste and found the 'class question' to be the primary issue that needed correction. While Gandhi spoke of the village as a community and advocated the need for its restoration, Nehru pointed to its irreconcilable class contradictions. While Gandhi desired a revival of the village community and a resolution of the class question through a spirit of trusteeship, Nehru advocated its social transformation through agrarian reforms and an economic change using modern technology.

The landlords were not to be 'trusted' but disenfranchized in free India. The kisans, the real 'masses of India', were being exploited and oppressed not only by the colonial state but also by the local landlords. Their difficulties 'in the main related to such questions as rent, ejectment and possession of lands'. 'Swaraj would be of little avail if it did not solve' the problems of the kisans, Nehru believed.[40] The Land Reforms introduced soon after Independence were a direct translation of such thinking. If agriculture was to develop, it was necessary that we put 'an end to *zamindari* and *jagirdari* systems. We must...eliminate all intermediaries and fix a limit for the size of holdings'.[41]

Nehru also disagreed with Gandhi on the value of modern industry and migrations of rural residents to cities. He had no desire to bring the presumed self-sufficient and autonomous village back. Industrial development and urbanization would be required for the building of a modern country, an integrated national economy. Addressing the Associated Chamber of Commerce in Calcutta in December 1947, he had said:

> ...while we want to help the peasants and agriculturalists, industry also is of dominant importance in India. Agriculture can produce wealth but it will produce more wealth (if) more people are drawn from agriculture and put in industry. In fact, in order to improve agriculture, we must improve industry (sic). The two are allied.[42]

The only point of his agreement with Gandhi was the need for a revival of rural handicrafts and cottage industry. However, for Nehru, this was to be more for pragmatic economic reasons and not for a cultural revival of the traditional craft. He did not believe modern industry would be able to employ all the surplus rural population and an increasing use of technology was bound to release labour from agriculture. Thus, in India, the need was to encourage 'the village and cottage industry in a big way'.[43] Though 'the village could no longer be a self-contained economic unit...but it could very well be a governmental and electoral unit, each such unit functioning as a self-governing community within the larger political framework and looking after the essential needs of the village.... I feel sure that the village should be treated as a unit. This will give truer and more responsible representation.'[44]

Thus, despite their differences on the possible futures of India's village, Nehru was not untouched by the influence of Gandhi. Or, perhaps, he was trying to accommodate the Gandhian world view by bringing it into the policy domain. As we have seen in the discussion above, despite his modernist outlook to nation building, Nehru did carry a positive view of the pre-colonial village community as had been presented by the colonial and orientalist writers.

It was left to B. R. Ambedkar to develop a critique of the idea of the 'village community', invoking his own personal experiences of caste hierarchy as an 'untouchable' himself.

Ambedkar, the 'Anti-village' Advocate

Gandhi and Nehru were the most prominent leaders of India's freedom movement. They also shaped the popular imaginations of the emerging nation, of its pasts and its possible futures. Though the core of their audience was the emerging urban middle class, their influence went far beyond. They emerged as the icons for a cross-section of Indian society and the post-Independence state system of India. While Nehru became the prime minister of the country and remained in the chair until his death, Gandhi too occupied an important symbolic space in the life of the new nation. His picture continues to appear on Indian currency notes. Their views of the village have also been critical in shaping policies and programmes of development and representation.

Perhaps the third most important leader who played a critical role in the making of modern India is B. R. Ambedkar. Though he was not a part of the Indian National Congress, he took up the task of drafting the Indian Constitution, helping the Constituent Assembly put together its proposals and also influencing it through his knowledge of law, as it had come to be practised in the democratic countries of the West. He was perhaps the most educated member of the Constituent Assembly, with two doctorates from two of the most prominent institutions of higher learning in the modern Western world— Columbia University and the London School of Economics. He was thus trained not only to practise law at the bar but also equipped with the skills of a social science researcher.

His vision of India, the social composition of its settlements (villages, towns, and cities), and possible pathways to take it forward on the road to becoming a modern democratic society were also shaped by his own experience, as a scholar and as a 'victim' of the prevailing order of caste. Over the years after his death, he has consistently grown in stature. As Eleanor Zelliot points out, he is perhaps the only pre-Independence leader who has continued to grow in fame and influence throughout the contemporary period.[45]

Village as the Den of Untouchability

Despite his exceptional educational accomplishments, Ambedkar was not allowed to forget his social background, his belonging to an untouchable caste. And despite his equally monumental contribution to the making of the Indian Constitution, he remains a leader with a specific caste identity, popularly viewed as a champion of Dalit rights. He indeed fought for their rights all his life, but his writings also provide a sociological perspective on the Indian society: on village life, caste, gender, law, and many other subjects.

Much like Gandhi and Nehru, Ambedkar too was born in an urban setting, in the cantonment town of Mhow in present-day Madhya Pradesh. His family too had been urban and hailed from Ambadawe, a town in the Ratnagiri district of Maharashtra. His father was employed with the colonial army and had earned the rank of subedar. However, despite having all the credentials that set him outside the rural order of caste, he had to frequently experience humiliation owing to his caste identity. These experiences significantly influenced his understanding of village life. The village, for him, was 'the working plant of the Hindu social order' where one could observe 'the Hindu social order in operation in full swing'.[46] Far from being a harmonious community, the village for him was a divided universe and caste was its basis:

> The Hindu society insists on segregation of the untouchables. The Hindu will not live in the quarters of the untouchables and will not allow the untouchables to live inside Hindu quarters.... It is not a case of social separation, a mere stoppage of social intercourse for a temporary period. It is a case of territorial segregation and of a cordon sanitaire putting the impure people inside the barbed wire into a sort of a cage. Every Hindu village has a ghetto. The Hindus live in the village and the untouchables live in the ghetto.[47]

The divisions that marked a typical village were not hard to see: it was divided into two sets of populations: the 'touchable' groups and the 'untouchable' groups. The touchables formed, what he called, 'the major community' and the untouchables 'a minor community'. The former lived inside the village and the latter were made to live outside the village in separate quarters.

> The touchables were economically the dominant community and commanded power; the untouchables were a 'dependent community' and a 'subject race of hereditary bondsmen'. The untouchables lived according to the codes laid down for them by the dominant 'touchable' major community. These codes laid guidelines regarding their habitations; the distance they ought to maintain from the 'Hindus'; the dress they should wear; the houses they

should live in; the language they should speak; the names they should keep. They could not build houses having tiled roofs; they could not wear silver or gold jewellery.[48]

Like Gandhi and Nehru, Ambedkar too wrote extensively on different aspects of Indian society and the colonial rule. The social structure of the village and caste appear very frequently in his writings. However, some of his arguments were best crystallized during the debates in the Constituent Assembly where some 'Hindu members' had passionately argued in favour of making the village an autonomous administrative unit with its own legislature, executive, and judiciary. Ambedkar had vehemently opposed such a move:

> I hold that these village republics have been the ruination of India.... What is the village but a sink of localism, a den of ignorance, narrow-mindedness and communalism?[49]

Such a recognition of the village as a unit of the legal structure of India would have been 'a great calamity' for those who lived on its periphery, the untouchables, he argued.[50]

While Gandhi and Nehru had accepted the colonial construct of 'village community' as a reality of India's past, Ambedkar looked at it more critically. Given his training in the social sciences, he was able to locate the source of this construct in the orientalist narratives of India. He also provided a sociological explanation for its uncritical acceptance by the middle-class elite of India. 'The average Hindu was always in ecstasy whenever he spoke of the Indian village. He regarded it as an ideal form of social organisation to which he believed there was no parallel anywhere in the world.' [51]

However, the 'realistic picture' of village life was very different. The so-called village community was nowhere close to being democratic. Life in the village was marked by cultures of exclusion, denials, and discrimination. 'When the whole village community was engaged in celebrating a general festivity such as Holi or Dasara, the untouchables must perform all menial acts which were preliminary to the main observance. These duties had to be performed without remuneration.'[52]

The Republic of Untouchability

Ambedkar underlined that besides their complete domination, the untouchables were also exploited and oppressed by the upper castes. They were not allowed to acquire wealth in the form of land or cattle; they could not practise agriculture. Even as labourers they could not demand reasonable wages and had to submit to the rates fixed or suffer violence.[53] They lived a life that was full of humiliation and dependency. There was only one source of livelihood open to them. It was 'the right to beg food from the Hindu farmers of the village. A large majority of the untouchables in the village were either servants or landless labourers. As village servants, they depended on the Hindus for their maintenance, and had to go from door to door every day and collect bread or cooked food from the Hindus in return for certain customary services rendered by them to the Hindus.'[54]

> This is the village republic of which the Hindus are so proud. What is the position of the untouchables in this Republic? They are not merely the last but are also the least.... (I)n this Republic there is no place for democracy. There is no room for equality. There is no room for liberty and there is no room for fraternity. The Indian village is a very negation of Republic. The Republic is an Empire of the Hindus over the untouchables. It is a kind of colonialism of the Hindus designed to exploit the untouchables. The untouchables have no rights.... They have no rights because they are outside the village republic and because they are outside the so-called village republic, they are outside the Hindu fold.[55]

Ambedkar extended his view of the village to his perspective on Indian society. Beginning with the village, he asserted that this culture of caste domination prevailed all over. 'From the capital of India down to the village level the whole administration is rigged by the Hindus. The Hindus are like the omnipotent almighty pervading all over the administration in all its branches having its authority in all its nooks and corners.'[56]

Ambedkar also rejected the popular anthropological theories of caste that highlighted the ideological unity of the Hindu society and claimed that the untouchables too subscribed to ideas of purity and pollution. There was no such cultural consensus or a willing acceptance of the hierarchical order.

> The four varnas were animated by nothing but a spirit of animosity towards one another. There would not be slightest exaggeration to say that the social history of the Hindus is not merely of class struggle but class war fought with such bitterness that even the Marxists will find it difficult to cite parallel cases to match.... It seems that the first class-struggle took place between the Brahmins, Kshatriyas and Vaishyas on the one hand and the Shudras on the other.[57]

Ambedkar, thus, had no great appreciation for the village. The ground realities of the actually existing villages were well understood by him and became a source of his critique of the undemocratic spirit of Indian society. The village, for him, was a 'model' of the Hindu society, a microcosm of the Hindu social order, marked by hierarchies of caste and a culture of exclusion and discrimination, best reflected in caste-based spatial divisions within the rural settlements.

Making of the National Common Sense

Thus, despite their different trajectories, Gandhi, Nehru and Ambedkar all began with the same construct of the Indian village. Each saw the Indian village essentially as a Hindu village, composed of caste groupings and marked by differences and inequalities. While Nehru foregrounded the realities of class, Ambedkar pointed to the divisions of caste. Gandhi recognized the presence of both caste as well as class. And while he acknowledged that these differences and inequalities were undesirable, he firmly believed that the collective spirit of the traditional community had the potential of overcoming them. He did not principally oppose the idea of caste-based divisions, but considered the practice of untouchability as unacceptable, and needing reform.

Similarly, class divisions within the village could be overcome through trusteeship. Both Gandhi and Nehru were in favour of preserving the village, albeit in a reformed version. Nehru was keen on modernizing its agriculture through technology and a redistribution of land, while Gandhi believed in a completely different paradigm of life, which was not driven by a desire for endless consumption. Village life, for him, was also a morally superior way of living, in which lay an alternative to capitalist modernity.

Ambedkar differed with both of them on a fundamental level. He had no sympathy for village life. Unlike Gandhi and Nehru, he did not accept the colonial view of the village community as a historical account of India's past. For him, it was an orientalist construct. The actually existing village had no community spirit. On the contrary, it was a site of caste-based oppression, exclusion, and exploitation.

Not only was there no place for Dalits to live in the village with dignity, the so-called spirit of village community was also antithetical to democracy. The Indian villages, thus, needed a radical transformation. For his fellow Dalits, his prescription was to abandon the village, and to move to towns and cities. Not that caste was absent there, but it was perhaps easier to escape it in the city than it was in the village.

Together, the writings and reflections of Gandhi, Nehru, and Ambedkar also became a source of popular common sense about the nature of Indian society and its pasts. Notwithstanding their differences, there are many ways in which the three seem to agree. They all spoke about the village in civilizational terms. The Indian village had a pan-Indian character, with no regional variations, of caste, community, or ecology. Villages of Punjab or Bengal were viewed as similar to those of Kerala or Kashmir. They also showed no awareness of the significant regional differences in the nature of caste hierarchies, or their dynamics across different religious and regional communities. They, thus, accepted the orientalist and colonial view that the village was the core of India and that it was the social universe of the Hindus. None of them made any reference to a Muslim or Sikh or tribal village in colonial India. By giving such credence to the orientalist view of India's past, they not only shaped the popular imaginations of the emerging urban middle classes but also of the social sciences.

Nevertheless, it should be remembered that though orientalist/colonial categories such as 'village' provided them with conceptual resources, these categories did not completely limit/determine their politics and world views. Their substantive notions of empirical reality were shaped by a multitude of factors, and the effects of their uses of such categories varied significantly. They were all unhappy with the existing state of affairs in the Indian village but had different prescriptions about the nature and modes of change required. Their ideas and visions for rural futures also shaped independent India's policies for social change and rural development, a subject I discuss in a later chapter of the book.

chapter 4

THE ACTUALLY EXISTING VILLAGES
HISTORY AND ETHNOGRAPHY

As was described in the previous chapters, the colonial construct of the Indian village had its uses for British rule in India. The Indian nationalist leaders too found the colonial framing of village useful, turning it around to claim cultural unity of India. If the Indian village had been a distinct reality across the subcontinent, it was proof enough of the oneness of India despite diversities of region, faith, and language. Their appropriation of the colonial view of village also made their narrative a part of the national common sense among the emerging middle-class elite. The popular constructs, however, have very little to do with the past and present-day realities of the Indian rural life, 'the actually existing villages'.

By now, we have a fairly good amount of historical and social anthropological research writings that provide us a clearer idea of the realities of village life in the subcontinent. They go far back in time and tell us how rural society and agrarian economy evolved in different parts of present-day India and how the country changed over time. They highlight diversities and fluidities of the rural landscapes across the subcontinent. They also tell us how the British colonial policies changed rural lives and social relations in quite a fundamental way. These popular/colonial ideas have even played a role in shaping state policies concerning rural society and economy, during the colonial period and after Independence.

Social scientists have been carrying out surveys and ethnographic studies of village life since the early decades of the twentieth century. A good number of social anthropologists carried out intensive ethnographic studies of Indian villages in different parts of the country during the 1950s and 1960s, soon after India's independence from colonial rule. Some economists and social anthropologists have even revisited a specific village or a set of villages, studied in the past by themselves or by others in their profession, and used similar tools as the ones used earlier to develop a temporal understanding of the changes that have taken place in the villages' social and economic life over time. This chapter is an attempt to provide a brief overview of the actually existing realities of village life, as we can discern from such research.

As discussed in the previous chapters, colonial writings depicted India's villages as self-sufficient communities which had stayed stable and stagnant since ancient times, enclosed within themselves and free from any influence of the happenings in the outside world. They were assumed to be simple communities with no sense of private property or internal differentiation of class, which presumably also kept them free from any kind of social conflict. Nineteenth century Western scholars such as Sir Henry Maine and Karl Marx took the colonial descriptions of Indian village as authentic accounts of the prevailing empirical realities of the region, assuming them to be a peculiar type of human condition, closer to the primitive state of being, and stuck in time. They were then presented as epitomes of a traditional social order, and the backward human condition.

They, thus, went on to commend the British rulers of India for their policies that were helping to disintegrate Indian villages, their sense of equilibrium, and thereby enabling them to move on the path of 'progress'. Such a view found currency even among the English-educated middle-class Indians and the later-day nationalist leaders. Even though they knew about the complicated nature of rural realities, saw how British rule had been a cause of their ruination, and demanded the ouster of colonial rulers, nevertheless, they accepted many presumptions of the colonial view of the 'rural' and of the larger Indian society, and agreed with the dire need for reform through development and modernization.

The colonial formulations of the Indian village were not based on any kind of empirical surveys or a reading of local histories or even direct observations of rural lives. They were mostly drawn from orientalist imaginations and their readings of select textual sources, mostly accessed through the local Brahmin elite. The view of the village they presented was not only a simplified version of the complex and diverse reality, but was also motivated to provide a justification for the colonial conquest of the region, suggesting that it was for the good of India. However, in reality, their primary concern in extending the Company's rule, and later British government rule, was to extract land revenue from cultivators.

The later historians of the region, through their arduous empirical work have clearly shown that the ideas propagated by the colonial rulers about the nature of pre-colonial rural and agrarian realities were completely unfounded.[1] Rural realities of the subcontinent were ecologically and socially diverse. They were also quite fluid, and far from stagnant. Recent historical research on the pre-colonial pasts of India have thus provided enough evidence for a comprehensive rejection of the colonial view of the Indian village.[2]

The assumption that there existed no notion of private property on land or that it was owned communally by the village community has been unanimously abandoned by historians. Though land was rarely bought and sold in the market, rights over it were clearly marked and transferred according to prevailing customs. The customary rights varied across region and often depended on the caste status and occupational identity of households. Similarly, historians of rural India have also shown that there existed a wide variety of rural settlements across the subcontinent. They were all integrated in the regional political economies and had active interaction with the outside world. Further, historians also agree that rural society was well-stratified much before the British established their rule in the region. Writing on northern India of the Mughal period, Irfan Habib, a well-known historian of medieval India says:

> ...economic differentiation had progressed considerably among the peasantry. There were large cultivators, using hired labour, and raising crops for the market, and there were small peasants, who could barely produce food grains for their own subsistence. Beyond this differentiation among the peasantry, there was the still sharper division between the caste peasantry and the 'menial'.[3]

Another historian of South India highlights in her work the presence of a sizeable population of landless agricultural labourers, who invariably all belonged to some specific caste groups, ranked lower down in the local hierarchy.[4] Additionally, pre-colonial villages were not isolated. They were linked to the central authority through revenue bureaucracy. The primary source of income for rulers of the time would have been the taxes they collected from cultivators, for which they created specialized classes, some of whom were part of the village. Pre-colonial rural and agrarian life was also not free from conflicts and tensions. Even though we do not have evidence of any widespread peasant revolts, there were cases of unrest in conditions of excessive oppression by the ruling establishment. A more frequent response to situations where the demand for taxes became unbearable was for the peasants to flee en masse to other territories where conditions were more favourable for land cultivation.[5]

More importantly, rural life and agrarian economy was dynamic in nature, constantly changing. Writing on the fourteenth and fifteenth century history of the region, historian David Ludden presents a very vivid account of this dynamism:

In the fourteenth century, South Asia became a region of travel and transport connecting Central Asia and the Indian Ocean. This redefined the location of all its agrarian territories.... New technology, ideas, habits, languages, people and needs came into farming communities. New elements entered local cuisine. People produced new powers of command, accumulation, and control, focused on strategic urban sites in agrarian space. By 1600, ships sailed between China, Gujarat, Europe, and America.... A long expansion in world connections occurred during centuries when a visible increase in farming intensity was also reshaping agrarian South Asia.... Regional formations of agrarian territory came into being, sewn together by urban networks....[6]

He goes on to show how certain communities moved across regions, bringing about significant change in the agrarian economies and their social composition. Speaking about the present northwest of India, he writes how the drying up of the Saraswati River forced the Jat farmers of the Rajasthan region to move 'into the upper Punjab doabs and into the western Ganga basin in the first half of the second millennium'.[7]

All these trends combined to open new agricultural territories from Panipat to Sialkot along very old trade routes running from Kabul to Agra. By the sixteenth century, Jalandhar and Lahore were thriving towns surrounded by lush farmland. Wheat lands expanded west of the Ganga and in Punjab doabs astride trade routes and around old trading towns where distinctively urban commercial and administrative groups were already prominent.... As farmland expanded in spaces between the plains and high mountains, new opportunities for trade arose at ecological boundaries, and this stimulated more commercially oriented production and processing. By the sixteenth century, tobacco, sugarcane, honey, fruits, vegetables, and melons fed Punjab commercial life, along with profits from sericulture, indigo, and all the elements of cloth manufacturing.[8]

Besides the north-western region, he shows other similar trajectories of increasing regional integration and growing trade in agrarian commodities with far-off lands. Contesting the popular colonial formulations of the autonomous and self-contained idea of village life, David Ludden describes how there existed a close relationship between the domain of agriculture with the dynamics of urban life in every region:

> The economic simplicity of the pre-modern countryside is largely a fiction of modern urbanites. We get a more accurate picture if we imagine many localities with urban economic, social, and cultural characteristics strung together by networks of mobility to form urban agglomerations of various sizes. Urbanism lay inside agriculture rather than being set apart and its internal transport system moved at a walk or a boat's pace.... Its manufacturing was closely connected with agriculture....[9]

However, the establishment of British rule during the second half of the eighteenth century did produce many far-reaching changes in the rural landscape and its agrarian economies, although very different from the professed objectives of their 'civilizing mission'.

The Colonial Assault: British Rule and Decline of Agriculture

As indicated above, the primary source of income for rulers in pre-modern times was land revenue, the taxes collected from cultivating peasants. This was not unique to India. Rulers invariably made claim over a share of the farm produce as, in principle, all land belonged to the king. For the common villagers or peasant cultivators, these rulers were all outsiders who lived in towns and cities. The villagers generally interacted with the agents of the rulers, who kept accounts of the cultivating peasants and the volume of land being cultivated by each one of them. Accordingly, they collected taxes from cultivators. Some of these intermediaries could also be from among the villagers.

It was important for the rulers that the peasants continued with their tasks so that taxes could be claimed from them. In times of crop failure, due to drought or flood, the rulers tended to be flexible with their tax demands, making it easier for the peasants to survive and to cultivate the next crop. Some of them even showed generosity and provided the hungry peasant with food grains and some form of loans. Others lured peasants from neighbouring kingdoms with such loans and better terms of taxation to expand their agrarian economies.

The British East India Company arrived on the western coast of India to pursue its mercantile interests. However, seeing the fragmentary nature of political power in the region, they also developed colonial ambitions. Robert Clive won the Battle of Plassey on behalf of the British East India Company and established control over a territorial region of the subcontinent as early as 1757, and the British government entered the picture through the Regulating Act of 1773 and the Pitt's India Act of 1784. Yet, it was only in 1849 after conquering Ranjit Singh's Sikh kingdom of Punjab that the British were able to extend their rule over a vast expanse of the subcontinent.

Quite like other rulers, the British too craved land revenue. Given that they had little knowledge of the local agrarian conditions and rural realities, they experimented with a range of land revenue systems, hoping to maximize their tax collections from the Indian cultivators. In the process, they introduced something called the systems of land settlements. Unlike the past rulers, the British worked with their own common sense and their knowledge of British realities. Unable to make sense of the local arrangements, they attempted a formalization of ownership rights over agricultural lands and tax obligations of individual cultivators. Though their intended objective was to make the collection of taxes easier and more effective, the reforms they introduced had many other far-reaching consequences. They created a new sense of individualized property ownership of land, changing the customary relationship that the cultivator had with land to a formal legal relationship, essentially making land a commodity that could be sold and bought in the market.

The first of these major 'reforms' was the Permanent Settlement introduced in the Bengal Presidency in 1793. The new settlement declared the tax collecting officials in the earlier regime, the zamindars, as the owners of the tracts. The local zamindars previously only had the right to collect revenues from tillers of the land. According to the American political sociologist Barrington Moore Jr., besides their intention of simplifying the process of tax collection, the Company rulers also saw in the local zamindars a counterpart of the 'enterprising English landlord', who, they believed, had the capacity to 'establish prosperous cultivation' if provided with secure and permanent ownership rights over land.[10] They perhaps also had a politico-strategic reason for doing so. Giving ownership rights over land to the local zamindars would make them beneficiaries of colonial patronage. This would go a long way in consolidating a loyal support base for the 'foreign rulers' in the local society of Bengal.[11]

However, the new settlement turned out to be a disaster, for almost everyone. For the common peasant, the new system just meant an increased demand for taxes. Introduction of a formalized system of landownership and a growing economic burden also weakened the relations of patronage and loyalty that the zamindars had with the cultivating peasants. Even though peasants had always paid taxes and experienced exploitation, their patron zamindars tended to also show a sense of care and concern for them. Anthropologist James Scott describes this relationship of patronage as the 'moral economy of the peasantry'.[12]

Its disintegration obviously increased the precarity of the common cultivator. Further, contrary to the expectations of the colonial rulers, the landlords showed no sign of entrepreneurship. Instead, they began to see themselves as 'feudal lords', who had the right to a share in the tax collected without having to do any labour or effort for it. They further appointed village level tax collectors and the system soon developed into a kind of 'parasitic landlordism'.[13] By the middle of the nineteenth century the entire area under Permanent Settlement was in a state of crisis. With the growing precarity of the peasant and the parasitic tendencies inherent in the system, agriculture saw a decline, and so did collection of land revenue.

Learning from the Bengal experience, the colonial regime tried different kinds of arrangements in the Madras and Bombay presidencies. Instead of giving formal ownership rights to the intermediary tax collector, they bestowed it on the actual cultivator and landholders, the ryots. This came to be known as the Ryotwari Settlement. The ryot, in theory, was a tenant of the state, responsible for paying tax directly to the state treasury and could not be evicted as long as he paid his revenue. Another variety of land settlement introduced in the United Provinces, Punjab, and the Central Provinces was called the Mahalwari or Malguzari settlement, where the village was identified as the unit of assessment for tax liability. As such the Mahalwari system was not very different from the Ryotwari system. Effective ownership of the cultivated land was vested in the cultivator here as well, but the village paid the revenue collectively. A villager of 'good social standing' was generally given the responsibility of collecting the revenue from individual cultivators and paying the assessment on behalf of the village. Eric Stokes argues that the growing influence of utilitarian philosophy in England during the time was also a factor that produced distaste for landlordism and led to the introduction of these new systems of revenue assessments.[14]

Despite the different settlements, the patterns of change experienced in the land relations were more or less similar in most parts of the empire. While the new settlements changed the formal structures of authority, the colonial policies did not in any way democratize the village or its agrarian economy. On the contrary, their policies strengthened the moneylenders and landlords—relics of a feudal social order. The new land revenue system also forced the peasants to get increasingly involved with the market, even when they did not have the capacity to produce surplus, leading to what came to be known as the commercialization of agriculture. This too, as described below, had disastrous consequences for the common people.

Commercialization of Agriculture

'Commercialization of agriculture' is an expression used to describe two related processes. The first, a shift in the agrarian economy from primarily producing cereals for consumption by the local communities, to an increasing tendency to produce cash crops to be sold in the market. The second, was a process whereby agricultural land itself became a commodity—to be sold and purchased in the market like other commodities.

A Shift in Cropping Patterns

Though production of crops for their sale or exchange in the marketplace was not an entirely new phenomenon for Indian agriculturists, it grew both quantitatively as well as qualitatively during the British rule. As Habib points out, during the Mughal period, cash crops such as cotton, tobacco, and sugar cane were produced by the big peasants.[15] However, these markets were generally local in nature and the demand for such things was limited. Establishment of colonial rule completely changed this scenario. The introduction of the railways and the opening of the Suez Canal made the Indian village a part of the global market.

Simultaneously, the Industrial Revolution in England generated fresh demands for specific agricultural products required as raw materials in the new industries. A manifold increase in the land tax at the same time compelled the peasantry to shift to crops that had better market value, which effectively meant switching over from food crops to cash crops. According to one estimate, in the Rayalaseema region alone of southern India, the area under food crops declined from around 78 per cent in 1901–1904, to around 58 per cent in 1937–49, while the area producing cash crops increased from 17 per cent to nearly 30 per cent during the same period.[16] Similar changes were happening elsewhere. For example, from the state of Punjab a large proportion of food and non-food crops began to be exported. While there was a rapid increase in the agricultural production of the region from 1921 onwards, per capita output of food crops experienced a decline. According to the estimates of George Blyn for the entire country, exportable commercial crops grew more than ten times faster, at 1.31 per cent annually, compared to only 0.11 per cent per annum for food grains during 1894 to 1947. He also estimated that per head availability of food grains declined by 25 per cent during the inter-war period. This decline was highest in Bengal, Bihar, and Orissa at 38 per cent, while the relatively prosperous state of Punjab also saw a decline by 18 per cent.[17]

One obvious consequence of this shift in cropping patterns and a growing involvement of the cultivating classes in the market was a significant increase in the vulnerability of the local population to famines. Forced commercialization of agriculture disintegrated the existing systems of food security.

India experienced a number of deadly famines, particularly during the second half of the nineteenth century and the first half of the twentieth century. Bengal was transformed from a prosperous region to a land of frequent famines. In one of its worst famines during 1943–44 nearly 3.5 million people died. Though the official reports and 'inquiries' by colonial rulers attributed the cause of these famines to scarcity of food due to crop failures, it was also a direct result of colonial policies and significantly greater levels of income inequality. As Amartya Sen argues, it was not always the scarcity of food but the changes in the 'exchange entitlements' that caused the 1943 Bengal famine.[18] Richa Kumar provides a poignant summary of the historical literature on famines and their relationship to the colonial rule:

> During the last 30 years of the 19th century the country saw the worst famines with 16.6 million to 30 million people dying.... Ironically, people died while food was being exported and banquets were thrown to celebrate the monarchy's rule. ...The immense loss of cattle and bullocks, and the destruction of the pastoral economy that formed the bedrock of maintaining soil fertility, had adversely affected agricultural productivity. Such eroded soils were more vulnerable to drought.... There was nothing to fall back on—water storage systems were in tatters; the commons were inaccessible and food stores were inadequate. The extant level of yield fell by a third to a half and that of the average life expectancy by 20% during this period....[19]

She goes on to show how the colonial and later developmentalist thinking tends to completely ignore such facts of history. 'However, this exploitative past has been quietly forgotten and replaced with a narrative of ignorant, unproductive farmers toiling away using ancient practices that had supposedly remained static over time.'[20]

Land Begins to Be Sold and Bought

The new settlements introduced by the British colonial rulers conferred formal and transferable/alienable rights over land and simultaneously increased tax demands. Increasing market orientation of agricultural production created conditions under which land began to acquire the features of a commodity. The new administrative and judicial system also introduced laws against default of legal dues that included default of rent, revenue, and debts. The moneylender, who until then lent keeping a peasant's crops in mind, began to see his land as a mortgageable asset against which he could lend money. Further, an increase in population during the nineteenth century made good quality cultivable land scarce.

As land became both scarce and transferable and the economic environment began to change, the moneylender started advancing many more loans than before, provided the peasant was willing to offer his land as guarantee against a possible default. At this stage the rich landowners also entered the credit market, more with the intention of usurping the lands of smaller peasants than to earn interest. The smaller cultivators began to lose their land irrespective of the system they were a part of: zamindari, ryotwari, or mahalwari. In most cases, they continued to cultivate the same plots of land but increasingly as tenants and sharecroppers. The number of those working as landless labourers also went up.

What was the long-term impact of these policies? Did they open up the way for modernization of Indian agriculture and village life? Did they weaken the system of caste-based hierarchies? A simple answer to these questions is, certainly not. On the contrary, agriculture experienced, what some historians describe as a process of 'traditionalisation', making it 'backward'.[21] The colonial rulers exploited the cultivating peasants without making any productive investments in agriculture. Some of the reformers, who lauded the colonial rulers for helping Indians overcome their social ills, criticized them for their economic exploitation of the region. In his well-known book, *Poverty and Un-British Rule in India* (1901), Dadabhai Naoroji had famously argued how the colonial policy of high taxation resulted in wealth being drained out to England, causing severe economic deprivation of India.

Similarly, nationalist historians have pointed to the process of de-industrialization that India experienced during the eighteenth and nineteenth centuries, as the British established their rule over the subcontinent. Some estimates suggest that around the middle of the eighteenth century, India contributed around 25 per cent to the total industrial output of the world, which was mostly in the form of handicrafts. This fell to a mere 2 per cent by 1900.[22] Though historians have identified a variety of factors that produced such a dramatic shift, its primary cause was India's colonization and the decline of its handicrafts industry. The decline of patronage due to the waning importance of the pre-colonial ruling elite, and increasing competition from machine-produced imports from Britain made it impossible for the artisans to survive in the industry. Many shifted to agriculture for survival, adding to pressure on agricultural land. This would have also implied an increase in the rural population. The fusing of landlordism and usury by colonial rule resulted in a tripling of the subjugation of the cultivating peasant: sarkari (of the state), sahukari (of the moneylender), and zamindari (of the landlord).[23]

While the Indian countryside was undergoing profound economic decline, a totally different view of the Indian village was being articulated by the British. As Ludden puts it:

Between the 1780s and 1820s, working in London and with urban intellectuals in Calcutta and Madras, Company officers developed the ideas that would create a unified theory of British rule and help the administration adapt to regional and local circumstances. Orientalist scholars saw Europe and India as comparable, related civilisations; so, as in Europe, also in India, classical texts held the key to basic cultural principles. William Jones and his contemporaries dismissed Muslim rulers as invaders and tyrants.... The Company established itself as the protective ruler of a land of Hindu tradition. ...Jones found the essence of India in Sanskrit texts, especially in texts on dharma.[24]

He goes on:

The principle was quickly established that diligent investigations could reveal all the salient facts about the real India to inform British governance, and it was determined that agrarian India was everywhere organised by the rules of caste society and by principles of *varn-ashrama-dharma* that represented traditional norms and a spiritually sanctioned social order.... [T]he rural population(s)...were subsequently compiled according to the rank order of castes (jati) within the varna scheme (Brahman, Kshatriya, Vaisya, and Sudra), even where this set of categories had not been applied in earlier English accounts and was not in vogue in local society.... Orientalism provided a flexible tool for weaving together revenue settlements and for adjusting colonial dharma to local conditions.[25]

Thus, the colonial imaginations of the village had very little to do even with their own policies and administrative experiences of working on ground in diverse agrarian regions of India. As we have discussed in previous chapters, these orientalist constructs eventually emerged as the hegemonic narratives of Indian realities, many of which also found acceptance among Indian nationalists.

Ethnographic Accounts of Village Life

India's freedom from colonial rule in 1947 was an extremely important moment for the village of the subcontinent and its agrarian economy. It was not simply a matter of foreign rulers being replaced by the native elite. Though India's freedom struggle was almost entirely led by urban professionals, rural masses had also participated in the movement in large numbers and with much enthusiasm. Beginning with the 1920s, India saw many popular movements of the peasant masses. While some of these were led by left-wing political actors, inspired by socialist ideology, others were part of the mainstream nationalist politics led by Gandhi and other prominent members of the Indian National Congress. The growing rural unrest also made agrarian issues an urgency for the nationalist movement, on which they promised to act on priority after Independence. The 'agrarian question' became a favourite subject of discussion during the annual sessions of the Indian National Congress during the years leading to Independence.

Given that nearly 85 per cent of all the Indians lived in the countryside and nearly 75 per cent of the working Indians were employed in agriculture, changing the rural landscape would have also been an obvious priority for the Indian state, committed to pursuing development through state planning. 'Development' during the early years after Independence, and later, was not merely a strategy of economic change but also an ideology of the new regime. It was the primary source of its legitimacy.

However, even though the political system had changed, the ground realities and the micro-structures that had evolved during the colonial period were still intact. The local actors that had acquired power through colonial patronage were still ruling the roost. Even if the cultivating peasant wished to work hard on his land and increase productivity, he would be unable to do so because of his loyalty to the local landlord, to whom he is indebted and to whom he is forced to sell whatever he produces at a price that is decided exclusively by the buyer. This left the cultivating peasant with no motivation to work.

Thus, land relations were to become one of the first major concerns for the Indian state, when it initiated the process of developing the rural and creating conditions conducive for economic growth by introducing land reforms. It also initiated many other schemes and programmes that were to create an enabling environment for rural development. It continues to be a major area of policy and state action even today. We shall continue to discuss this in more detail in Chapter 6.

Social Life of the Village

Besides questions of poverty, deprivation, and agrarian distress, the villages in India also had their social and cultural life, which has undergone many changes during the post-Independence period. Independence from colonial rule and the formation of India as a nation state also generated a great deal of academic interest in understanding the complex realities of Indian society. The popular stereotypes emanating from the orientalist imaginations of the region were of very little value for making sense of the vast country that was trying to move on the path of democracy, and aspiring to modernize its economy and cultural values.

It was also the time when a new phase of social science research was emerging. Some of it emanated from the West through the newly opened departments of 'area studies' in the American universities, for example, and some of it was prompted by the local need for empirical details required to initiate policies and programmes of development. There were also independent scholars motivated by the revolutionary changes taking place across the world after World War II and the extensive decolonization of Asia, Africa, and Latin America.

Though political colonialism had ended, its influence

persisted. As we have discussed earlier, the ideas of development and modernization were part of the Western imagination, which visualized regions like South Asia as 'backward'. These ideas and narratives had also been accepted uncritically by a large majority of the Indian nationalists. Thus, at the time of India's independence, almost everyone agreed that India lived in its villages, spread across diverse regions of the subcontinent. Living in the village also implied that the villagers shared a way of social organization and a belief system, which reflected a pre-modern or 'a traditional way of life' with some obvious similarities that living in the village presumably entailed. Even when they spoke different languages, ate different kinds of food, held different religious beliefs, and had varied kinship practices, they were all believed to subscribe to some common values and social practices. They were expected to be practising the caste system and lived in joint families with a patriarchal/traditional belief system.

For the professional sociologist or social anthropologist, the Indian village was not merely a demographic reality or an administrative unit. It was also a cultural tradition and a social institution by itself. It was seen as a useful methodological category, an entry point to access the ground realities of the vast lands that had come to be organized in the framework of a nation state.[26] The economists and political scientists held similar views. There was virtually no disagreement among them on the assumption that everything in the village—its agrarian economy, its caste system, its patriarchal kinship and political order—needed to change for India to move forward on the path of development.

However, notwithstanding their developmentalist preoccupation, they did produce very rich accounts of village life, which contradicted popular assumptions. The world-renowned sociologist and social anthropologist M. N. Srinivas, for example, questioned the binary of 'conservative rural peasant' and 'modern man of the city'. 'The conservatism of the peasant was not without reason. His agricultural techniques are a prized possession embodying as they do the experience of centuries. His social and cultural institutions give him a sense of security and permanence'.[27] The Indian villages also had a considerable degree of diversity. This diversity was both internal as well as external. The village was internally differentiated in diverse groupings and had a complex structure of social relationships and institutional arrangements. There were also different kinds of villages in different parts of the country. Even within a particular region of the country, not all villages were alike.

The Indian villages had never been autonomous or sovereign republics, as presented in colonial literature. The stereotypical image of the Indian village as a self-sufficient community was a myth. Speaking about his village, Sripuram in Tamil Nadu, the sociologist André Béteille argued 'at least as far back in time as living memory went, there was no reason to believe that the village was fully self-sufficient in the economic sphere'.[28] Similarly, M. W. Smith argued for the need to look at village life in the wider context, to make sense of social life in Punjab.

However, villagers interacting with the outside world did not mean that the village did not have a design of its own. Many anthropologists reported that the village had a sense of solidarity across castes and it provided its residents an important source of identity and a sense of pride.

> The village settlement, as a unit of social organization, represents a solidarity different from that of the kin, the caste, and the class.... Each village is a distinct entity, has some individual mores and usages, and possessed a corporate unity. Different castes and communities inhabiting the village are integrated in its economic, social, and ritual pattern by ties of mutual and reciprocal obligations sanctioned and sustained by generally

accepted conventions. Inside the village, community life is characterised by economic, social, and ritual co-operation existing between different castes....[29]

Typically, a village tended to have two sets of castes, the landowning jajmans and a set of service providing castes. They ranged from Brahmins, who provided ritual services, to the caste groups of potters, blacksmiths, carpenters, barbers, cobblers, and scavengers. While the landowning jajman enjoyed the most critical position, the service providing groups had a set of entitlements. The nature of the relationship among them has been a source of contention among students of Indian society. Several scholars argued that village life was marked by a sense of 'reciprocity' across different caste groups. One group argued that even though they were ranked hierarchically, they did not see their relationships as being exploitative.[30]

However, many disagreed with such claims of complete social cohesion and reciprocity being the core feature of village life. The missiological anthropologist Paul Hiebert, for example, reported in his study of a South Indian village that although the caste system provided a source of stability, 'deep seated cleavages underlie the apparent unity of the village, which fragmented it into numerous social groups'.[31] Béteille too agreed. His village was clearly divided into three 'well-defined communities of Brahmins, non-Brahmins, and Adi-Dravidas'. The Brahmins and Adi Dravidas rarely interacted with each other directly.[32]

The American anthropologist Oscar Lewis too did not find any 'sense of a cohesive and united village community' in the Delhi village he studied. He too found 'caste and kinship to be the organizational pillars of village life. Caste divisions clearly weakened the sense of village solidarity. Like ethnic groups, castes had their own history, tradition, and identification. Each caste group lived in more or less separate quarters of the village; each caste formed a separate little community'.[33] Even the so called 'village common land' was not the common property of everyone. Far from working as a 'source of village unity, it had often been a source of dissension'. Rights to use the common lands were confined to the landowning dominant castes, generally determined by the amount of private land a Jat family held.[34]

Speaking in a similar vein, the British social anthropologist F. G. Bailey too rejected the notion of 'reciprocity' as the organizing value of village economy and social life. He offered an alternative perspective and emphasized on the critical role of the monopoly of dominant castes over the 'coercive sanctions.' The so-called 'reciprocity' was not a matter of choice for 'the dependent castes'.[35]

It is clear from the empirical literature that though the Indian villages during the 1950s and early 1960s exhibited a sense of unity, a closer view revealed underlying schisms and inequalities, a subject we will return to later, in Chapter 9, which deals with the changing dynamics of power in the Indian village.

Caste and Status

Caste and hierarchy have long been seen as the distinctive and defining features of Indian social life. While caste was a concrete structure that guided social relationships in most of India, hierarchy was its ideology. The idea of hierarchy pervaded almost every aspect of village life. An individual in the caste society lived in an unequal world. It was not just the people who were divided into higher or lower groups, but also the food they ate, the dresses and ornaments they wore, the customs and manners they practised—all were ranked in an order of hierarchy.

However, there was no single model or framework of hierarchy that characterized village life everywhere, as the idea of varna presumes. Rather, there existed a considerable variation in different regions. There were several socially autonomous castes, which did not easily fit into the textually prescribed order of the chaturvarnas (the four varnas and the outcastes, the untouchables). The empirical studies pointed out that in fact only the two opposite ends of the hierarchy were relatively fixed; in between, and especially in the middle region, there was considerable room for debate and negotiation regarding mutual position. The ranking order of castes was not as fixed or closed as popularly believed. In other words, status ranking at the local level was negotiable. As Srinivas puts it:

> The articulated criteria of ranking were usually ritual, religious or moral resulting in concealing the importance of secular criteria. The influence of the latter was, however, real. For instance, while landownership and numerical strength were crucial in improving caste rank, any claim to high rank had to be expressed in ritual and symbolic terms. But at any given moment there were inconsistencies between secular position and ritual rank.[36]

He described this process of upward mobility as Sanskritization, where an ambitious caste group, or a local section of them, tries to borrow the customs, rituals, and lifestyle of the higher castes in an effort to move up. However, it was not a simple process of claim-making through ritual and lifestyle imitation. It had to be preceded by economic mobility and collectively negotiated with the local power structure. The locally dominant caste was an obstacle to mobility for several reasons. In the first place, such mobility had the potential of threatening its own ambition, if not position. Second, it could result in a chain reaction which could then lead to the suspension of the flow of services and goods from dependent castes.[37]

Besides the ranking of castes and community, individual status also mattered in the Indian village. In the Telangana village of Shamirpet, the anthropologist and sociologist S. C. Dube found several factors that determined the position of an individual in the village community: caste and religion, landownership, wealth ownership, government job, office held in the village panchayat, gender, age, and personality traits.[38] Similarly, stressing on secular factors, Dube pointed to the manner in which the caste panchayats of lowly ranked menial castes worked as unions to secure their employment and strengthen their bargaining power vis-à-vis the landowning dominant castes.

As is evident from this discussion, landownership was closely tied to the social order of caste. Land was mostly held and cultivated by the so-called dominant castes. However, as mentioned above in the historical discussion of land settlements, patterns of landownership and frameworks of land relations varied across regions. Though economic class often overlapped with caste, they were not always the same thing. Not everyone who belonged to a dominant caste, such as Jats (in Haryana) or Reddys (in Andhra or Telangana), or Patels (in Gujarat), was an owner of an equal amount of land. Some of them could also be landless. Similarly, they were not the only ones who owned land in the village. Non-dominant castes, Yadavs (in Bihar, UP, and parts of Haryana) and even Chamars (in UP) could own land and cultivate it on their own.

Kinship Systems and the Myth of the Patriarchal Joint Family

Village studies by social anthropologists also looked at questions of kinship and family. India did not have a single kinship system. Dravidian kinship followed a different set of rules when compared with the north Indian kinship system. Some communities in the Tamil speaking region permitted marriages within the proximate kinship, such as a maternal uncle marrying his niece, but the same was prohibited elsewhere. Villagers in North India also avoided marriages within the village and, among some communities, even among inhabitants of nearby villages. Such a practice would have implied a much larger sphere of kin networks extending to far-off settlements.

There has been a popular view that the traditional family in the Indian village was a joint household where married sons lived with their wives and children in the houses of their parents, at least as long as they were alive and often even after that. Such a system of joint family begins to decline with the process of urbanization and/or westernization. The joint households give way to nuclear households where only unmarried and non-working children tend to stay with their parents. Nucleated households are thus much smaller in size. This presumption of rural families being all joint households was merely a speculative hypothesis.

The field studies reported that in reality, however, a large majority of rural households were relatively smaller in size. Only a small proportion of rural households had married brothers living with their wives and children in the house of their parents. Working in Gujarat, the sociologist A. M. Shah showed that in one of the villages he studied, 'there was no case of two or more brothers living in a single household after the death of their parents'.[39] Of the forty-one cases where parents had two or more married sons, only in twelve cases (29.26 per cent) did they live together.[40] He also looked at the available census data on the average household size in Gujarat and found little variation over time. Further, the joint households were possible only when families had large enough houses. The landless poor rarely had such luxury.

Systems of family and kinship also influence gender relations. Though social anthropologists who conducted village studies during 1950s and 1960s did not have a gender focus (the category had not become a part of the social science lexicon until the 1980s), they did write in great detail about the man–woman relationship in their monographs. Some regions and communities of the subcontinent also practised matrilineal systems of kinship and continue to do so even today. I discuss questions of gender, kinship, and that of land or class in greater detail in Chapter 8.

chapter 5

RURAL DEVELOPMENT
STATE POLICIES AND THE VILLAGE LIFE

'Development' has been a very attractive and popular idea, and why not? As the term has come to be understood, it implies the expansion of common resources to enhance the possibility of a better life for everyone. This is, after all, a worthy goal, one which can be achieved by universally fulfilling people's basic needs and making services required to lead a 'decent life' easily available. Nearly everyone asks for access to quality education: schools, colleges, and universities. Almost every country in the world today has a state/public-funded healthcare system, and in places where it is poorly funded or badly run, there is demand for its improvement. Provision of safe drinking water and a working sewerage system have become common expectations across regions of the world. Similarly, people expect that their state systems will make available the infrastructure required for connectivity with the rest of the world, through roads, rails, and airports, and, in recent times, even the installation of mobile towers/Wi-Fi networks that make digital communication easier and faster.

Interestingly, most of these were not common practices until around the middle of the twentieth century. Digital communication was not even known to most people in the world until the later part of the 1990s. However, by the second decade of the twenty-first century, it had come to be seen as a basic necessity required by almost everyone everywhere in the world for leading a decent human life. To put it differently, digital communication has become a citizenship entitlement, just like 'roti, kapda, aur makan' (food, clothing, and housing). The state system is expected to provide them to all, even to those who may be economically poor and/or staying in peripheral areas.

Further, citizenship entitlements are not simply a fixed set of basic needs required for human subsistence. They keep changing and growing with the changes taking place in the larger ecosystem. For human life, the notion of subsistence is also shaped by culture and social context. A good example of this is how digital connectivity became an essential need even for accessing school education when the Covid-19 pandemic resulted in a complete national lockdown in 2020 and educational institutions remained closed for nearly two years. All classroom teaching was moved to online platforms and only those who had mobile connectivity could access it.

Thus, on the face of it, development sounds like a simple idea or a process. Its realization, however, has been difficult to achieve, marked by contests, conflicts, and failures. The reasons for these difficulties lie in the prevailing social and political realities on the ground, which are not just incidental facts that can be easily taken care of but are produced by a long drawn historical process, often sustained by vested interests and supported by the prevailing power structures.

Contestations over Development

As is evident from the above discussion, the idea of development has come to be accepted as a desirable value across the contemporary world. Why should anyone stay hungry? How could anyone have problems with asking for a society free of social prejudice? What could be wrong with building good infrastructure? There should hardly be any disagreement on these issues. However, beyond such obvious positives in favour of the idea of development, it also has a tricky and complicated history. For example, a closer look at its history and ideology would show that the popular textbook view of development is firmly grounded in a Eurocentric understanding of the contemporary world. It assumes that the evolutionary history of the modern world culminates in Western Europe during the nineteenth and twentieth centuries with the growth of industrial capitalism.

Such a view assumes that it was only in Western Europe that science and reason emerged as popular values and practices, eventually producing an industrial society and democratic politics. The rest of the world was either 'primitive' or trapped in 'traditional cultures' with little possibility of change happening from within. It proposed a linear vision of human evolution, which placed countries of the Western world as being ahead in time than countries of Asia, Africa, and Latin America, i.e., the Global South.

Proponents of this view thus argued that the challenge before the 'less developed' countries was to catch up with 'advanced' countries of the West. Even the naming of some regions as less developed or underdeveloped produced a consensus on such a view of human history. In other words, the very notion of development, premised on a linear evolutionary view of human history, which sees countries of the Western world as developed and those of the rest of the world as developing, is fundamentally fallacious and ideologically constructed to produce a narrative of power that privileges the West.

This evolutionary developmentalism was not simply a marginal view among a section of white supremacists or Eurocentric intellectuals. It emerged as the mainstream perspective in the social sciences during the post-war period. Economists worked out theories of 'development as economic growth' laying emphasis solely on domestic national output (GDP), per-capita income, and consumption as indicators of its realization. Achieving a high growth rate became an end in itself, as it would presumably help the developing countries move out of poverty and catch up with the developed regions of the West.

The most popular and influential economists whose theory came to be seen as a common-sense view of economic change were W. Arthur Lewis and Walt W. Rostow. Both underlined that the key to economic growth was capital accumulation, the need for large-scale investment in the modern sector, such as industry and infrastructure.[1] They emphatically argued that there was no need to worry about poverty and inequality. Economic growth would take care of poverty through its 'trickle-down effect'. In their view, inequalities were not necessarily bad and their extreme forms would mend themselves over a period of time.

Besides the economists, sociologists and political scientists were also proposing new theories during the 1950s and 1960s and offering prescriptions to the elites of the newly independent countries of the Third World to 'modernize' their 'traditional' modes of life. Working mostly from American universities and concurring with the 'development economists', they claimed that the 'developing nations', marked by 'traditional cultures' were left behind because of their own incapacity to modernize. They argued that the elite of these countries needed to persuade their people to abandon their past traditions, values, and institutional practices and replace them with the Western type of institutions and 'progressive' values. This, they proposed, could be best done simply by imitating the developed countries of the West through introducing Western-style education, technology transfer, and propagation of individual entrepreneurship.

Though these formulations coming from the West have been very influential and, in some ways, they continue to be treated as 'scientific' ideas and theories of economic change, they have also been extensively criticized and contested by a wide range of scholars and activists. The most obvious problem with them is their wilful disregard of the history of colonialism. As discussed in the previous chapters of the book, the colonizing powers of Western Europe had enriched themselves through the plunder and loot of the colonized regions of Asia, Africa, and

Latin America. Simultaneously, they had provided charitable explanations for their actions by emphasizing that they introduced modern science and reason to the colonized people and thus paved the way for their future progress.

However, this was far from the truth. As scholars such as Andre Gunder Frank from Latin America have shown, the colonial plunder that fed the material prosperity of the European powers was, in fact, responsible for the state of 'underdevelopment' in the colonies. As he argues, development of the Western countries and underdevelopment of the developing countries were two sides of the same coin, implying that the present situation of the latter was a direct consequence of their exploitation by the former, producing a global structure of dependency and economic inequality.[2]

As indicated above, the underlying assumption of the development theories that treat nation states as naturally evolved economic units for measuring/ascertaining their comparative developmental status also defies history because it is based on a fallacious view of evolution, wrongly applied to the discussions of economic growth across countries in the present time. Nation states, as we know them today, came into being only in the middle of the twentieth century. As geographical regions they have had fluid boundaries and fluctuating political histories including the present-day nation states of Western Europe and North America.

Similarly, the binary of 'traditional' and 'modern' is neither historically valid nor is it sociologically sustainable. Such a view also assumes that a given society or a country is either 'traditional' or 'modern'. However, the fact is that all societies have a notion of their pasts, which they construct as their tradition. These so-called traditions are also constantly changing, being reinvented and reworked by each generation and over time.

Countries of Western Europe too have their own past traditions. Great Britain, for example, continues to be a political monarchy. Similarly, the 'less developed' countries that are marked as traditional have also had diverse histories, including those of the growth of science and technology. Countries like China and India have had immensely rich pasts, with their own cultures of science, technology, and formal education. They have been home to some of the greatest scientific discoveries and technological innovations in the fields of mathematics, astronomy, architecture, linguistics, agriculture, metallurgy, medicine, and textiles, to list a few.

Rural Development

In its obvious meaning, 'rural development' should simply imply development of rural areas. Given that agriculture is generally the most important aspect of the rural economy, developmental efforts should help increase productivity of land by investing in the required infrastructure that provides assured irrigation and helps the cultivating farmers save their crops from floods. It would also imply provision of institutional credit that helps them purchase farm machines and other requirements for cultivation, such as quality seeds, fertilizers, and pesticides, etc., that help increase productivity of land.

Besides agriculture, rural residents also pursue a range of other occupations, most important of them being fisheries, animal husbandry, and a variety of artisanal work. In addition to promoting their economies, rural development should also include making provisions for extension of basic services such as healthcare, safe drinking water, quality education, construction of roads, and provisions of mobile telephony that help in attaining a decent quality of life. As discussed in the opening section of this chapter, rural development should imply extending citizenship entitlements to rural residents that are normally available to urban residents.

However, this is not how classical theories of development would visualize rural realities. The evolutionist and 'accumulation-centric' thinking assumes that the processes of development and modernization would also be accompanied by urbanization, a migration of rural residents to urban centres, and a shift in their employment from agriculture to modern industry and the service sector. These processes were presumed to gradually bring about a decline of the 'rural' and its eventual disappearance. Modern and developed societies are assumed to entirely urban. This is why it is assumed that development would 'trickle down' to the rural and to its poor residents. As we have discussed in the earlier chapter, such thinking tends to counterpose the 'rural' with the 'urban' where the former is ipso-facto assumed to be 'backward'.

Thus, as also mentioned in the previous chapters, the classical development thinking had an inherent 'urban bias'. The Eurocentric thinking and overemphasis on capital accumulation implied a much higher share of developmental allocation to urban centres. This was supposed to enable the growth of the urban industrial sector, which in turn was to pull the rural residents out of villages and agricultural employment, paving the way for their urbanization. Despite a much larger proportion of the total population in most of the developing countries living in rural centres, the allocation of developmental investments was largely urban-centric.

However, by the late 1960s, it was becoming quite evident that the proposed trickle down of development benefits to rural residents was not happening. Even when the pace of industrialization accelerated, it did not generate large-scale employment. On the contrary, this gave rise to 'rural neglect', the perpetuation of poverty and deprivations in rural settlements. The loudest voice that articulated this phenomenon was that of Michael Lipton who in an influential book, *Why Poor People Stay Poor: A Study of Urban Bias in World Development* published in 1977, emphatically argued that in the name of development, the political regimes in developing countries extracted resources from rural areas and invested them in urban centres. It may be worth citing him at length here:

> The urban bias comes about as a result of the economic and political dominance of a relatively small urban elite. This elite, comprising businessmen, politicians, bureaucrats, trade-union leaders and a supporting staff of professionals, academics and intellectuals, effectively controls the institutions of power: government, political parties, law, civil service, trade unions, education, business organisations etc. They are far better organised than the rural majority. The elites use their power to allocate resources...in ways that are heavily biased towards urban needs. This bias is both inequitable and inefficient, since resources allocated to rural areas often generate greater benefits in terms of poverty reduction and economic returns. It is also self-reinforcing, as the more economic resources are devoted to urban areas, the more skills and human capital will concentrate in urban areas....[3]

Along with many others, Lipton went on to argue that state investments in rural areas are likely to produce much greater rewards in terms of poverty alleviation. There were others too who criticized the idea of a centralized top-down mode of planning and advocated for a bottom-up decentralized approach to development. It was in this context that 'rural development' emerged during the 1970s as a separate subject for policy engagement in the global narratives on development.

UN affiliated development agencies began to work with national governments around a range of new policy prescriptions. In a sense, the beginning of this shift happened in the late 1960s with the introduction of Green Revolution (GR) technology, the aim of which was to specifically target agricultural growth. While the GR was focused on increasing productivity of land, the later programmes, such as Integrated Rural Development and those focusing on livelihoods, were mostly equity-oriented.

Defining Rural Development

Rural development was defined as a set of policies which focus directly on the problem of rural poverty. While the importance of pursuing the task of economic growth was not undermined, it was no longer seen as being enough for rural areas, and the basic needs of survival and sustenance of the rural residents. As John Harris puts it:

> 'Rural Development' has emerged as a distinctive field of policy and practice, and of research.... This strategy came to be formulated as a result of the general disenchantment with previous approaches to development planning...and is defined by its concern with equity objectives of various kinds—especially the reduction of inequalities in income and employment, and in access to public goods and services, and the alleviation of poverty....
>
> The term...is at once broader and more specific than 'agricultural development'. It is broader because it entails much more than the development of agricultural production.... It is more specific in the sense that it focuses...particularly on poverty and inequality.[4]

Though conceptually it evolved in cosmopolitan centres of the Western countries, the practice of rural development also followed specific trajectories across regions and countries of the developing world, depending upon their specific histories, requirements, and politico-economic dynamics. For example, the history of rural development in India goes far back to the concerns of the British colonial rulers in the late nineteenth century. Indian imaginations of rural development also have their own nationalist trajectory and can be located in the movement for Independence.

Rural Development in India

State efforts to develop rural lives began soon after Independence. The union government designed specific programmes targeting rural poverty and lack of economic vitality. However, the idea of 'rural development' acquired a new focus in the 1970s. Following the global trends, the Indian government set up a separate Department of Rural Development in October 1974, which was elevated to the status of a full ministry of rural reconstruction in 1979. In 1982, its name was changed to the Ministry of Rural Development. Over the years, its identity, portfolios, and scope have kept changing, partly reflecting the shifting political orientation of the union governments and the global development agencies towards the issues of 'rural poverty' and 'agriculture'.

Nomenclature and global trends aside, changing or improving the social conditions of rural life through state policy has had a long history in India. It was a concern with a range of external actors, much before India's Independence. The most prominent of these was obviously the colonial state, but there were also others, like the Indian nationalists and the American missionaries, who engaged with it. As Subir Sinha points out:

> From the late nineteenth century, Indian villages began to figure, for quite different reasons, as objects of interest and intervention in the agenda of colonialists, cosmopolitan capitalists, nationalists, American philanthropists, and reformist missionaries.[5]

As discussed in the second and third chapters of this book, it was during the colonial period that the 'rural' became a subject of political and policy discussions. Imagined as autonomous communities, the British colonizers also treated the village as the 'unit of administration'. Village headmen were delegated power to collect land revenue on behalf of the colonial rulers.

Though their early interventions and reframing of land revenue systems resulted in agrarian mess and decline, they also propagated a kind of developmental agenda. As David Arnold argues, the 'discourses of deficiency' circulated from the late eighteenth century in colonial writings, against which was posed the capacity of the English to enhance agricultural production and rural prosperity. This was an important underpinning of British assertions of moral superiority, of 'their self-determined obligations to improve India, and hence their entitlement to rule over it'.[6]

Some of the colonial administrators also undertook empirical studies of the changing conditions of cultivators and initiated measures to enhance productivity. This was particularly the case with Punjab from where they recruited a large proportion of men for the colonial army. They undertook large-scale investments in developing canal networks for improving irrigational infrastructure. Large tracts of semi-arid lands were brought under cultivation in the western pockets of Punjab. They also initiated the establishment of new institutions for the development of agriculture. As Subir Sinha notes:

> Between the late nineteenth and early twentieth centuries new institutions were created concerned with forestry, fisheries, irrigation, cooperatives, credit, livestock, dairy and animal husbandry, and specific crops such as cotton, sugarcane, and tobacco. The Pusa Institute hosted agricultural scientists from abroad to work in rural India. These colonial institutions linked rural India with transnational development expertise.[7]

Many of these institutions continued to function after Independence and became models for the post-colonial developmental regimes.

Besides the colonial rulers, the Indian nationalists also saw the Indian village as being in need of desperate intervention from outside. As discussed in Chapter 3, even when they disagreed on politics and ideology, they all recognized the need to change the village through external intervention. While Nehru looked at the Indian village largely from a developmentalist perspective as 'a site of backwardness', Ambedkar too provided a critique of its social structure, as 'a site of oppression' for his fellow Dalits living on its peripheries. Even Gandhi, who celebrated the idea of Indian village and saw in it the possibilities of building a truly independent nation, was disappointed when he encountered the actually existing rural settlements and advocated for radical reforms to make the village a viable site for swaraj.

Though he propagated the need for a revival of the true spirit of the village, his ideas and roadmap for its reconstruction were also influenced by his contemporaries in the West, and several other 'experiments' of community-making underway elsewhere. Subir Sinha provides an elaborate list:

> [H]is project of national renewal through community reconstruction drew heavily on...[the] associational tendency that was emerging worldwide. In 1906, Gandhi visited the Union of Ethical Societies...and model communities in England that were based on the writings of Tolstoy and Ruskin.... Ruskin's *Unto this Last* (1862) inspired Gandhi's Phoenix Farm in Natal...and Tolstoy's *The Kingdom of God is Within You* (1953), which championed non-violence, communal living, and peasant wisdom, became the basis for his next experimental commune.... To achieve self-sufficiency in his communes, Gandhi gained ideas for small-scale leatherworks and bakeries from a Trappist monastery near Durban. The German naturopaths Kuhne and Just, and the British vegetarian Henry Salt, informed the health and food regimes in the communes....[8]

Another important way in which nineteenth-century Western thought seems to have shaped the imaginations of the 'rural' in India in the framing of policies of rural development post-Independence was through the idea of 'community'. In the Western context, the term acquired a specific meaning when it began to be used in the social sciences as a counterpoint to the idea of 'society'.[9] The term 'society' was defined by sociologists as 'a collective' marked by the complexity of its organization with significant internal differentiation of class and residence. It increasingly began to be used to denote the social life of the 'urban', where individualized subjects presumably formed collectives based on choice and reason within the framework of a modern nation state.

In contrast, the idea of 'community' was invoked to refer to the past of 'society', an earlier, simpler form, which was smaller in size, undifferentiated and worked with a 'collective mind'.[10] It was inherently conservative because its action, presumably, was not guided by reason and self-interest but by the demands of the existing normative and communal order. Peasants, for example, were seen to be living together as communities in their small-sized rural settlements. The ideas of community and society also worked well for the traditional–modern binary that was popularized by the above-mentioned modernization theories of social change. It was in this sense that the term 'rural communities' came to be used in 'rural sociology' when the sub-discipline first emerged in the United States (see Chapter 2).

Such a view of 'community' also worked very well with the Gandhian notion of the Indian village, particularly his idea of reform and rural reconstruction (see Chapter 3). Even though he was aware of the existing differences of caste and class in the village, they were to be dealt with through his idea of trusteeship. The Indian village, for him, was indeed a community, or that is how he wished to see it evolve for the realization of his ideal society, the swaraj.

Besides the challenge of developing and/or reforming the village, the 'backwardness' of Indian agriculture also emerged as an important subject of deliberations and concerns with the nationalists during the 1930s and 1940s. The annual sessions of the Indian National Congress passionately discussed possible pathways of improving the lives of poor cultivators and helping them move out of the vicious cycle of debt, bondage, and poverty. I discuss questions related to agriculture in detail in the next chapter of the book. In the following sections of this chapter, I discuss programmes that focused on the 'rural', generally.

Community Development Programme (CDP)

As indicated above, after recovering from the disruptions of Partition, the first government of independent India initiated a process of planned development, which was partially inspired by the experience of rapid economic growth achieved by the socialist countries, such as the then USSR. The first Five-Year Plan took off in 1951. Though the planning process did have some focus on agriculture and rural issues, its perspective was larger, geared towards transforming India into a modern and developed economy, for which the obvious focus had to be on industrial growth and development of modern education, science, and technology.

However, at the time of India's independence, nearly 85 per cent of the total population of the country lived in rural settlements. More importantly, the moral imperative of the freedom movement had been largely shaped by Gandhian reformist politics and his emphasis on the need for village reconstruction. As discussed above, though his notion of an ideal Indian village was shaped by a variety of intellectual currents, drawn from different parts of the world, he believed that such a community existed in the Indian past and it was possible to revive and recover it. Besides the obvious influence of Gandhian imaginations of swaraj, Barrington Moore Jr. argues, the CDP also drew its intellectual and institutional inspirations from two other sources: first, the American experience with agricultural extension services, and second, British paternalism, as had been presented by F. L. Brayne in his book named *The Remaking of Village India.*[11]

Introduced a year after the initiation of the First Five-Year Plan and around nine months after the first general election, on Gandhi's birthday, 2 October 1952, the Community Development Programme was an extremely ambitious initiative. It began with fifteen pilot projects spread across all the major states of the country. Each of the projects covered 300 villages. By early 1960s, the programme had been extended to most parts of the country.

Though the programme was expected to develop the rural economy by enhancing employment opportunities and productivity of land, it was not visualized through economic variables, such as land or asset ownership. It was conceived assuming that the Indian villagers had no inherent divisions or conflicts of interest. Stated otherwise, the underlying philosophy of the programme advocated the need for approaching the village as a culturally evolved social and communal universe, rather than a politico-economic formation.

Further, the programme underlined that 'the changes must and will come about democratically, that is, in response to the "felt needs" of India's villagers',[12] who will somehow be able to participate in the planning of a better life for all. The underlying assumption was that any lasting change required that the villagers themselves were eager and determined to improve their lot. The need was to exploit the huge reservoir of popular energy and enthusiasm on behalf of a new and rather vaguely defined social ideal. The core of its philosophy was 'to help the people to learn to help themselves'. Questions of caste, class, and gender even when acknowledged were seen to be of little significance for the functioning of the programme. The need was to boost and revive their sense of community and spirit of collective well-being. This was to be done through a village level worker (VLW), a gram sevak.

The governing assumption of the programme was that once external impetus and the basic services required for improved rural craft, agriculture, and allied activities were made available, the villagers would collectively want economic progress and they would sustain it through their own efforts as soon as they had been shown its advantages. The programme also gave consideration for the development of infrastructure for rural development, transport, education, healthcare, housing, and sanitation. Another point of action was developing minor irrigation projects and encouraging farmers to use better seeds and scientific methods of cultivation and crop selection.

Besides the VLWs the programme was run and supervised by block development officers (BDOs) and the district level bureaucratic set-up. The central government also created a separate ministry of community development, which allocated funds and oversaw its functioning. In 1957, a special committee was appointed under the chairmanship of Balwant Rai Mehta. Besides evaluating its functioning, the committee famously recommended the need for a democratic decentralization of its working and the setting up of a three-tier Panchayati Raj system.

Within a decade of its launch, the CDP came to be viewed as a failed experiment. Its assumptions turned out to be its bane. The Indian village was not a community without any divisions. Its emphasis on a non-political approach toward rural change and a non-recognition of caste and class divisions ended up helping only those who were already powerful in the village. Even though it celebrated the idea of community, it was managed bureaucratically from above. The VLW was also employed by the state and worked under the command of the block and district level bureaucratic system. Non-recognition of social divisions within the village resulted in its benefits being cornered mostly by those who were already well-off, the rural elite.[13]

More importantly, it failed to help in increasing India's food grain production, which the country desperately needed at that time in order to feed its rising population. The decade of the 1960s saw new innovations in agriculture. Though these innovations were taking place in North America, they appeared promising for raising agricultural productivity. The Government of India soon shifted its focus and turned to the new package of agrarian change, the Green Revolution. The CDP was soon forgotten. Though initially tried only in select pockets of the country, the package programme began to show encouraging results by the end of the decade and it blossomed during the following decade. The sociology and political economy of the Green Revolution is discussed in greater detail in the following chapter.

The questions of caste, class, and gender as aspects of rural development policies too found recognition in due course. The question of class appeared prominently in the parallel interventions through the various land reforms legislations. Though their impact varied quite significantly across states, land reforms were a significant state-induced legal intervention with far-reaching developmental implications. The story of land reforms too will be a part of the next chapter focusing on the changing modes of agrarian lives. While land reforms visualized rural economy as structured around 'class' and patterns of landownership, questions of caste and gender remained largely peripheral to the legal interventions. However, they did acquire centrality in the making of the Panchayati Raj institution, but could not acquire centrality in policies relating to the economic life of the Indian village.

Besides the CDP, land reforms, and Green Revolution, there are several other policies and programmes that have attempted to change rural lives through state intervention. Perhaps the most important of these was the promotion of credit cooperatives.

Credit Cooperatives

Credit is not merely a matter of economic transactions. It has been an important aspect of social life in the making of human history and across cultures and societies.[14] There has also been a great deal of discussion on debt and credit in the literature on rural life and agrarian relations. Credit played an important mediating role in the structuring of social and economic relations in rural India. Its relevance increased significantly during the colonial period, with increasing commercialization of agriculture and the associated changes introduced by British rulers in the land revenue systems.

The idea of cooperation and working together has been and continues to be part of all cultures. Kinship based communities did not even have a notion of the 'individual' as an economic agent. Communities tended to live together as socially integrated collectives. Even in caste-divided societies like India, individual jati groups had a sense of collective welfare, though generally confined to the members of one's own castes. Caste groups of a village did come together on some occasions.

The modern idea of 'cooperation' was born in England in 1844 when a group of twenty-eight artisans working in cotton mills of Rochdale town in Northern England came together to form a cooperative society with the name Rochdale Equitable Pioneers Society. Individually, they were all poor and found it hard to manage their household economies. Pooling their resources helped them manage their economies better. In a context where older bonds of community and kinship had been weakened by the rising tide of individualism, cooperatives appeared on the scene as an alternative mode of collective economic life.

Drawing from the history of cooperatives in Britain, some of the colonial bureaucrats proposed its introduction in India to deal with the growing indebtedness of cultivators and poverty in the countryside. In 1901, the Famine Commission recommended the establishment of Rural Agricultural Banks through the establishment of Mutual Credit Associations. Soon after, in 1904, the colonial government provided the cooperatives a legal status through the enactment of the Cooperative Credit Societies Act, which was further amended in 1912 and 1914. The setting up of the Reserve Bank of India in 1934 further helped the cooperatives acquire a formal status in the emerging banking system.[15]

The evolving nationalist movement also supported the idea of cooperatives and it received a significant boost after Independence. With a view to map the situation of rural credit, the Indian government appointed the All-India Rural Credit Survey Committee in 1951 and it submitted its first report in 1954. The committee observed that:

> ...large parts of the country were not covered by cooperatives and in such areas where it had been covered, a large segment of the agricultural population remained outside its membership. Even where membership did exist, the bulk of the credit requirement (75.2%) was met from other sources. The Committee recommended introducing an integrated system of rural credit, partnership of the government in the share capital of the cooperatives and also appointment of government nominees on their boards, thus participating in their management. The Committee emphasized the importance of training.[16]

Over the ensuing years, the cooperatives became an important component of India's development planning. The Five-Year Plan documents carried a separate discussion on them. A good deal of effort was put into expanding their network. Over the years, almost every village was connected to a Primary Agriculture Cooperative Society (PACS). Though PACSs invoked the idea of cooperation and its organizational structure included office bearers, elected by its members, who oversaw their functioning, the institutions were also financed and regulated by the state system through the district and state level 'cooperative banks', which also supported PACS financially.

Those writing on India's development efforts also began to examine the working and impact of cooperatives. The early evaluations of the rural cooperatives tended to resemble those of the CDP. Their benefit tended to be monopolized by those who were already resourceful and enjoyed positions of domination in the village setting. Their credit thus tended to help them further reinforce their local power. This was best summarized by Ronald J. Herring:

> The prevailing system of land tenures tends to be reproduced as a hierarchy of differential rights to institutional credit, after preserving the very distinctions which were the core of the 'traditional' agrarian system. ...[T]he flow of credit tends to follow the lines of power in the village in the case of primary societies; power in the village typically is a mirror image of the land tenure system. ...In summary: (1) tenants are less likely than owners to be members of co-operatives; (2) small owners are less likely than large owners to be members; (3) small holders in co-operatives are less likely to receive loans and the co-operatives meet a smaller percentage of their total credit needs compared to large owners.[17]

The internal evaluations too confirmed these assertions of social scientists, leading to changes in governing norms over the years. More importantly perhaps, the changes that came about in the rural economy during the 1960s and 1970s also altered the nature of demand for credit. Following nationalization of commercial banks in 1971, private banks too began to lend to the agricultural sector on priority basis. Their lending capacity was significantly higher than those of the PACS's. This was very clearly evident during my fieldwork in three villages of Karnal district in Haryana conducted during the late 1980s.

The success of the GR technology had helped the big farmers owning more than 15 to 20 acres of agricultural land generate sizeable surplus of their own. They no longer needed the short-term and limited amount of crop-loans that the PACSs offered. They could generally take care of their short-term requirements from their savings. Most of them had opened their accounts in the local branch of a commercial bank. Since they mostly sold their surplus grains to the local mandis, the grain markets, and sold it through the arhtiyas (commission agents), they could also borrow from them for their cropping needs, such as buying seeds, fertilizers, and pesticides. The arhtiyas invariably also doubled up as suppliers of such inputs required for farming. For capital investment, such as buying a tractor, they borrowed from the commercial banks for long-term loans, which advanced them such loans at low or reasonable rates of interest.

Around the same time the PACSs came under increasing external regulation, resulting in their bureaucratization. By the late 1970s, the de-facto power of managing the PACSs had shifted from the elected president of the managing committee to an officially appointed 'secretary' of the society, who was an employee of the District Cooperative Bank. The office of the president no longer offered a source of power and patronage, leading to growing indifference of the locally influential or politically aspirational individuals. This steady depoliticization of the institution transformed the PACSs into what I described as 'mini-banks' marked by corruption and bureaucratic indifference.[18] They mostly served the smaller and marginal farmers but did not play any critical role in sustaining their economic life and the power dynamics of the village.

By the 1990s, the significance of credit cooperatives as developmental institutions has steadily declined. However, the idea persists, and cooperatives continue to be a source of various economic activities, seen as being able to articulate a range of economic policies across ideological spectrums. In fact, the union government even set up a separate ministry of cooperatives in 2021.

Integrated Rural Development

As indicated above, the decade of the 1970s saw a rethinking of the 'rural' and its possible development trajectories by the global development agencies. The earlier assumptions of the benefits of economic development trickling down to the poor, and the view that the urban-centric models of economic transformation would be accompanied by a process of urbanization that would nearly end the village and make it part of the urban economy and city life, proved to be premature.

Proponents of 'rural development' thus argued for a target group-oriented programme which would identify the rural poor and provide them with income and employment generating assets, that in turn would eventually help them come out of poverty. The rural poor were identified as those with small and marginal land holdings or those who worked as agricultural labourers, using a purely economic criterion. During the early 1970s, the Indian government began with two specific programmes: the first targeted the small cultivators, and the second was for those with marginal sized land-holdings and the landless. The two programmes were named the Small Farmers Development Agency (SFDA) and the Marginal Farmers and Agricultural Labourers (MFAL).

By the late 1970s, the Indian Planning Commission decided to merge the two in a more comprehensive effort to target poverty. A new Integrated Rural Development Programme was launched in 1978–79, merging SFDA, MFAL, and a few other ongoing programmes. The vision of the IRDP was spelt out in Sixth Five-Year Plan 1978–83 document:

Rural Development now contemplates a multi-pronged attack on the problem of rural development. 'Integrated' here covers four principal dimensions: integration of sectoral programmes, spatial integration, integration of social and economic processes, and above all the policies with a view to achieving a better fit between growth, removal of poverty and employment generation. More specifically, it involves a sharp focus on target groups comprising small and marginal farmers, agricultural labourers and rural artisans, and an extremely location-specific planning in the rural areas.[19]

The underlying assumption of the planners was that the cause of the economic condition of the poor was their lack of possession of any productive asset other than their labour. Providing them with income generating assets would promote their employment and help them come out of poverty, which translated into helping the identified rural household with an income generating asset, a subsidized bank loan. The beneficiary was required to return back a part of the loan over a period of time, presumably from the income that the asset generated.

Though it soon became a major programme of rural development, it also attracted a lot of criticism. Even the internal evaluations of its implementation process found it wanting. The most obvious problem was in its working through the local bureaucracy and other vested interests. The subsidy component created scope for corruption.

A wide range of empirical studies of the programme also reported on its practice from different parts of the country. More importantly, the programme did not factor in the local dynamics of power and patronage. Identification of the poor using purely economic criteria could be easily manipulated. No one keeps accounts of incomes in rural India. A person from a big landowning household could also identify themselves as poor provided no agricultural land was registered in their name. The agricultural economist M. L. Dantwala put it quite sharply:

> Equity-oriented policies and programmes pursued within the cast iron iniquitous economic structure will not only be self-defeating, but may prove counterproductive through a 'trickle-up'. More simply, a direct attack on poverty without an equally direct attack on the structure, which has bred poverty and continues to do so, is an illusion at best, fraud at worst.[20]

By the 1990s, IRDP had begun to lose its sheen. The problems it encountered in the process of implementation and the criticisms it attracted were hard to ignore. This was also the time when the global perspectives on development began to shift towards what has come to be known as the 'right-based approach to development'. It was in this context that the next major programme of rural development was born.

Mahatma Gandhi National Rural Employment Guarantee Act

Formally notified on 7 September 2005, the Mahatma Gandhi National Rural Employment Guarantee Act (MGNREGA) has come to be one of the biggest programmes of rural development in the history of India. The programme was envisioned with a right-based perspective and passed as an Act by the Indian Parliament, which gave it legal status. Its legal status makes employment a 'right' of those who seek it, and providing it becomes a responsibility of the government. The provisions and processes of the programmes were mostly worked out by a group of civil society activists, who had themselves been involved in different ways with the well-being of the rural poor.

The core component of the programme is to provide up to 100 days of guaranteed wage employment in a financial year to the rural households (not persons) who seek it. Unlike the earlier programmes, the MGNREGA does not 'target' the poor and is conceptually open to every rural household, the only condition being that they have to ask for it. The underlying assumption of the programme is that there is a lot of disguised unemployment in rural India. Even if someone was to seek employment, it was hard to find it within the village, given the seasonal nature of employment being made available in agriculture. The guaranteed 100 days of employment are supposed to add to the work they may already be getting in agriculture or as rural casual workers. Additional employment would help them earn extra income and thereby support their livelihood.

Besides providing an immediate livelihood security through gainful employment, the Act also envisages the creation of sustainable assets in rural areas. This is achieved through the work that workers carry out while employed under the MGNREGA. These typically include working on local level projects that would help in water conservation through renovation of water bodies, drought proofing, building roads that improve rural connectivity, or any other relevant projects identified by the rural communities themselves.

How does this actually work on the ground? What makes MGNREGA right-based and demand-driven? This is done by making the local communities participate through their elected bodies, the Panchayati Raj institutions (PRIs), at all levels of its implementation. Its concrete planning or project identification begins at the village level where, in an open meeting of the village panchayat, villagers register their interest in obtaining work. This information is consolidated by the panchayat officials. They also deliberate on the nature of projects to be proposed for the village. The project is then submitted to the intermediate panchayat at the block level for sanction. It, thus, abandons the idea of a bureaucratically imagined 'targeting' and identification of the poor. By making it a legal right, it makes the poor a party to the process of implementation.

The PRIs are also involved in the implementation process.

The Act mandates that at least half of the funds allocated for the programme be spent/managed by the PRIs. The PRIs are required to spend at least 60 per cent of all the funds on wage payments. Some state governments have given the PRIs even more than 50 per cent of allocated funds for the programme. Given that all the planning and implementation is done through elected bodies and through open meetings, it is assumed that they are likely to be more accountable than the bureaucratically run systems by the 'outsiders' and from above.

The right-based approach to rural development thus visualized poverty very differently from the earlier perspective that defined it primarily in 'caloric' terms, with the poor being those who are unable to generate enough income to avail the required volume of food. As summarized by James Manor:

> The concept of 'poverty' is...defined...not in narrowly economistic terms. It is not just a severe shortage of funds, incomes and assets, but also includes a severe *shortage of liberties, opportunities and the capacity to operate effectively and to exercise influence in the public sphere*. In other words, 'poverty' consists in part of a severe shortage of 'political capacity' which implies four things; poor people's political awareness; confidence; skills; and connections to other poor people and to allies among the non-poor.[21]

As Manor argues, by giving them the 'right' to take advantage of what it offered, it turned a state-funded programme of poverty alleviation into a kind of 'self-targeting' programme that 'sought to inspire demands from the poor, by inculcating in them an awareness of their rights'.[22]

How has the programme been doing? Evaluations carried out by independent scholars tend to suggest that this has been one of the more successful programmes of rural development in independent India. Though non-poor households too seek employment in the programme, it is mostly sought by the rural poor and has been of significant help to them in overcoming their poverty. Besides aggregate poverty levels declining, the programme has helped rural households lessen the burden of debt from informal moneylenders. It has also helped the rural poor to send their children to schools.[23]

Besides helping the rural poor households, the programme also strengthened the PRIs by keeping large volumes of funds at their disposal. By involving PRIs in the process to envision and implement, the programme also strengthened their institutional capacity and social acceptability within the communities. The regions and villages where the programme worked well have also been able to develop their infrastructure for larger development of the community.[24] It also provided a kind of safety net to the rural poor during the Covid-19 pandemic when they returned to their villages upon the Indian government's announcement of the national lockdown in 2020.

However, this is not to deny the obvious problems that programmes like this encounter. Not every state government has been equally enthusiastic about its implementation, partly because of the bureaucratic inertia and partly because of the lack of political will and the vested interests blocking it. Even when PRIs have been given an important role in implementation, funds have to be dispersed by the state bureaucratic system. The functionaries and officials of PRIs are also not immune to corruption and bureaucratic behaviour. There have been reports of the bigger landowners and urban contractors complaining about the shortage of labour because the rural poor are no longer desperate for work, either as agricultural labourers in large farms or as footloose labourers in the urban markets. Most critically, a programme like this is susceptible to sabotage by local vested interests and the internal power dynamics of caste, class, and gender in the Indian rural setting.

While the MGNREGA remains the most funded and important programme of rural development at the national level, the central and state governments also have many other programmes designed for rural development, with some targeted at specific categories, such as women, youth, children, or SCs and STs, and others with a generic focus, such as skill development and building infrastructure for sustainable rural livelihoods. Even though the Indian state has been steadily shifting its focus to 'urban', given its demographic size 'rural' is hard to ignore in a democratic political system.

Besides the union and state governments, rural development has also been popular with a wide variety of social activists, working through non-government organizations (NGOs). Some of them also collaborate with official agencies and help them implement programmes at the local level. Their programmes are invariably focused on specific social categories, such as children, poor women, or environment and sustainability. Their activities are spread across specific areas, such as education, healthcare, and credit. One of the areas where their work has been quite extensive is the formation of self-help groups among rural women and of their own thrift societies. Many of those who run these NGOs are urban activists, motivated by Gandhian ideas of rural reconstruction. Some are also faith-based, while others are formed by left-wing activists.

The Afterlives of Development

The disintegration of the erstwhile socialist bloc led by the Soviet Union in the late 1980s also revived the older theories of economic growth, now known as neoliberalism. Advocates of the neoliberal perspective aggressively argued for the withdrawal of the state from the sphere of economy and its reduced intervention as a regulator of markets. Free flow of global trade and markets was supposed to help reduce corruption within the state institutions and promote growth, which in turn was to presumably also generate resources for dealing with problems of poverty and hunger in countries of the Global South, the term that is currently used for the nation states that were earlier seen as part of the Third World.

However, it was also to a large extent ideologically inspired, reflecting the pro-market and small-government philosophy of neoliberalism, driven by the vision of a unified global capitalism. The International Monetary Fund (IMF) and the World Bank played a central role in promoting neoliberal policies in developing countries. These involved market liberalization, privatization, and government spending cuts; they were considered necessary to restore the confidence of international lenders and place borrowing countries back on the path of sustainable economic growth.[25]

While global agencies and local corporate interests have been able to push for neoliberal policies through national governments, 'development' continues to be a popular idea as well as state practice across countries of the Global South. Notwithstanding the ideology and history of the term, a large majority of the poor and deprived in these countries continue to view development as offering something positive to them. As discussed in the opening section of the chapter, development has come to be seen as an aspect of citizenship entitlements, which helps in expansion of the rights of the poor and the marginalized, and promises them a good life. Eradication of poverty and social prejudice, which produce a variety of exclusions and discriminatory practices, are processes that every society has begun to pursue in the emerging global political order. They are also seen as important developmental goalposts by global agencies like the World Bank, UNDP, and IMF. Growing economic disparities as an outcome of neoliberal policies are increasingly becoming a source of worry for global agencies. Thus, some economists who initially promoted neoliberal reforms have come to realize that the idea of the withdrawal of the state from welfare measures as a strategy of growth has its limitations.

More importantly, development is increasingly also

embedded in democratic politics. As Nobel Prize-winning economist and philosopher Amartya Sen rightly argues, it is only in democratic societies that the government policies tend to take the issues of the poor and socially excluded with some seriousness. In democratic countries, these issues often become part and parcel of the electoral political process and find reference in election manifestos across political parties, irrespective of their ideological positions on economic policies. Even when governments subscribe to neoliberal policies in principle, they continue to intervene in some critical spheres of economy and income distribution in order to provide some solace to those living on the margins.

It is in this context that contributions of the Nobel laureate Sen have been significant. Development, as he argues, is not simply a natural process of growing up or an evolutionary unfolding of the inherent potentials of an organism, a human person, or a nation state society. In the social context of present-day societies, it also has a political dimension and could produce profound political effects. It ought to be seen as a process that creates an enabling environment for common citizens, helping them 'to lead lives they have reason to live'. Development, as he argues, should be seen as a kind of 'freedom'.[26]

Such a framing of development takes it beyond the conventional economic notion of the phrase, which defines it simply in terms of growth measured through the volume of 'gross domestic product' or the gross income of a country and the per-capita income of its inhabitants. More crucial than the volume and value of economic goods and services that the working population of a country produces is the need to focus on enhancing their capabilities, which would require the removal of major sources of unfreedom: poverty as well as tyranny, poor economic opportunities as well as systemic social deprivation, neglect of public facilities as well as intolerance or overactivity of repressive states.[27]

What people can achieve (their capabilities) is influenced by economic opportunities, political liberties, social powers, and the enabling condition of good health, basic education, and the encouragement and cultivation of initiatives.[28]

He goes on to identify 'five types of interrelated freedoms, namely, political freedom, economic facilities, social opportunities, transparency and security'. As mentioned above, the agency that can enable the common people to overcome these hurdles is the state or the political system. Normally, it is only the state that has the resources, the legitimacy and the authority to 'provide public education, health care, social safety nets, good macroeconomic policies, productivity and protecting the environment'.[29]

Such ideas of development that advocate a focus on expanding human capabilities helped the UNDP to turn its focus towards 'human development', including the introduction of the Human Development Index (HDI), a composite system of measuring the average achievements of a country in terms of three basic dimensions of human development: a long and healthy life, as measured by life expectancy at birth; knowledge, as measured by the adult literacy rate and the combined gross enrolment ratio for primary, secondary, and tertiary schools; and a decent standard of living.[30] This approach culminated in the formulation of the Millennium Development Goals (MDGs) by the United Nations in the year 2000. The MDGs put forward a challenge to the global community of nations to achieve some basic standards of living for their populations by 2015.

The goals and targets were concerned with reducing extreme poverty and hunger; achieving universal primary education; promoting gender equality and the empowerment of women; reducing child mortality; improving maternal health; combating HIV/AIDS, malaria and other diseases; ensuring environmental sustainability; and developing a global partnership for development.[31]

Besides governments, different agencies of the United Nations also called upon the global funding agencies and the civil society organizations (the NGOs) to involve themselves with the global agenda of achieving the basic development goals encapsulated in the framework of MDGs. Their participation generated a good deal of discussions and dialogue across a range of actors, which resulted in a reworking of the UN development goals and their 'expansion' into 'sustainable development goals' (SDGs). The revised set of goals placed a greater emphasis on environmental challenges than had been the case with the MDGs.

Given its size and spread, development of the rural remains a significant challenge for policymakers, economically and politically. It is going to remain so for decades, if not centuries to come.

chapter 6

RURAL LIVELIHOODS
AGRICULTURE AND NON-FARM ECONOMY

Rural economies have traditionally been seen as being woven around agriculture. Even those who did not own any land or were not directly engaged in its cultivation tended to be employed in occupations allied to agriculture. For example, besides the full-time cultivators and farm workers, a traditional village in India would have specialists like carpenters and blacksmiths, who made and repaired ploughs and other equipment required for cultivation of land. At a broader level, a typical Indian village also had a range of other service providers whose primary clientele or patrons were the cultivating farmers, though they also served members of the larger village community. These included the local traders or shopkeepers, moneylenders, tailors, weaver, barbers, potters, masons, cobblers, priests, and a few others.

Their numbers, or proportion in the total population of a given village varied, depending upon the size of the village, the nature of its agrarian economy, and its general prosperity. In a bigger village with prosperous agriculture, they could make up almost half of its population, or even more. They tended to also double up as farm labourers during the peak cropping seasons. In smaller settlements their numbers would tend to be lesser. In some cases, smaller and poorer villages did not even have households of such service providers. These villages tended to depend on those living in the neighbouring villages for such services.

In some regions and ecological conditions, the primary economic activity of rural residents could also be different from agriculture. For example, in coastal villages of fisherfolk, the primary occupation of its residents revolved around fishery. Similarly, horticulture, dairy farming, and rearing of animals or poultry farming have also been viewed as intrinsically rural economic activities. While some pursued them as full-time occupations, others practised them along with agriculture, as sources of additional income and economic security. The common uniting factor among these activities is that they all involve working directly with 'nature', primarily using human labour power in the processes of production. Economists tend to club all these activities together and describe them as the 'primary sector' of a national economy.

In comparison, 'urban' settlements are viewed as being different from the rural not only because they are bigger in size and denser in population, but because the nature of their economy is seen to be very different. In the popular imaginations of the urban economy, livelihoods in the cities and towns are predominantly drawn from commercial activities and industrial production, often described as the 'secondary sector' of a national economy.

In addition, the urban economy also employs a large number of people in modern and specialized occupations described as 'services'. The service sector includes a very wide variety of diverse economic activities, ranging from garbage collection to medical services and healthcare; from banking and insurance to mass media, software engineering, scientific research, and general education. They also include activities allied to the state and the political systems, such as legislature, police and civic bureaucracy, judicial services; and those working for civil society welfare, such as NGOs and faith-based institutions.

Such activities are seen as being substantively or sociologically different from those of the 'primary' sector of the economy. As the popular view or assumptions go, the pursuance of such activities requires individually acquired specialized skill and training through formal education. The nature of work and responsibility in urban occupations is also individual-centric. In contrast, the traditional rural occupations tended to be collective in nature. The skills needed for land cultivation and pursuance of other 'traditional occupations' were all culturally acquired while growing up in the community, as members of a family or a kin group.

The two sets of settlements are thus visualized as if their economies and livelihood patterns are mutually exclusive and fundamentally different from each other. They have also come to be valued differently, as if they represent two different stages in human evolution and processes of economic growth. Furthermore, the description of the rural as 'traditional' is also suggestive of a 'conservative' nature, as if it were continuing unchanged and completely insulated from any kind of outside influence. Starting from the orientalists and colonial administrators to the nationalist ideologues, popular stories, and even in social science theories, rural economiesare usually represented as being stuck in time, reproducing themselves over centuries without much change in technology and productive capacity. Their authoritarian social organization, structured around hierarchies of caste, class, and gender, tend to prohibit change from within.

In contrast, the 'urban' is often envisioned as the site of modernity. Its livelihood patterns are viewed not only as being inherently diverse but also ipso-facto dynamic, open to change and experimentation. While the rural economy is 'informal' in nature, the urban economy is presumed to be mostly 'formalized', operating within a rationally framed set of rules. Its social organization and hierarchies are also claimed to be formally structured within the value frame that is grounded in individual entrepreneurship and achievement. Extensive use of modern technology, the flexible nature of its social organization, and its rational orientation makes it adaptive to change, constantly evolving into enhanced productivity, prosperity, and social differentiation.

While spatial qualities, such as size of a settlement, are indeed important in the shaping of social and economic patterns of a place, the view that presents 'rural' and 'urban' economies as being fundamentally different has many limitations. As discussed in the opening chapters of this book, such a binary framing of the rural and urban has its origin in a Eurocentric view of the world. Human history has not followed a universal pattern of linear evolution with 'rural' and 'urban' being two stages in the process of human progress.

Historical evidence found in different regions of the world, including South Asia, clearly suggests that the 'rural' and 'urban' economies have tended to co-evolve, as regional social, economic, and political formations that are internally fluid and dynamic, constantly changing and evolving through mutual interaction and influence, almost everywhere in the world. As I have tried to argue in Chapter 4 while discussing the history of the South Asian regions in medieval times, the rural and agrarian economies of the region actively participated in trans-regional/ global mercantile activities and trade. Economies of the South Asian region were as much shaped by influences coming from the outside as by those emanating from within.

Persistent Notions of Traditional Rural Economy

As mentioned above, irrespective of the conflicting evidence, the notion of a static rural economy persists in common-sense narratives, as well as in textbooks of social sciences. The reasons for this persistence are not simply because of ignorance or an intellectual inertia. Of the many reasons, the most obvious is the manner in which the popular self-image of India's economy came to be shaped during the colonial period. There has also been a persistent influence of Western and Eurocentric theories propagating a similar view on the patterns of economic growth, the making of which goes back to classical social science writings emerging from nineteenth-century Europe.

Such framings of the rural economies have also been found useful by the political establishment and powerful elites. As has been argued by Bernard Cohn (discussed in Chapter 2), British colonial rulers intentionally produced and propagated a view of India as a land of self-contained villages, existing for centuries without any foreign influence and internal change, to justify their presence in India. Based on such a view, they presented themselves to their fellow countrymen as benevolent agents of change and progress.[1] These colonial writings also became a source for thinkers attempting to formulate grand theories of human progress where the Indian village economy conveniently appeared as an example of a 'type' of traditional/pre-capitalist social and economic formation.

Against this simplistic view of rural economic life, this chapter, along with a subsequent chapter, presents a more nuanced and differentiated picture. The realities of caste, class, and gender have to be the obvious points of focus for such a discussion, with an examination of them as structuring categories that shaped rural economies and differentiated livelihoods. This is followed by a contemporary history of change in the rural economies of India.

Scholars with different theoretical persuasions and Western-educated Indians have often used the category of 'peasantry' to describe the rural people of India. However, its use has several limitations. First and foremost, it fails to recognize how caste functioned as an organizing principle of landownership and distribution in the village. In other words, caste was not merely a system of ritual hierarchy but also an aspect of the rural economy. It shaped occupational monopolies and economic entitlements. Like other systems of domination, the everyday life of caste evolved into a normative system to which most consented.

However, that did not mean that it was a harmonious system that treated everyone equally and fairly.

Unfortunately, mainstream academic literature on the Indian caste system has mostly tended to describe it purely in cultural terms, as a system of religious hierarchy emanating from the Hindu faith, as if strictly following the prescriptions inscribed in a few classic or canonical texts. One of the core implications of such a religious view of caste is to imagine it as an integrative and harmonious system of social relationships: since the hierarchy of caste is prescribed as a religious value in Hinduism, anyone claiming to be a member of the faith is bound to uphold its practice, without any reservation or discontent. Belief in the idea of karma or destiny ensured that even those located at the lower end of the social hierarchy subscribed to its normative order and worked hard to live up to its prescriptions for an inter-life mobility, hoping to be born in a 'higher' caste and better social conditions in their next life. We will return to a longer discussion of caste, class, and gender as structuring realities of rural India in Chapter 8.

Changing Rural Economy

India is a large and diverse country. The social, economic, and political histories of different regions and diversities of ecological conditions makes it difficult to visualize the changes occurring in these regions in a simple or a singular narrative. However, despite these variations there have been some common patterns of change experienced across the subcontinent, particularly since the colonial period. First, the British colonial rulers brought together most of present-day India into a common administrative system. Even though there were significant variations in the manner in which they restructured systems of land revenue collection across regions of the subcontinent, there were also many underlying similarities in their approach to Indian agriculture. This is clearly evident from the many similarities in the 'destructive legacies' they left behind. As Richa Kumar puts it:

> ...the backbone of Indian agriculture was broken during the eighteenth and nineteenth centuries through colonial policies that sucked the vitality out of the land and channelled the wealth to Great Britain. In collaboration with some social groups who became beneficiary intermediaries, colonial interests created pathways of unparalleled exploitation of natural resources. Cash crops like opium, jute, wheat, cotton and indigo were grown on prime agricultural land with food crops relegated to marginal areas. This was coupled with a systematic neglect of customary water harvesting and storage structures, and state takeover of the forests to harvest timber.[2]

As discussed in Chapter 4, the changes they introduced in land revenue systems across regions intensified commercialization of agriculture, including transforming land into an alienable commodity. These policies produced far reaching implications for rural/agrarian social relations. The increasing indebtedness of the smaller cultivators unleashed a process commonly described by historians as 'land alienation'. They lost their agricultural lands to moneylenders and big landowners, who often tended to be one and the same individual. Though money lending and debit/credit were not unknown in pre-colonial India, the local sahukar, the customary source of cash during special occasions, such as a wedding in the family, worked within the constraints imposed by the local communities and cultures. He functioned as a 'crude balance wheel to even out periods of scarcity and prosperity'.[3] Moneylenders generally did not disrupt the customary arrangements.

The colonial policies completely changed the local economic environment. Land became both scarce and transferable. Since colonial law made land a saleable commodity, the moneylenders began to advance higher amounts, with the intention of usurping a cultivator's land. The bigger and richer landowners also began to eagerly advance cash to smaller landowners with the same intent. Tenancy and landlessness grew. So did social and political unrest. Nationalist leaders like Gandhi and Nehru provided a voice to the growing anger in the countryside. In some regions, this also came out in left-wing mobilizations by the Communists.

Independence from colonial rule was an important turning point for the rural economy. As discussed in the previous chapter, 'rural development' became a major priority with the post-colonial Indian state. Thanks to state policies and direct legislative interventions, such as the Land Reforms, patterns of rural livelihood have undergone some significant changes.

Developing Indian Agriculture

The idea of development has its origin in the European and Eurocentric imaginations of the world. As discussed in the preceding chapters, such an imagination has been a source of many difficulties in engagement with rural realities of a country like India. However, the idea of development, quite like democracy, has acquired a life of its own and has a very wide appeal, particularly among the poor and the marginalized.

The nationalist political elite, who inherited power from the British colonial rule, were thus confronted with the challenge of responding to popular aspirations for a better life as promised by the freedom movement. However, at the time of India's independence, Indian agriculture was an example of everything that could have been wrong with the economy of an 'underdeveloped' country. Even when nearly three-fourths of its working population worked on its vast farmlands, served by an extensive spread of rivers and a wide range of climatic conditions, India could not produce enough food for its own population. The newly independent country had to import a considerable amount of food grains from the 'developed' countries of the First World, with the United States being the chief supplier. While the food-surplus countries of the Western world were eager to sell, or even give away food as aid, their supplies came with 'conditions' unfavourable to a nation whose new political elite were trying to restore its lost dignity.

Given their first-hand exposure to the ground realities of rural life during the nationalist struggle, the new rulers recognized that the challenge was not merely of low productivity of land, but also of transforming the social framework of agricultural production. Independence from colonial rule did not by itself change the local conditions. The local level class relations continued to persist. Speaking at the Delhi School of Economics in 1955 after his extensive tours of rural India, Daniel Thorner was among the first social scientists to conceptualize such a reality. He highlighted the prevailing situation of land relations as being intermeshed with debt dependencies. A small section consisting of a few landlords and moneylenders, who usually belonged to the local upper castes, controlled virtually everything in most of rural India. They had stakes in keeping agriculture backward and perpetuating stagnation, 'a built-in depressor'.[4] This was not very different from what the left-leaning members of the Indian National Congress had been pointing out. There was near unanimity that the way forward for Indian agriculture was to enforce a change in land relations from above, through state legislations, in the form of land reforms.

The Land Reforms

Soon after Independence, a wide range of reforms were proposed. They were all designed to help strengthen the effective control of land in the hands of actual tillers. They included abolition or de-recognition of 'intermediary tenures', regulation of land rent and tenancy rights, and conferment of ownership rights on tenants over the lands they had been cultivating for a long time. These initial proposals were followed by more radical reforms, such as a ceiling over the volume of land a person could own, and identification and acquisition of the surplus lands for redistribution among the landless rural poor. Legislations were also passed to facilitate consolidation of land holdings, which enabled the farmers to swap their scattered plots of land to bring them together in one place.

Collectively these legislative interventions by the government to regulate landownership and related arrangements, in order to democratize effective cultivation of land, were called Land Reforms. The policy was visualized by the union government, but given that the Indian Constitution has listed 'agriculture' as a 'state subject', they were implemented at the provincial level.

Though the state governments followed directives from the union government and enacted the required legislations, their implementation was rather lethargic. Many among those sitting in the state legislatures were themselves big landowners, and they worked to sabotage the initiative by intentionally keeping loopholes in the texts of the new laws, thus escaping the legislations and retaining their lands. Evidently, there was a clear absence of 'political will' on the part of the local ruling elite.[5] Effective reforms could happen only in regions where there was a strong political pressure from below, i.e. political mobilizations of the prospective beneficiaries.[6]

However, despite the sabotages and compromises, the Land Reforms did succeed in weakening the hold of the big feudal lords who had no direct interest in cultivation of land. With the decline of the hold of such 'absentee landlords', the number of those directly involved in the farming of land grew.[7] Even when the legislations were not directly effective, the fear of losing land induced many potential losers to sell or rearrange their holdings in a manner that effectively reduced their hold over the agrarian/rural economy.[8]

For example, in a state like Rajasthan, where the traditional Rajputs have been very influential, anthropologist Anand Chakravarti found that even though the 'abolition of *jagirs*' (intermediary rights) was far from satisfactory, the legislations made considerable difference to the overall landownership patterns, and to the regional power structures. Most of the village land had moved into the hands of those who could be called small and medium landowners. In qualitative terms, most of the land began to be self-cultivated, and the incidence of tenancy declined considerably.[9]

Yet, Land Reforms could not make much of a dent in the problem of landless-ness. A large majority of landless labourers in the Indian countryside have traditionally been from the 'Untouchable' and other 'low' caste groups. They could rarely exercise much political influence in regional politics. The beneficiaries, by and large, belonged to the middle level caste groups who traditionally already cultivated land as a part of the callings of their castes. Otherwise also, the holding structure continued to be fairly iniquitous, though the proportion of smaller and medium size landowners has been expanding over the years, a subject I discuss a little later in this chapter. While the decline in absentee landlordism created positive conditions for agricultural growth and rural development, inequalities and caste-based differences persisted.

State Investments in Agriculture

As discussed in the previous chapter, besides the land reform legislations, the Indian state has also been spending a good deal of resources on a wide range of programmes for rural development. Some of these have also been targeting agricultural sector. Nearly three-fourths of the working Indians depended on agriculture, directly or indirectly, when India began its development planning. Their well-being was closely tied to the agrarian economy, at least in the short and medium term.

Growth in the agriculture sector was also seen as being a requirement for India's industrialization. A more productive agrarian economy could produce surplus, which could be harnessed for laying infrastructure for industrial development. It was in this context that India's first Prime Minister, Jawaharlal Nehru, said that agriculture was the 'basis of all our development work'.[10] Even though India's development planning was modelled to take the country towards industrialization, 'the first three Five Year Plans allocated over 22 per cent of the total investment to agriculture while Industry accounted only for 17 per cent'. The government invested a great deal in laying irrigation networks and setting up agricultural universities. These have also had a long-term impact on the sustained growth of Indian agriculture.

As a consequence of these initiatives, the productivity of land began to steadily increase, from a mere 0.4 per cent during the first half of the twentieth century to 2.6 per cent in the first fifteen years after Independence.[11] This was obviously not enough to feed the hungry Indians, whose numbers were also consistently growing. One of the biggest challenges for the government was ensuring that enough was available for all. This could be done only by importing food grains from countries such as the USA, which had surplus and were willing to sell it. Besides the obvious costs of buying food grains from the international market using scarcely available resources, the terms of trade were often defined conditions amounting to political dependencies.

The Green Revolution

Food scarcity was not merely a local or a national problem for countries like India. It had also emerged as a major geopolitical challenge internationally in the post-World War II period.

Countries like India were being seen as 'Malthusian time bombs'.[12] According to this view, a rapidly growing population in a newly independent nation state like India could not be sustained by the slow pace of growth in its food production. The Western political powers saw this as a source of 'worry' in a world marked by the Cold War. Hunger could lead to political upheavals. Thus, the idea of the Green Revolution was proposed as an alternative to a possible Red Revolution.

The GR was to be a technological solution to enhance productivity of land and remove persistent food scarcity. At the centre of the new proposal was the ongoing research in North American labs since the early 1950s on hybrid seeds which were being touted as the major solution to enhance productivity of land. But the GR was not just about using the new high yielding variety (HYV) seeds. It was a package programme, which also required fertility enhancing chemical fertilizers, use of chemical pesticides and weedicides for protection of plants from pests and weeds, assured irrigation, and a larger use of machines.

The success of the programme also required some institutional support in the form of cheap institutional credit to cultivating farmers, providing them some kind of price incentives, and stable markets. The programme was also to be backed by further research, innovations, and dissemination. This could be done by setting up specialized research institutes and agricultural universities, which, along with teaching and research, would also offer their extension programmes for reinvigorating farming practices.

Given that many of the early programmes for rural development introduced by the post-Independence state did not produce the desired outcomes, the idea of GR was easily sold to the Indian government. The initial support promised by the USA in its implementation would have also been an added incentive. The HYV seeds arrived in India in the early 1960s. The USA-based Ford Foundation was directly involved in the introduction of the Intensive Agricultural Development Programme (IADP) in 1961 in fourteen districts of different states of the country on an experimental basis. It was extended to 114 districts (out of a total of 325) in 1965 with a changed nomenclature, Intensive Agriculture Areas Programme (IAAP).

As proposed by its advocates, the programme came with a variety of incentives for the cultivating farmers. Besides providing them with new seeds and chemical fertilizers at subsidized prices, the programme also offered cheap credit through commercial banks for investments in machines, and funded the development of irrigation infrastructure. The state governments were also encouraged to put in place marketing networks, such as the mandis, to ensure that farmers receive adequate prices for their produce. In order to build its own stocks of food grains for the public distribution system (PDS), the central government began to procure food grains through the newly set up mandis at a pre-declared minimum support price (MSP), which was decided after calculating all the costs incurred by the cultivators, including the costs of labour with an added amount as profit for the cultivating farmer. The new technological revolution in agriculture was to be supported by a scientifically trained mass of professionals who were to be educated in the newly set up agricultural universities.

Though its initial success was limited to some regions of the country, the GR has been widely seen as a successful programme. It was celebrated the world over and has been studied and debated upon quite extensively in academia. The new technology has since been extended even to those regions and crops that were initially not a part of the package programme. Policymakers often speak about the possibilities of its 'second' and 'third' waves, and it has come to be seen as a 'model' for all agrarian futures envisioned in the country.[13]

Speaking purely in quantitative terms, India's agricultural sector that had been nearly stagnant during the first half of the twentieth century began to grow at the rate of 3 to 5 per cent per annum[14] and the momentum has since been spreading across regions of the subcontinent, including those seen as agriculturally 'backward' states. This has had a direct bearing on the availability of food grains.

A close look would reveal that India's food grain production had begun to increase soon after Independence, even before the introduction of GR technology. It went up from mere 50.82 million tonnes in 1950–51 to 82.02 million tonnes in 1960–61, and then steadily grew, going up to 108.42 by 1970–71. In 2016–17, India produced 275.68 million tonnes of food grains, over five times its food output in the early years after Independence.[15] The most spectacular increase has been in production of wheat, from a mere 6.46 million tonnes in 1950–51 to 98.38 million tonnes by 2016–17. The corresponding figures for rice were less impressive, going up from 20.58 tonnes in 1950–51 to 110.15 million tons in 2016–17. The growth rate for oilseeds and for pulses during this period was also in the same range. While the total output of oilseeds went up from 5.16 to 32.10 million tonnes, production of pulses saw an increase from 8.41 to 42.95 million tonnes.[16]

Most of this growth has been due to the increasing intensity of agriculture, and not due to the extension of cultivation to uncultivated lands. India's net sown area has not seen a very dramatic increase. It went up from 118.75 million hectares in 1950–51 to just 140.13 million hectares in 2016–17, whereas the area sown more than once went up by 4.5 times, from 13.15 million hectares in 1950–51 to 59.52 in 2016–17.[17] This has obviously been made possible by the growing use of machines and by expanding irrigation. India saw a significant increase in gross irrigated area, from 22.56 million hectares in 1950–51 to 96.46 million hectares in 2016–17.

This growth in agricultural productivity within the framework of the GR has also introduced some serious problems and imbalances. Growing use of chemical fertilizers and pesticides in food grain crops have impacted the quality of food, causing serious health issues for cultivators as well as for consumers. The new seeds and greater intensity of cultivation requires greater exploitation of groundwater, with some areas experiencing serious problems of declining water tables. This has particularly been the case in states like Punjab and Haryana where paddy was introduced as a major crop.[18]

The growing commercial orientation has also shifted the focus to certain crops which can be easily marketed, resulting in declining diversity of crops. For example, the number of crops produced in Punjab declined from twenty-one to nine during the GR period. Lower diversity of crops could have serious implications for the health of the soil besides causing other long-term environmental issues. Some of these issues of 'sustainability' have also been responsible for what has come to be described as 'agrarian distress', resulting in growing cases of suicides among farmers (to be discussed in the following chapter).

Agrarian Change and Social Life

Agrarian change is not only about increasing the productivity of land. It is also about the changing social framework of agricultural production. Adoption of new technologies and increasing integration of agriculture with the market economy also changes social relations across the classes, castes, and genders engaged in agricultural production. These changes also have implications for aspirations and orientations of different categories of rural society, the institutional matrix of rural life, cultural values, and power relations.

Even though popular middle-class narratives tend to view rural residents as conservative and resistant to change, the new technology was quickly adopted by almost everyone. This was particularly true of the regions where GR technology was first introduced during the 1960s. When I first went to do primary fieldwork in three villages in Haryana during the late 1980s, I found that nearly every single cultivator used HYV seeds and chemical fertilizers.

Mechanization too had spread across different categories of cultivators. Even though smaller cultivators did not have the resources to invest in machines, they found it cheaper to hire-in tractors for ploughing their fields than to maintain a pair of oxen for the purpose. When the combine harvester became available a little later, most showed little hesitation in hiring the machines. These machines could harvest the entire crop of a village within a week or so, thereby efficiently performing a task that previously required over a month of manual labour. This immensely helped farmers save their mature crops from the vagaries of weather.

Even though smaller cultivators did not show much reluctance in accepting the machines, the new technology was certainly not 'resource-neutral'. Intensive cultivation using machines, HYV seeds, and other chemical inputs required much greater use of cash and credit, all of which had to be bought from the market. The bigger farmers had resources, or could access credit at cheaper interest rates from commercial banks and credit societies. On the other hand, not only did the small farmers not have much savings of their own, they also found it harder to access credit. Even when they managed to raise credit from the local traders in the newly set-up mandis, it was done on the promise of selling the farm yield through the crediting trader.

Thus, it became an even bigger compulsion for the smaller cultivators to orient their crops to the nature of markets. This is how the farmers of Punjab and Haryana shifted nearly entirely to the cultivation of wheat and paddy, because these crops could be easily sold through the mandis at a secure price, the MSP.

On the whole, farmers too saw an increase in their incomes from farming during the early decades of the GR. However, such market systems with a system of assured MSP are not present in every state, MSP is not offered for all crops, and rice and wheat cannot be produced all across the country at all times of the year.

As mentioned above, the early decades of the GR saw the farmers with substantial holdings benefitting a great deal from the new technology and their better access to the credit network. Thus, they were the major beneficiaries of the system. This enabled them to expand their holdings by improving their banjar (unproductive) and forest lands. These farmers invariably also belonged to the numerically large middle-level caste groups, whom Srinivas had called the 'dominant castes'.[19] Their social and demographic position in the village was crucial in helping them consolidate their political position, even beyond the village.

A new social class of 'rich landowners' thus emerged in the GR pocket, which came to dominate the regional/state level politics. Their adoption of new technology and intensification of agriculture helped them accumulate economic surplus, which they began to invest outside agriculture. Perhaps the initial investments everywhere were in the education of their children, which helped the households diversify into urban occupations, including commerce and industry.[20] Some began to enter agricultural trade.[21]

Expanding railways, road transport, increasing availability of jobs in modern industry and the urban informal economy opened up many new avenues of mobility and the newly well-off rural families benefitted from them. A new class of mobile, rich farmers emerged on the scene. As the Hyderabad-based human rights activist Balgopal put it:

> ...a typical family of this class has a landholding in its native village, cultivated by hired labour, *bataidar*, tenant or farm

servants and supervised by the father or one son; business of various descriptions in town managed by other sons; and perhaps a young and bright child who is a doctor or engineer or a professor.[22]

As I have indicated above, the GR was not merely a productivity enhancing programme, it also had a political side to it, a kind of ideology. It shifted the focus away from questions of distribution and relational structures, and towards 'a narrative of ignorant, unproductive farmers toiling away using ancient practices that had supposedly remained static over time...[o]verlain upon the thesis of the timeless, unchanging village'.[23] Such a narrative also worked well for the richer landowners, who began to be celebrated as 'progressive farmers' who had helped India overcome its crisis of hunger.

What needs to be acknowledged here is also the fact that the GR brought in its wake many imbalances in the farming practices with implications for the health of the soil since a much greater emphasis was placed on wheat and paddy at the cost of the rich diversity of crops. Unregulated use of chemical fertilizers and pesticides also affects the quality of grains being produced. It has solved the problem of hunger, but has given rise to others.

More importantly, the larger process of economic growth did not shift India's workforce from agriculture to manufacturing, as it was supposed to as per the classical theories of economic growth. The prosperity brought about by the new technology during the early years of its introduction did not last. On the contrary, the prevailing inheritance cultures resulted in the steady division of land holdings. The new technology could not generate an internal dynamic of growth within the rural economy. On the contrary, it appears to have soon become a story of unmet aspirations.

The excitement produced by the GR did not last for very long. In less than twenty years the surplus producing farmers of the GR regions were on the streets, demanding a better deal for agriculture and a protection from the dominant players in the urban markets. The decade of the 1980s saw the rise of powerful farmers' movements. This was also an indication of their declining influence in national politics and a looming 'agrarian crisis'.

The neoliberal reforms of the early 1990s fundamentally changed the orientation of the Indian state towards agriculture and its farming populations. The broader orientation of the Indian economy also began to change. However, unlike the 'classical' growth trajectories of the industrialized nations of the Global North, even when the share of India's agriculture declined rather rapidly, a much larger proportion of the workforce remained employed in agriculture. Such a decline in the relative size of an agrarian economy in terms of its value addition has produced many imbalances, going beyond the sphere of income and employment. To put it differently, the decline of agriculture is also ideological, as a value and a valued occupation.

The following chapter explores this process of the decline of agriculture, and its possible futures.

Rural Livelihoods Beyond Agriculture

Though rural India always had a section of its population employed in non-farm occupations, they tended to be subsumed within the agrarian economy. Given the hegemonic position of categories such as peasantry and its uncritical use in the Indian context, the macro data collected by the state agencies perhaps did not even have columns for the enumerations of the wide range of artisan communities in rural India, who mostly functioned outside agriculture, though supporting its operations. It was with the growing visibility of newer forms of rural non-farm occupations, such as construction and manufacturing, that the economists began to take note of the rural non-farm economy (RNFE).

Besides increasing productivity of land through the introduction of new technologies of cultivation, the post-Independence developmental state also expanded the reach of education. It invested in developing communication networks and increasing connectivity across regions and settlements. Those who prospered with the GR and acquired formal education also developed aspirations for mobility beyond agriculture. The decline of the traditional jajmani occupations and an increasing use of machines and other inputs for cultivation also began to alter the rural economy. Growing cultures of consumption also created demand for a range of goods. Over time, villages saw a growth of local markets.

Prosperous rural residents began to invest in building pukka houses. The state development programmes, such as assured rural employment for a certain number of days under the MGNREGA of 2005, also encouraged investment in rural infrastructure. Besides construction, a much larger number of rural residents are employed in petty shopkeeping and providing urban style services to rural residents. These ranged from shops that sell locally required farm inputs and consumer goods to beauty parlours and tuition centres.

Changing Structure of Indian Economy and Employment

Despite the significant pace of growth of its economy since the early 1990s, India continues to be predominantly rural. This is not simply about its demographics. Even in 2011, nearly three-fourths (72.4 per cent) of its workforce resided in rural settlements, larger than the share of rural population, which stood at 68.8 per cent. As one would expect, a large proportion of those who live in rural areas also work locally, within the rural settlements. Interestingly, however, the proportion of those working in agriculture has been steadily declining, shifting their livelihood to other rural non-farm occupations, completely or partially. Some rural residents also go to the neighbouring town to work while continuing to live in the village with their families.

What is new about the rural non-farm occupations? What implications does it have for rural livelihoods and the well-being of rural residents?

The available official data points to some very interesting trends. Besides the steady decline of agriculture, which we discuss at length in the next chapter, the rural non-farm economy has been growing in terms of its value addition to the national income mostly because of the growing practice among urban industrialists to set up their manufacturing units in rural areas. Though this trend has been there for a long time, it seems to have picked up after the introduction of economic reforms in the early 1990s. For example, the share of manufacturing units located in rural areas in the year 1993–94 contributed less than 30 per cent to the net national domestic product. By 2011–12 it went up to 51 per cent.[24] In other words, a larger proportion in the net domestic product (NDP) contribution of the manufacturing sector came from industries located in rural areas. The share of factories located in urban centres was lesser than those located in the rural areas.

However, this is not an indication of any kind of internal economic dynamism of the rural economy. It merely points to the growing spatial spread of Indian manufacturing. The newer manufacturing units are being set up in rural areas as urban land would have been far more expensive. More importantly, this migration of manufacturing to rural areas did not translate into a significant shift of rural workforce from agriculture to manufacturing. In fact, nationally the share of workforce employed in the manufacturing sector 'declined by 4.1 percentage points during the forty years ending with 2011–12'.[25]

Further, the official data also shows that the share of agriculture in the rural NDP has declined quite substantially during this period, from 64.36 per cent in 1980–81 to merely 35 per cent in 2009–10.[26] In other words, agriculture contributed to only around one-third of the total rural economy.

Table 6.1. Share of rural areas in total Net Domestic Product (NDP) and workforce

Year	Share in NDP	Employment
1970–71	62.4	84.1
1980–81	58.9	80.8
1993–94	54.3	77.8
1999–00	48.1	76.1
2004–05	48.1	74.6
2011–12	46.9	70.9

Source: Ramesh Chand, S. K Srivastava, and Jaspal Singh, 'Changing Structure of Rural Economy of India Implications for Employment and Growth', New Delhi: NITI Aayog, 2017, p. 3.

However, such a statistical representation of the status of agriculture in the rural economy is not free from problems. Despite its relative decline in the national economy, agriculture remains the mainstay of the rural economy, more so in some regions than others. Even more importantly, it continues to be the primary source of livelihood for a much larger proportion of the working population. While the NDP generated by rural manufacturing is added to the gross number for rural areas in official data sets, it hardly belongs to the rural residents. As discussed above, in most cases, rural areas only provide space for the manufacturing units. Their ownership would lie with the urban residents. Often, much of the workforce too comes from the urban settlements.

Table 6.2: Rural Employment in Agriculture and Rural Non-farm (RNF) sectors

Workers	1983		1993		2004–05		2011–12	
	Agri.	RNF	Agri.	RNF	Agri.	RNF	Agri.	RNF
Total	81.45	18.55	78.38	21.62	72.65	27.35	64.10	35.9
Rural male	77.71	22.29	74.00	26.00	66.50	33.50	59.36	40.64
Rural Female	87.7	12.30	86.20	13.80	83-34	16.66	74.94	25.06

Source: Himanshu, 'Rural Non-farm Employment in India: Trends, Patterns and Regional Dimensions', *India Rural Development Report,* Hyderabad: Orient Blackswan, 2015, p. 87.

The available official data also provides some interesting evidence of the growing number of rural workers being employed in the non-farm sector. As is evident in Table 6.2, the share of rural workers employed in the rural non-farm sector has been steadily growing and it went up from 18.55 per cent in 1983 to 35.9 per cent in 2011–12. There are obvious regional and state-wise variations. The proportion of rural workers employed in the non-farm economy is much larger for some states, such as Kerala where they were 70.9 per cent, followed by Tamil Nadu (52.7 per cent), Punjab (48.2 per cent), and West Bengal (48.1 per cent). On the other extreme are the states of Chhattisgarh (15.9 per cent) and Gujarat (26.1 per cent).[27] More importantly, the nature of this employment is not in the form of well-paid regular jobs. A large majority of them tend to be either self-employed or find employment in the local informal economy, which is mostly precarious and low paying.

In the absence of internally generated dynamics of economic growth, RNFE is likely to remain a rather fragile alternative. Ownership and cultivation of land still carries a sense of dignity and pride, while the precarious employment in the local non-farm economy does not. Its growth could be seen as a sign of decline of agriculture and as well as a general desperation. Further, its substantive nature significantly varies across regions of the country. A more nuanced understanding of its value addition would require a 'revisit', conceptual and empirical.

chapter 7

RURAL TRANSFORMATIONS
DECLINING AGRICULTURE AND
THE CRISES OF VILLAGE LIFE

The question and the framings of 'rural transformation' have had a rather peculiar trajectory. Classic social science writings and the later-day theories of modernization do not discuss it merely as a process of change within the 'rural'. They tend to view it as a course that should alter the very nature of the settlements. A near complete end of the 'rural' and its metamorphosis into 'urban' is ipso-facto taken for granted in such conceptualizations. This, interestingly, is done despite the common knowledge that cities and villages have existed parallelly for centuries, as I have repeatedly argued in different chapters of the book. The history of human settlements shows that while occasionally some rural settlements did indeed grow in size and become viewed or classified as 'urban', in most cases and in most places the two together constituted the regional economies and political/state formations. In other words, the two have always been simultaneous and integral components of nearly every social, economic, and political system.

But there is no denying the difference between the two. Villages and cities have never simply been demographic realities. Not only do they differ in the natures of their economies, they also differ in how their social, political, and cultural processes operate. The relationships between different forms of settlements have often been marked by hierarchy and power, with bigger cities often being the centres of domination.

The rise of industrial cities in the early nineteenth-century

Europe was, however, an important turning point in human history. It gave rise to a new form of economic regime, where cities could emerge as the primary sites of production, overtaking and eventually marginalizing agriculture. This was not simply an economic change. It ushered in a new regime of capital.

Karl Marx famously described it as the arrival of capitalist society. His influential writings on the larger social and political impact of the new 'mode of production' also speculated an eventual subsumption of rural communities and agrarian economies by the logic of the capitalist system. The pre-capitalist 'peasant' and feudal agrarian system were to simply melt away, giving way to an industrial urban society structure formed around the logic of commodity exchange. This was to happen everywhere and with everything. The spirit of capitalism was to become a global reality. Karl Marx even commented on India and the possible futures of its village life. As we have discussed in the opening chapters of the book, he uncritically accepted the colonial constructs of the presumed insulated and static nature of the Indian village economy, and rather enthusiastically predicted that the British rule would successfully destroy its ancient social order and its internal equilibrium, for all times to come.

Influenced by his projection, the Marxist economists of India deliberated for nearly a decade during the 1970s over the larger meanings of changes that were taking place in the Indian countryside, and whether the process of agrarian change in rural India was also paving the way for the emergence of a capitalist 'mode of production' in Indian agriculture.[1] Many found that such a change was indeed underway, though many others questioned the claim. However, they all agreed that for India to move on the path of progress, its rural social order had to disintegrate and pave the way for a capitalist form of economic regime. Its inability to do so was attributed to the persistent power of the 'semi-feudal' lords and their ability to enforce a regime of coercion over labouring hands and, thereby, reproduce a kind of 'backwardness'.

Karl Marx and the later Marxists are not the only ones who were hoping for and speculating upon the path of change for rural settlements and agrarian economies. Even those politically and ideologically opposed to the Marxist prognosis tended to passionately advocate for a structural change in the social and economic organization of the Indian village. In fact, they too proposed a roughly similar road map of rural futures, albeit in a different language. For example, the dualistic model of economic growth proposed by economist W. Arthur Lewis or the idea of 'modernization' popularized by several American sociologists during the 1950s, takes the end of 'rural' for granted. For them, the process of industrialization, modernization, and urbanization were coterminous, as if each needing the other, each producing the other, each following the other.

No one will doubt that the regime of capital and commodities exchange has indeed conquered most economies; it had already spread across most regions of the world by the early twentieth century. Modern industries and services today have become sites of economic innovations and expansion. The steady rise of industrial economies and modern services, in terms of their value addition to the economies, have long bypassed the agrarian economies. By 2018, the share of agriculture in the global gross domestic product (GDP) had declined to a mere 4 per cent.[2] Even in less developed regions of the world, in countries of the Global South, where it continues to engage up to half of the working population, the share of agriculture has been sharply declining, often measuring below 20 per cent of the national GDP.

Yet the 'rural' persists and the story of its survival is both complex and fascinating. As the available data suggests, while globally the size and proportion of the urban population has indeed been steadily growing, particularly since around the beginning of the nineteenth century, the corresponding trajectory of the rural demographics has been very different from that of the trajectories of agrarian economy, both in terms of its value addition to the national income as well as the number of full-time workers employed in the sector. Even at the beginning of the twenty-first century, nearly half of the world population lived in rural settlements of various descriptions. It was only in 2007 that the balance began to tilt in favour of the 'urban'.[3]

The absolute numbers make the story even more complex and interesting. Globally, the absolute number of rural residents has not seen any decline over the past two centuries. On the contrary, it has only been growing. For example, according to the available data, the total or absolute number of people living in rural areas across the world even in the year 2021 was 3.42 billion, which was nearly four times their number at the beginning of the nineteenth century, and double their number in the year 1950 (1.79 billion).[4] More importantly perhaps, the global story of urbanization is internally very different. The nature and trajectories of change have been significantly diverse across regions of the contemporary world. Even within countries and regions of the world, the patterns and nature of urbanization have been quite varied.

As discussed in Chapter 1 and shown through Table 1.1, the Indian story of urbanization is similarly complex and does not appear to affirm any predictable proposition suggested by theorists of rural transformations. The Indian village has never been a static or stable reality. As we have discussed at length in the initial chapters of this book, this was the case even in the pre-colonial period. This chapter focuses on contemporary processes, with a primary focus on the 'decline of agriculture' and its marginalization as a source of rural livelihoods. Such a process is not merely an economic change. It also has wider social and political implications, one of which has been the widespread 'agrarian distress'.

We begin with a brief discussion of the wider historical

context of shifts in India's economic policies in the recent past. Introduction of 'economic reforms' during the early 1990s has had significant implications for India's agriculture. This is followed by a brief presentation of the rural working population of India. How many of them are employed in agriculture, and in what form? How have their numbers been changing over time? The next section provides a detailed discussion of the changing patterns of landownership, and how these patterns reflect a process of the decline of agriculture. This is followed by a discussion of the ensuing agrarian crisis/rural distress, and the accompanying changes in some aspects of everyday rural life.

Rural Workers, Emerging Trends

The decade of the 1990s was an important turning point for the Indian economy and its popular self-image. It was also a critical moment in the history of the contemporary world. The neoliberal economic reforms initiated by the Government of India in response to the rapidly changing global scenario significantly accelerated the pace of economic growth. The end of the Cold War and the growing use of internet technology for communication and business outsourcing emerged as important opportunities for the Indian software professionals and companies for participation in the 'new' economies in the rapidly globalizing world.

While India's urban economy, particularly its service sector, began to grow at an unprecedented rate, the pace of its agrarian economy began to slow down, resulting in a steadily increasing gap between the urban and rural incomes. The rapidly growing urban economy also translated into an expansion of the urban middle classes, who increasingly began to be seen as the new face of India in the global economy. Their influence grew locally as well. Though their numbers were still merely around one-fourth of the working Indians, by the turn of the century, those from the urban middle-classes began to emerge as a 'moral majority'.[5] They were the 'new normative' that everyone aspired to be!

On the other end, the farm sector was seeing a comparative decline in its share in the national economy. According to the available official data, the share of agriculture (including allied activities such as forestry, horticulture, and fishing) in the national income (GDP) came down from more than half of the national income in the early 1950s to 17.8 per cent in 2019–20. This could easily be viewed as a positive change from a development perspective as it reflects a growing diversification of the Indian economy.

Interestingly, however, the shift in the working population moving out of agriculture has been far slower and its nature has been rather complex. As the official data shows (see Table 7.1) for the first twenty years, from 1951 to 1971, there was no decline in the percentage of workers in the sector. Given the overall increase in the population, including the rural population, the absolute number of those working in the agricultural sector would have actually seen a significant increase. However, during the post-1971 period, it began to decline and came down from nearly 70 per cent of the total workforce in the early 1950s to 54.6 per cent in 2011.

Table 7.1: Rural population and changing nature of workers employed in agriculture

Year	% Rural Population	% Rural workers in Agriculture	% Cultivators	% Agricultural Labourers
1951	82.7	69.7	71.9	28.1
1971	80.1	69.7	62.2	37.8
1991	74.5	59.0	59.7	40.3
2011	68.9	54.6	45.1	54.9

Source: Adapted from *Pocket Book of Agricultural Statistics 2020*, Government of India, p. 13.

The official data also reported a significant internal shift within those working in the agricultural sector. As shown in Table 7.1, among those working in the sector, the number of workers reporting themselves as cultivators saw a significant decline, from 71.9 per cent to 45.1 per cent, but the number of those reporting themselves as agricultural labourers saw a substantial increase, from 28.1 per cent in 1950 to 54.9 per cent in 2011. At the national level, the aggregate proportion of farmers (main and marginal cultivators) accounted for around 25 per cent of all workers, while the corresponding proportion of agricultural labourers was 30 per cent.[6]

These numbers are even more striking when we calculate their proportion in the total population of 'main workers'. As per P. Sainath, 'in the main "worker cultivator" category of the 2011 census data...farmers made up only for 7.8 per cent of India's working population'.[7] Another interesting fact about this decline is that during the first decade of the twenty-first century, the number of those reporting themselves as cultivators declined even in absolute terms, from 127.3 to 118.8 million.

By themselves, these numbers could be quite misleading, suggesting that the shrinkage of agriculture is for real, as was predicted by the dualistic model of economic growth, and might suggest that the workforce was indeed moving out of agriculture. The reality however, is very different and complex. As is evident from Table 7.1, as many as 54.6 per cent of the rural workers continue to identify themselves as being employed in agriculture. In fact, figures collected by the Agriculture Census of 2015–16 tell us that even when the numbers of those who identify themselves as being farmers is declining, the number of land holdings is not. On the contrary, it shows a slight increase, 'from 138.35 million in 2010–11 to 146.45 million in 2015–16, an increase of 5.86 per cent' even when 'the total operated area in the country decreased from 159.59 million hectares in 2010–11 to 157.82 million hectares in 2015–16, a decrease of

1.1 per cent. The average size of operational holding declined from 1.15 hectares to 1.08 hectares during the same period'.[8]

It is not hard to explain or reconcile these apparently conflicting figures. They, in fact, reveal the complicated nature of the situation on ground. As is shown in Table 7.1, the decline in the number of cultivators during the twenty-year period (1991 to 2011) is accompanied by a corresponding rise in the number of those who identify themselves as 'agricultural labourers'. The decline in the number of those who identify themselves as agricultural workers is only 4.4 per cent over a period of twenty years. Not all of those who reported themselves as agricultural labourers were completely landless, or had become rural proletariat. Though their proportion vary across regions or states of the country, many continue to own tiny plots of agricultural land, which they mostly self-cultivate, and the land continues to provide them with subsidiary income. In other words, their association with land continues even when a major proportion of their income is derived from wage work. The shift is merely a reflection of the fact that many of those who had worked in the past as cultivators had to significantly supplement their incomes by moving to wage work. As the size of their holdings shrank over time, they needed to diversify into other occupations for mere survival.

This takes us to a discussion of the nature of landownership and the shrinking size of land holdings.

Changing Patterns of Landownership

The Indian agrarian scene has historically been dominated by small and marginal cultivators. Over time, land holdings have become even smaller. As shown in Table 7.2, even in 1961 as many as 63 per cent of all the operational holdings were in the size category of 'marginal' and 'small' cultivators (below 2 hectares or 5 acres). Together, they cultivated less than

20 per cent of the cultivated land. In contrast, more than 80 per cent of the land was cultivated by cultivators with more than 5 acres of land. The medium and big farmers, who made up only 18 per cent of the total cultivators, cultivated more than half of the total land. The big farmers whose holdings were above 25 acres held nearly 31 per cent of the total operated area. They made for only 4.7 per cent of all the holdings.

This has undergone substantial change. Even though the relative numbers of agricultural labourers have gone up and the number of cultivators has come down, the change does not reflect what the Marxist theory had proposed. There seems no tendency towards a greater concentration of land with the big farmers possessing capital. Even though disparities persist, the proportion of small and marginal cultivators has only been growing. More importantly, they also cultivate a much larger proportion of the land. As is clearly evident from Table 7.2, by 2015–16, the proportion of small and marginal farmers had gone up to 86 per cent of all the cultivators, and they held a little less than half of the cultivated land, around 47 per cent, which is much higher than the 1961 figure when it was less than 20 per cent. On the other end, the number of large-size cultivators had come down to a mere 0.57 per cent, and they held only around 9 per cent of the cultivated land, which is less than one-third of their share in 1960–61.

As I have been repeatedly arguing in this book, agrarian realities of the Indian subcontinent are also marked by significant regional variations and diverse trajectories of change. This is also true of landownership patterns. The average size of holdings in some regions, such as Punjab and Haryana, have historically been bigger than some other regions, such as Bihar and West Bengal. This is partly a result of varying demographic and settlement patterns, such as density of population, and partly because of contemporary political histories. Similarly, the nature of disparities in landownership in the regions that saw radical

Table 7.2: Changing holding size of operational holding and area operated

Year	1960–61		1976–77		1990–91		2015–16	
Size-class (Hectares)	% Holdings	% Area operated	% Holdings	% Area operated	% Holdings	% Area operated	% Holdings	% Area operated
Marginal (Below 1)	40.70	6.70	54.60	10.70	59.00	14.90	68.45	24.03
Small (1–2)	22.30	12.20	18.00	12.80	19.00	17.30	17.62	22.91
Semi-medium (2–5)	18.90	20.00	14.30	19.90	13.20	23.20	9.56	23.83
Medium (5–10)	13.40	30.40	10.10	30.40	7.20	27.20	3.80	20.16
Large (10 plus)	4.70	30.70	03.00	26.20	1.60	17.40	0.57	9.07
Total	100	100	100	100	100	100	100	100

Sources: Surinder S. Jodhka, 'Agrarian Structures and their Transformations', Veena Das (ed.), *Oxford India Companion to Sociology and Social Anthropology: Volume II*, New Delhi: Oxford University Press, p. 1242; *Pocket Book of Agricultural Statistics 2020*, Government of India, p. 2003.

land reforms, such as Kerala, is much lesser than those that were largely able to avoid any redistribution of holdings. However, regional variations notwithstanding, land holdings have been getting smaller everywhere in the country.

The obvious explanation for this process of marginalization of holdings is the growing population and the nature of inheritance cultures in Indian families. Across most communities, land or assets are equally distributed among the sons. Almost every son in an Indian family would claim his share of land. More importantly, despite a steady growth of the Indian economy, its ability to generate viable employment for rural workers to move to cities, leaving behind agricultural been rather limited. Even those who move out are not able to find dignified employment. Thus, a majority of them tend to keep their families in the village and hold on to the small plots of inherited agricultural land.

There have also been other reasons, which are context and region-specific. For example, working in villages of Haryana during the early 1970s, economist Sheila Bhalla had reported that the prosperity brought about by the new technology had also encouraged members of joint households to divide their holdings. Increase in productivity made even smaller holdings viable.[9] Over time their holdings become even smaller. However, once divided, it is hard for families to come together and form a joint household to make their land holding economically viable. At another level, the shrinking size of land holdings also reflects and represents a larger process, which I describe as the decline of agriculture as an economy, as an occupation, and as a value.

Decline of Agriculture, as a Value

The introduction of Green Revolution technology, though confined only to a few pockets of India, generated a great deal of interest among a wide range of people. Even though its critics pointed to its limited spread and its possible social and ecological 'side effects', it generated a great deal of excitement during the early decades of its implementation. It produced a visible sense of pride in the Indian development community and among the rural elite. The new technology had presumably solved India's problem of food scarcity—absolute hunger and famines were a thing of the past!

Looking back, it appears as though it was a surprising thing to have happened. Deliberations on Indian agriculture in development circles until the middle of the 1960s were hopelessly negative, and mostly focused around subjects like technological backwardness of Indian agriculture, and the social conservativeness of the Indian peasantry. Since the British colonial rulers had left, the responsibility of feeding the Indian masses lay at the doorstep of the new ruling elite. Even though production of food grains had begun to pick up soon after the colonial rulers left, the urgency of providing food to the hungry masses was extremely pressing, and any help was welcome. The early initiatives taken by the Government of India after Independence to ameliorate the depressing scenario had not been very successful. As discussed earlier, the Land Reform legislations had by and large been thwarted by vested interests, and the Community Development Programme had almost completely failed to achieve its professed objectives.

It was in this background that the success of the Green Revolution, as the British economist T. J. Byres put it, brought the discourse on Indian agriculture out of the 'limbo of cow dung economics' and the 'dismissive contempt' with which development professionals saw it.[10] Indian agriculture began to show some degree of dynamism. Scholars and journalists began to extensively write on the changes taking place in the countryside. Though everyone did not turn into its admirer, or become a 'green revolutionary', the fact that something hitherto unknown was happening in the pockets where the new agrarian technology had been introduced was widely recognized. Many saw this as a moment of India's modernization going beyond its urban centres. In less than two decades, this euphoria was to recede and another narrative of hopelessness was to take its place.

In its heady days, GR had generated a new-found impatience among the rural elite in the countryside. This was particularly pronounced by the early 1980s in the pockets that had enthusiastically taken to the new technology. The most vocal were the surplus producing farmers who began to mobilize themselves into unions demanding subsidies on farm inputs and higher prices for their produce. The increased integration of agriculture with the market economy, prompted by the shift to cash crops, was inherently against the farm sector and favoured the urban industry and middle-class consumer, they argued. They pointed to unequal power relations between the town and countryside and to the fact that the agricultural sector suffered from unequal terms of trade. The evidence of this, they argued, was the rapidly growing indebtedness among the farming classes.

These 'new' farmers' movements emerged nearly simultaneously in different parts of the country in all those regions where the new technology had become popular and had changed the cropping pattern in response to the demands of the market. Though their movements were regionally specific in terms of the leadership and strategies of mobilization, they coordinated their activities across the country. These movements could be viewed as an early indicator of the impending 'crises of Indian agriculture'. The primary focus of the farmers' movements was around the questions of 'prices' and 'terms of exchange' between what they sold and bought from the market. Farmers demanded subsidies or lower prices for farm inputs such as seeds, fertilizers, and pesticides, and higher and stable prices for what they took to the market to sell, i.e. the farm produce. They also organized themselves through self-led unions, similar to that of the urban workers. Even though these movements were generally led by better-off farmers, all categories of cultivators joined them. Given that even smaller cultivators had taken to the new technology, shifted to new seeds, and were nearly as integrated into the market as the bigger farmers, they too were equally affected by the market processes.

The Crises

The initial prosperity that came with the new technology also began to change their lifestyle. It unleashed a new kind of consumerist aspiration among farmers. For example, in regions like Punjab, farming households began to spend a lot on weddings in the families. Many bought tractors by taking loans from banks even when they did not have big enough holdings. Owning a tractor became a new status symbol. However, uncertainties of the agrarian economy persisted. As the state subsidies began to recede in the late 80s and early 90s, incomes from agriculture began to decline.

An obvious, and much talked about implication of this has been the growing indebtedness of farmers. Normally, debt and credit are common aspects of economic life. As they compulsively participate in the market processes for carrying out cultivation of their fields, many farmers end up in chronic debt. While some decide to sell their land and join the ranks of agricultural labourers or move to casual labour in towns, many find it hard to come to terms with their imminent downward mobility. This anxiety of losing status makes many choose death by suicide over loss of face in their family and larger community. The worst affected by this syndrome are the men who come from socially dominant and high-status caste communities but have relatively small land holdings. This is not simply an economic crisis but also a serious social and human tragedy.

By the late 1980s, farmers' indebtedness began to emerge as a serious problem across regions of the country. However, it came to be discussed by the mainstream media at around the turn of the century when different regions of the country began to report a nearly sudden rise in the numbers of cultivating farmers killing themselves. Among those who flagged the issue of farmers' suicides was *The Hindu* journalist P. Sainath. Reporting from the Yavatmal district of Maharashtra he claimed the number of farmers killing themselves had gone up manifold. The official data on the state of Maharashtra showed that the reported cases of suicides by farmers went up from a mere 62 in 2001 to a staggering figure of 3,228 in 2015.[11] Similar stories were being reported from other states as well, particularly from regions where farmers had taken to the new technology. These included states of Andhra Pradesh, Karnataka, Tamil Nadu, Madhya Pradesh, Gujarat, Punjab, and Haryana.

Most commentators find a close connection between the story of 'agrarian distress'/growing incidence of farmers' suicides and the shift in India's economic policy post the 1990s. This has been well-presented by author Jaideep Hardikar in his book, *Rama Rao: The Story of India's Farm Crisis*, in the context of cotton farmers in the Vidarbha region of Maharashtra. Describing the fast-changing realities of agrarian lives during the post-liberalization period, he writes:

> Around the mid 1990s, a liberalised and globalised economy engulfed many unsuspecting farmers in problems that were beyond their comprehension.... Landed farmers, once among the respected classes in a village economy, were now unable to meet their ever-growing needs....
>
> There was a growing perception among the rural peasantry in Vidarbha that the new economic realities were doing them more harm than good. Cotton farmers, for example, saw their production costs multiply many times as energy, input and fertiliser prices soared.
>
> The growing market orientation of the agrarian economy also unleashed a social change in the village society.... While generally the cost of living...went up,

their real incomes stagnated. Government subsidies were
tweaked or withdrawn.[12]

Some of the leading economists too argued on similar lines.
They too pointed to the growing neglect of the rural society and
its agrarian economy. With an increasing focus on promoting
private capital and integrating India into the emerging global
markets, the policy focus on agriculture rapidly declined. The
emerging corporate lobbies began to increasingly influence the
policy priorities of the Indian state. Agriculture became a losing
enterprise. With declining incomes from land, many argued
that increased indebtedness and misery of the cultivators was
inevitable.[13] According to the calculations made by Hardikar,
nearly 4,00,000 farmers killed themselves between 1995 and
2018.[14]

However, some scholars have questioned the validity of such
claims and have argued that farmers' suicides should not be seen
in isolation. They also need to be seen in the wider context, i.e.,
the prevailing suicide rate in the given state and the patterns of
their rise or fall, they argued. Dipanjana Roy, for example, argues
that the 'data collection and reporting process for farmer suicides
is wrought with flaws (and)...lacks transparency when it comes
to the definition of a farmer suicide'.[15] She also shows through her
analysis of the available official data that when farmers' suicide
went up in a given state, suicides among other social groups,
the non-farmers, also went-up.[16]

However, official data are not the only evidence of growing
desperation and despondency among farmers. A large volume
of journalistic reportage from rural India and a wide range of
field studies by social scientists have clearly shown that there
has been a significant increase in farmers' indebtedness across
regions of India. They have also shown, with primary evidence
and individual biographies of cultivators, that farming in India
has increasingly become a precarious occupation. A connection

between the suicides of individual farmers and their being in chronic debt has also been reported by a wide range of researchers from different parts of the country.[17]

Furthermore, the crisis of agriculture is not merely economic, emanating from the shifting balance of different sectors, or its greater state of neglect during the post-1990s period. It could be seen as part of a much wider change taking place in the Indian countryside which also has a social and political dimension. The weakening of older structures of patronage, partly made possible by the new technology but also accentuated by a growing democratic assertion of the marginalized caste communities, has weakened the hold of rural patriarchs and the landowning dominant castes over village life. To put it differently, the 'agrarian crises' of the post-1990 period is also a crisis of social and power relationships. We need to approach it as a social and political process. As a process of change, it is not only about the agrarian economy but also about rural society.

To elaborate on this point, I would like to introduce some of my own empirical work that made me aware of these processes. During my field studies in villages in Punjab, selected from different parts of the state and carried out during 1999–2000 and 2005–2006, I found a lot of evidence that the smaller farmers were struggling to make ends meet. Some had even quit farming and were engaged in odd jobs in the village or in neighbouring towns.

On the other hand, the bigger farmers stayed invested in agriculture, while simultaneously diversifying their economies as well as their habitations. Many of them had moved part of their families to cities, where their children studied in private English medium schools. Concurring with Staffan Lindberg, I had argued in a paper published in the *Economic and Political Weekly* that 'most agricultural households in Punjab had become economically diversified. They were increasingly becoming "pluri-active", standing between farming and other activities whether as seasonal labourers or small-scale entrepreneurs in the local economy.'[18] 'Agriculture and farming were no more an all-encompassing way of life and identity.'[19]

These changes also brought about an element of instrumentality to everyday life in the village. Collective resources of the villages, such as the common land and village ponds began to wane. Disappearance of such commons also made it difficult for the poor to survive in the villages. Their absence increased the economic vulnerabilities of all agrarian households. The declining practice among rural households of keeping milch cattle is directly linked to it. When I revisited two villages of Haryana in 2008 where I had first done fieldwork in 1988, the evidence of such a change was starkly visible.

People of Haryana, particularly those who live in rural areas have traditionally been very proud of the region being a land of milk and ghee (clarified butter). As a popular slogan goes:

'Deshan mein desh Haryana, jit doodh dahi ka khana.'
(Haryana stands apart from other 'nations',
as this is a land where milk and curd are consumed as common food.)

During the late 1980s almost everyone in the village kept buffaloes or cows. The landed households with substantial holdings kept a large number of cattle, ranging from five to forty. Apart from being a source of nutrition, milk produced at home was also sold to the milk vendors who sold them in the nearby town or city. Farmers also raised calves and sold them when they matured, adding to their incomes. Cattle also worked as a buffer in times of crisis. If a crop failed, or the family needed additional cash for a wedding in the family, they sold a few of their cattle, which helped them escape indebtedness to the local moneylenders. Even the official development programmes for the poor, such as IRDP, recognized its importance and provided landless households subsidized loans to purchase milch cattle, to help them raise their income. Some of the poor households also raised sheep and made a living out of it.

Twenty years later this had changed. None of the households in the two villages kept sheep. Cattle ownership had also come down significantly. While only around 10 per cent of the rural households kept no cattle during the late 1980s, their number had jumped to 42 per cent by 2008. This figure was even larger for the Dalit (69 per cent) and the other so-called backward castes (57 per cent). More importantly perhaps, even among the landed households, a large majority (around 90 per cent) kept only one or two animals.

While there were several reasons for this change, the most critical was the disappearance of the commons, the grazing grounds around the villages, and the village ponds.

'Where do we take them for grazing? There are no open lands left any more around the village'.

Those who did not have their own fields and had no holdings of their own complained about the economic unviability of keeping cattle in the absence of the grazing grounds.

'Where do we have the money to buy fodder? It makes no sense to buy and keep a buffalo if we have to also spend money on the fodder.'

The changing position of women in the landed households was also a factor.

'Our wives and daughters-in-law no longer like working in the cattle shed.'

Some also referred to the changing nature of caste relations and their waning authority; the fact that they no longer had any Dalit households tied to them.

These changes were obviously resulting in a growing disenchantment with agriculture. It has become increasingly hard for agricultural households to hope for any kind of economic mobility by working on the land, and living in the village. Even in a state like Punjab where the average holding size is much larger

(3.62 hectares) than the national average (1.08 hectares), there has been a growing sense of disenchantment with agriculture. During a primary survey, carried out in six villages selected from different pockets of the state, we found that as many as 63 per cent of the non-Dalit respondents did not want their wards to pursue agriculture. Only 12 per cent of them chose agriculture as a preferred occupation for their coming generations. These numbers were even lower in the village of Jethumajra, selected from more the urbanized Doaba regions of Punjab, where only three per cent wanted their future generations to pursue farming.

This disenchantment was also reflected in the way they viewed the future status of farming communities. Our non-Dalit rural respondents, many among whom have traditionally practised farming and taken great pride in being farmers, sounded cynical. Only around 9 per cent were sure of a bright future for agriculture. Another 20 per cent reported that it is likely to remain stable. In contrast, nearly half of them had no hesitation in reporting it as being dismal.[20]

Ontological Insecurities

It was not only the physical commons that had disappeared, social ties too had become shaky. To put it differently, the 'emotional-commons' too were rapidly disappearing from the rural landscapes. 'I do not feel so great being in the village any more. The old respect that we had is no longer there', a bigger landowner told me in a Punjab village during my fieldwork in 1999–2000.

The Indian village was never a community in the sense in which the category is popularly invoked and understood. However, despite the persistent hierarchies of caste, often marked by violence and exclusion, the villagers did share a sense of collective destiny. The disintegration of the jajmani ties and caste ideology obviously has very different implications for different sections of rural populations. Even for outside observers, these changes could mean different things. For those on the margins, particularly members of the Dalit community, this change had only been for the better. They had worked to weaken the oppressive normative order of caste and the value frame of hierarchy. Even women from the dominant caste communities would not complain.

However, for the men of the dominant and upper castes, these changes meant an end to their power and privilege. Not surprisingly, they were the ones who complained the most, about the village and working on the land. As indicated above, some of them had already begun to visualize their futures outside the village. They made the move by normally first investing in an urban house. Their younger generations were very eager to move out.

At another level, these changes also created a new kind of individualization among the villagers and their everyday social life. Growing uncertainty of agrarian life, absence of viable economic opportunities outside the village, and rapidly changing relational frames in the local society had also generated a new sense of anxiety of being and identity. In a different context, sociologist Anthony Giddens invokes the idea of 'ontological insecurity',[21] which seems to apply well to sections of the post-Green Revolution rural contexts of India. One of the visible manifestations of this process was a growing urge among the local villagers towards newer forms of religiosity.

I was made aware of this towards the end of my fieldwork in 2008 in two villages of Haryana. I found a large number of local residents going to a wide range of deras and the passionate devotion among them for their newly adopted gurus and their shrines. The two most popular religious sects in these villages were the Dera Sacha Sauda located in Sirsa town of Haryana, around 100 kilometres from the villages, and the Radha Soami Dera located in Beas in Punjab, around 350 kilometres from the village. However, these deras had local branches, located within a distance of around 10 kilometres. Some of the villagers had also become part of the organizing team of the local branch of the deras. I found as many as 500 followers of the Dera Sacha Sauda in Village-1. There was something interesting about their social profiles. While nearly all of them were relatively poor (though not abjectly poor), in terms of caste identities they were a mixed lot. Even though caste was rarely forgotten, the new-found common religiosity seemed to provide them a sense of community. This became particularly evident when they travelled together to a shrine, or organized a satsang in the local dera.

The growing popularity of deras and the gurus also had a more practical explanation. As indicated above, the prosperity brought about by the growing use of new technology and HYV seeds ushered in a new kind of consumption culture among the cultivating households. This also encouraged alcohol consumption to become more widespread. One of the two villages also had a local liquor vend. Liquor consumption among the men in rural areas in different parts of the country is described as a major social problem. It has the potential of creating a serious crisis in the economy of the household and produces conflicts within the family, often resulting in greater incidences of domestic violence. Politicians have gone to the extent of promising/introducing prohibition, hoping to win over women voters for their parties. Though the deras and their gurus were popular both with men as well as women, it was the latter who tended to show more enthusiasm for going there. One of the motivating factors for women of these villages to go to the deras, with their men, was the hope that the guru would convince the men to give up alcohol.

During his fieldwork in villages of western Uttar Pradesh, sociologist Satendra Kumar too observed a similar process of growing religiosity across members of different religious communities. Rituals and festivities that had hitherto been popular only in urban centres were increasingly becoming part of the rural landscape of the region.

> ...an increasing number of Jats are shifting away from their Arya Samaj roots and joining religious and spiritual sects such as the Dera Sacha Sauda, Radha Soami, and Kali Kholi Wale (Lord Krishna's incarnation) which are urban and have spread to rural Muzaffarnagar, Meerut, and western UP. With the agricultural and village festivals on the decline, they are embracing Hindu rituals and festivals such as Navaratri, participating in kirtans....[22]

Such a process was not confined only to the agrarian dominant castes of the Hindus. Even among the poorer Muslims religiosity was growing.

This neo-religiosity is almost always communitarian and demonstrative, easily politicized. In some cases, the right-wing religio-political/communal organizations have also been actively promoting this trend.

Growing religiosity was not the only emergent social and cultural process. At another level, such a 'disintegration' of the communitarian ethos and consequently increasing individualization is also producing a kind of neoliberal sensibility. Desire for mobility, growing reach of electronic media, cell phones, and culture of consumption brings the lifestyles of the urban middle classes to the village, a subject of much significance with multiple implications—social, economic, and political. We will return to this in the following chapters of the book.

Crisis of Ecology

Accompanying the economic distress is also a serious, if not currently severe, crisis of ecology and environment. Though the nature of emerging ecological challenges varies across regions, it is visible almost everywhere. For example, the most serious challenge being faced by the farmers of north-western states of Punjab and Haryana is the over-exploitation of groundwater and rapidly declining water tables. The main reason for this is the shift to paddy cultivation during the early years of the Green Revolution.

Given that the logic of the Green Revolution was about feeding the growing population and the production of food grains, the initially introduced HYV seeds were of wheat, the staple food of the local people of the region. However, a large proportion of the Indian population ate rice. Though rice cultivation was not unknown in the region, it was a marginal crop as it needed a much greater volume of water than was available in the region at most times of the year. With new sources of irrigation becoming available, cultivation of rice was no longer a difficult proposition. It also turned out to be an economic and ecological boon for perpetually water-logged pockets of the state, a problem which had only worsened with the laying of canals in these regions. The tube wells that irrigated paddy took care of the problems created by water seeping in from canals and left the fields ready for the rabi crops later in the year.

Since paddy was eagerly procured by the Food Corporation of India (FCI), it quickly became a profitable commercial crop for Punjabi farmers. Given paddy's wider market, locally and abroad, farmers could often also sell it at high prices to private traders. Some varieties, such as Basmati, continue to be sold at a much higher price in the open market than the MSP available in the mandis. By the early 1970s, wheat and rice emerged as the two most popular crops in the region. This had a direct implication for the crop diversity of the region. As mentioned in a previous chapter also, besides replacing the native varieties and locally cultivated seeds with the commercially available HYV seeds, the number of crops sown in the region also came down. The crisis of ecology being confronted by rural India has diverse manifestations. In addition to the declining water tables and impoverishment of the soil, there are also local level issues in each region of the subcontinent. The process of global warming is likely to only heighten the challenges of ecology being confronted by rural cultivators and the population at large.

As is evident from the discussion above, the claims and assumptions proposed by the classical conceptions of rural transformation, popular among social scientists and also among a section of policymakers and social activists, have major flaws. The source of their limitation lies in their uncritical acceptance of the Western experience of change as a generalized model of economic and social transformation and their presumption that every normal economy ought to undergo similar stages of growth. However, trajectories vary across regions and countries of the world. A closer historical view would show that such variations have been present even within the countries and regions of the West. Differing trajectories ought not be interpreted as 'anomalies' or 'deviations'. There can be no single idealized model of social or economic transformation. The Indian experience is as real as any other.

The discussion presented in this chapter also clearly shows that while India's agrarian economy has undergone major changes overall and across regions, it does not conform to a single model of economic growth. It clearly presents a range of patterns without necessarily moving in a specific direction. In a way, the India story shows the value of a non-teleological perspective. Even when agriculture significantly declines in terms of its share in the national GDP, it continues to matter. In terms of employment, it remains the largest sector of the Indian economy. It also continues to matter in electoral politics and in everyday social life. It remains a source of self-identification for many, even for those who are no longer fully engaged with it. As mentioned in the previous chapter, the quality of occupations that they seem to be diversifying into remain economically unattractive as they offer rather low incomes and remain precarious.

Agriculture also continues to be an important source of economic and social security. Rural residents tend to hold on to their land, even to marginalized holdings. Economists might find it irrational, but that appears more like a convenient and lazy explanation. The challenge before us is to develop a context-specific and meaningful understanding of the rural realities of the subcontinent, which can help the relevant actors to effectively engage with its diverse dimensions.

chapter 8

CASTE, CLASS, AND GENDER
CHANGING SOCIAL LIFE

Social life in rural settings is popularly imagined as being very different from its counterpart, the urban milieu, in its nature and patterns. As discussed earlier, such an understanding of the difference in the modes of living between the two types of settlements has been popular not only among social scientists but also with laypeople, a part and parcel of our common sense. Most middle-class urban Indians, for example, would assume that villagers always live in joint households where married brothers and their families live together with their parents, often under the command of an authoritarian patriarch, a father or grandfather. Simultaneously, most educated middle-class Indians would also endorse the view that in urban settlements everyone lives in nuclear households, where a husband and wife live with their unmarried children, and without the presence of other kin or an overarching patriarchal authority.

According to this popular view, life in the Indian village is also organized around the institution of caste. The village provides an ideal and appropriate ecosystem for caste divisions and hierarchies to function effectively. As is popularly assumed, caste curates and conditions nearly everything in an Indian village. Everyone grows up within the habitus of their caste and kinship community, from where they acquire notions and sensibilities of what is good or bad and what is right or wrong. The patriarchs in families arrange marriages as per the rules and restrictions of caste endogamy and exogamy. Its patriarchal social order very neatly demarcates the roles and statuses of the two genders as per the rules handed down over centuries.

In this commonsensical view, economy and occupations too are determined by caste. Everyone learns the craft and skills required for performing their caste occupation while growing up within their families and the larger kinship circle to which they belong. Cultivators, potters, barbers, carpenters, blacksmiths, shoemakers, sweepers, toddy tappers, sweet makers, moneylenders, priests, healers and midwives, all acquire the skills of their craft while growing in their households, from their elder kin, and they join them as full-time workers once they are old enough to do so.

Rural social lives are thus presumed to be lived and organized collectively. Questions of individual choice or taste are simply irrelevant to them; so is the idea of individuality or an individual's identity. Such a patriarchal social order could also be oppressive, particularly for rural women, young children, and for those living on the margins of the village society.

However, as is suggested in these presumptions, rarely do people complain about caste divisions or contest the authority of the male heads of the households or that of the village patriarchs. Such situations of conflict normally do not arise because everyone in the Indian village lives by their tradition. They grow up imbibing its values and norms. An absence of such existential anxieties and individual choices also makes their way of life simple and fairly predictable.

Even though such stereotypical images of rural social life are often constructed and invoked by middle-class urban Indians to convey the superiority of their lifestyle, they may occasionally also attribute a positive value to such an imagination of the village society: the villagers may often be ignorant and rustic but their lives are simpler and easier to live because they have a kind of stability, which urban folks have lost and often long for. Rural residents are also seen as living closer to nature, in consonance with its flows and without any conflict with it. They are viewed as being free from an excessive greed for material goods. Enticed by such a stereotype, many urban Indians long to go and live in the village, away from the hustle and bustle of urban life.

In preceding chapters of this book, I have repeatedly questioned the validity and value of such a contrasting view of rural and urban societies. The size of settlements and spatiality in general are indeed significant and they do play a role in shaping or structuring social relations and ways of thinking and being. Further, villages, towns, cities do differ in distinct, definable ways. For example, the size of a settlement would have implications for the way in which identities of caste, kin, and community tend to function in everyday life. The anonymity available to those living in the bigger urban centres also brings about a different kind of social and cultural diversity, which is generally absent in a smaller settlement. However, a contrasting view of rural and urban settlements, or an idealized imagination of the Indian village as having been ever stable and harmonious or of a farmer as a 'simpleton' is completely flawed and ahistorical. Its counterpoint, the popular stereotype of the city being free of ascription-based hierarchies, lived solely through individualized identities and rationally organized economic life, and above any kind of active identification with ethnicity, caste, or religion in public life is equally flawed.

As noted earlier in the book, such a view of the Indian village, or this binary mode of framing rural and urban settlements is also not very old. It has its origin in the evolutionary theories of human species, applied uncritically to human society by functionalist sociology and some romanticist Western thinkers who did not like the changes produced by modernity and industrialization in their societies. Gandhi's romantic view of the village was also drawn from a similar imagination.

As I have discussed in the previous chapters, such a view of the Indian village was also invoked and popularized by the

British colonial rulers. Such a view also presented the Indian village as having been static for ages and an undifferentiated form of social reality, which helped them legitimize their presence in India as benevolent rulers, who were working hard to introduce a spirit of change among the Indians, particularly among those living in its innumerable village communities. As the British claimed, the Indian villages had been eternally stagnant and had no capacity to change on their own; they had to be invaded and disrupted from outside for their own 'progress'.

This also made it easier for them to persuade members of the emerging middle class in India about the superiority of the Western way of life, which was also the urban way of life. The Western city emerged as a model of modern life. The contrasting imaginations of the Indian village on one side and Western city on the other became a source of theorizing social and economic change. This imagination underlay much of the development thinking with which the native elite of India visualized its future after freedom from colonial rule. Even when the nationalists mobilized popular opinion for Independence, they accepted the colonial framings of India being a backward country, a land of never changing villages. Besides accelerating economic growth, state policies and programmes were to also change the presumed social organization of the village, developing it and making it more like the city.

Social Life in the 'Actually Existing Villages'

As mentioned above, social life in villages indeed tends to follow a different pattern when compared to that in the towns and cities. This difference at times could also be quite significant in terms of their institutional arrangements and cultural values. However, as also alluded to in previous chapters of the book, the two—village and city—have evolved together and they tend to shape each other. This has been the case almost everywhere. Thus, the 'actually existing villages' need to be seen in their regional context, in relation to the larger historical processes of power, economy, and ecology.

These broader processes also shape the local institutions, social arrangements, and cultural values. For example, joint households have never been as common among rural residents as is popularly believed. The poorer labouring households, who have always been nearly half of the rural population, always lived in nuclear families. Only those with big land holdings and large houses lived jointly. Joint households are also not uncommon in urban settings, particularly among the large business families. Likewise, while caste has indeed been important for the organizational structure of the Indian village, the Indian city was also structured around caste.

The social and economic life of the village was actively influenced by the land revenue policies of the pre-colonial regimes of power. Furthermore, urban commerce was also mostly structured through the logic of the prevailing hierarchies of caste in the given region. When the dynamics of caste changed during the British colonial period, it changed everywhere, in the village as well as the city. Such a rural–urban synergy in the functioning of caste continues in twenty-first century India even as it has been undergoing radical changes. Using a few empirical case studies, this chapter provides an overview of the changes in rural social life that have taken place in the past century or so with a focus on the relational structures of caste, class, and gender.

Given the diverse nature of different regions of India, trajectories of change have also been significantly varied across regions. However, inter-regional integration has been growing, particularly after the formation of India into a democratic nation state, which often works with a common policy regime at the national level.

Framing Caste

Any mention of caste in the context of the village in India is likely to immediately invoke some obvious images. After all it is in the Indian village that caste is assumed to function most evidently and effectively. As mentioned above, it is popularly viewed as configuring virtually everything in Indian rural life. While there is indeed an element of truth in such a framing of village life, it tends to also simplify and overgeneralize the prevailing realities. It may be worth our while to examine the popularly understood notions of caste and their relevance for an understanding of realities of the rural context. In social science writings, the idea of caste in the rural context is invoked at least in two different modes: the varna model and the jajmani system. The imaginaries of social organization these frames invoke are not congruent with each other.

The Varna Model

The most popular view of caste tends to describe caste on the framework of varna hierarchy, which simply refers to the four or five-fold classification of Hindu society. The evidence used in its support is always the ancient Hindu text of *Manusmriti*. As is popularly understood, such a framework of hierarchy places the Brahmin at the top, followed by the Kshatriya (warrior), the Vaishya (trader), and the Shudra (peasant/artisan/labourer). Beyond the four varnas were/are the avarnas/achhoots (the untouchables). The underlying assumption of this view would also suggest that such an order of hierarchy emerged sometime in the ancient past, or that it was founded by Manu, the author of *Manusmriti*. These divisions and the corresponding normative order presumably continued to be practised across the subcontinent until India was pushed into the path of Western-style modernization by the British colonial rulers. The Indian state continued with such a policy of modernizing/westernizing

India after Independence and caste has since been waning.

This popular varna theory tends to reduce the reality of caste to a single variable and sees it as a Hindu religious value. The order of caste hierarchy is thus viewed as corresponding to the religiously assigned ritual status of every group based on the ideas of purity and pollution. The dialectics of purity and pollution thereby produces an all-encompassing system of inequality, inherently legitimate, and universally accepted. The absence of any kind of contestation presumably kept it going, without change, for centuries and millennia.

Given that the everyday practice of caste was reproduced through a neatly worked out hierarchy of occupations, sanctified by religious belief, and produced a mutually exclusive division of social groups, everyday life acquired a kind of self-regulating equilibrium. The mundane realities of economic life were also reducible to religious beliefs, the ideology of caste. Notions of karma (worldly action) and dharma (ethical duty) implied an otherworldly orientation of the Hindu mind whereby every Hindu is preoccupied with their life after death and not with their material welfare during the life being lived. In other words, for the Hindus of India, economic well-being and political power have been of secondary value.

While this view of caste is almost universally accepted, in reality, it is extremely problematic and has also been widely criticized by scholars. The reality of caste, they argue, needs to be also looked at historically and empirically, at how relations of caste are practised on ground and what changes have occurred over time.[1]

As discussed at length in Chapter 4, the ground realities of caste have always been very diverse and fluid. The available empirical writings, by historians and social anthropologists on the pasts and present social organizations of the region, clearly show that the five-fold theoretical classification of the caste system holds very little value on ground. Each region of the subcontinent has an innumerable number of caste groups and communities, in hundreds. Some sociologists and social anthropologists suggest that these are jatis and they are subdivisions of different varnas and could be accommodated into the overarching framework of the system. However, in reality it is hard to do this. Thus, hierarchies of caste can be best understood in their regional contexts.

Boundaries of caste kinship also follow a regional pattern. The Brahmins of Tamil Nadu have no corresponding jati anywhere in north India with whom they could intermarry. Likewise, the Ahirs or Jats of Haryana have no corresponding status group anywhere in southern India. The nature and order of hierarchy also varies across regions. The Brahmins, for example, do not occupy the highest position in caste hierarchy in many regions of the country. This is particularly true of the rural context, where landownership also determines status hierarchies. Most importantly, such a framing of caste is blind to history. As the rural economies changed, caste relations and hierarchies also experienced significant changes; they have done so in the past and continue to do so in the present.

The Jajmani System

The rural caste system has also been widely discussed through the category of jajmani system, also known by other names, such as the baluta system in parts of Maharashtra. Unlike the varana model, where the Brahmin occupies centrality and is at the top of the hierarchical order, at the core of the jajmani system are the big landowners, the dominant caste. The literal meaning of jajman is the patron, who derives his status from the position he occupies in the local agrarian economy by the virtue of his control over agricultural land. Given the critical significance of farming and agricultural production as a source of livelihood, every other caste is dependent upon the patron. These are typically the caste communities whose services were viewed as being essential for carrying out farming. They included the carpenters, potters, barbers, leatherworkers, sweepers, and even the Brahmin priests. While the servicing castes provided all the required services to the patron castes, the patrons too reciprocated and took care of their clients by sharing with them a part of their farm produce, and ensuring that the livelihood and social needs, such as providing resources or credit for a wedding, of the dependent castes were met. The Brahmin priest may enjoy a degree of respect when compared with a barber or potter but he too becomes a dependent service provider to the patron. Writing about his Punjabi village, Prakash Tandon provides a useful description of the system in his famous autobiographical text, *The Punjabi Century*:

> We had a family barber, whose father before him had been our family's barber, and so the barber's family and ours were indissolubly bound. Good or bad we could not get rid of him, nor could he refuse to serve us, unless we went to live in another place and adopted a local barber family. But whenever we returned to our hometown the old barber was there, and there was no changing him.[2]

Speaking about the Brahmins of his village, he goes on to show their marginal position in the social life of his village:

> With us brahmins were an underprivileged class and exercised little or no influence on the community.... Our brahmins did not as a rule even have the role of teachers, because until the British opened regular schools, teaching was done by Muslim mullahs in the mosques or by Sikh granthis...in the *gurdvārā*s. Our brahmins were rarely erudite; in fact, many of them were barely literate, possessing only a perfunctory knowledge of rituals and knowing just the necessary mantras by heart.[3]

The idea of the jajmani system has also been very popular with social anthropologists and other social scientists who have studied village life empirically. Early social science conceptualizations of the jajmani relations presented them as a harmonious system of interdependence and reciprocity. In his book *The Hindu Jajmani System*, published in 1936, W. H. Wiser, for example, emphasized the presumed spirit of a communitarian bonding, arguing, 'Each served the other. Each in turn was a master. Each in turn was a servant.'[4] Such an emphasis on 'reciprocity' also suggested a cooperative or a non-exploitative nature of caste relations. Wiser's account of the system was obviously influenced by the then popular colonial stereotypes of Indian village life having been devoid of any conflict, or even a notion of private property.

Closer empirical studies provided a very different view of the jajmani relations. Some saw it simply as a system put in place by the locally dominant to ensure a stable supply of labour for agriculture and other requirements. Even when different caste groups depended on each other, their occupations were rarely assigned equal status. The relationships were also not free of coercion. Some scholars have gone to the extent of saying that its normative of hereditary obligations and caste-related occupational duties served to legitimize the local variety of slave labour.[5]

Writing on the South Indian village he studied, André Béteille provides a vivid account of the coercive side of this inter-caste relationship that existed in the village even during the 1960s, victims of which were the untouchable Adi-Dravidas.

> ...traditionally Brahmins did not have much direct connection with Adi-Dravidas. They gave their land to non-Brahmin tenants who, in turn, engaged Adi-Dravida labourers. In other ways also Brahmins were often dependent on non-Brahmins for dealing with Adi-Dravidas. When an Adi-Dravida misbehaved, a Brahmin *mirasdar* might ask his non-Brahmin tenant to fetch the

miscreant from the *cheri*, tie him to a tree, and give him a beating. Physical force...was one of the most effective sanctions against the Adi-Dravidas....[6]

The popular beliefs that jajmani relations existed almost everywhere in the Indian subcontinent and that it has been in existence since the ancient period have also been questioned by scholars. Historian Sumit Guha, for example, did not find any traces of it in the eastern part of Uttar Pradesh.[7] Likewise, Peter Mayer traces its origin to the later part of the nineteenth century, and argues that it came into existence in response to some of the policies introduced by the colonial rulers.[8]

The Lived Realities of Caste

The above brief introduction to the two frames of discussions on caste popular with students of rural India clearly show that it is nearly impossible to talk about caste in the manner in which it is generally understood. Caste is neither simply about ritual status, nor is it a system of reciprocal ties where caste groups live in harmony, doing their jobs generation after generation. Control over cultivable land remained a critical dividing line across caste groups. Those who had control over agricultural land also dominated over others. The dependence of the landless on the big landowners was a crucial feature of rural life and it expressed itself both in terms of class as well as caste.

There also existed other common features of caste across regions, such as the practice of untouchability, hierarchy, exclusion, and segregated settlements and caste exogamy. For example, across the subcontinent, some groups in the village were identified as untouchables and they were made to live away from the main village. Interestingly, this was true not only of the Hindu villages. The Muslim villages of Punjab (including what is now western Punjab in Pakistan) or Gujarat where the landowning patron groups are Muslim also have caste-segregated settlements. The same holds true for the Sikh dominated villages of the Indian Punjab. Most untouchable caste groups also tended to be landless and poor. However, the specific features of inter-caste relations significantly varied across regions.

Perhaps a better way of conceptualizing caste would be to look at it as an ascription-based system of hierarchies or 'ascriptive hierarchies' that institutionalizes relations of dependencies through humiliation. In other words, caste is a system of domination, discrimination, and denials/exclusions. It institutionalizes violence in everyday social life.[9] More importantly, in the context of this chapter, like all social relations, caste is not a reality frozen in time.

A large majority of scholars working on rural India agree that even in the twenty-first century caste continues to persist in most parts of rural India. Some would even insist that it has become more coercive and violent. The number of reported cases of caste atrocities continues to be very high and the practice of untouchability has also not gone away.[10] However, the social science researchers working on the ground also underline the point that the nature of caste relations has undergone significant changes after Independence, over the past seventy-five years or so. Some would even go to the extent of describing these changes as being radical.[11]

For a meaningful discussion of the changing nature of caste relations, it will be useful to also recognize the critical significance of the prevailing economic realities, often framed in the language of 'class'.

Class in Rural India

Seen in terms of livelihoods and economic life, caste divisions closely correspond with divisions of class. The two reinforce each other in a variety of ways. As discussed above (and in the fourth chapter), even the pre-colonial village in India was far from a homogenous community. It was internally differentiated and unequal, both socially and economically. The rich and the dominant almost always belonged to the so-called upper castes, and the poor to the so-called lower castes. Those from the untouchable groups were among the poorest in the village. The system of caste hierarchy clearly served to perpetuate inequality, legitimize discrimination, and reinforce exclusions or denials.

This appears to be evident even in the social anthropological village studies of the 1950s. Even while working broadly with a functionalist perspective, M. N. Srinivas had underlined the point that the social framework of patron–client relationships in his Mysore village also had a class dimension. It was structured through vertical ties between landlord and tenant, between master and servant, and between creditor and debtor, and these relationships did not always correspond with the prevailing structure of caste hierarchies.[12]

Some scholars have also highlighted the native conceptions of class, which were as much a source of identity and social organization in Indian rural and agrarian life as caste was. The most well-known of such an argument is that of Daniel Thorner who, after extensive tours of the Indian countryside during the early years after Independence, had suggested that on the basis of (i) the form of income derived from the soil; (ii) the type of right in the soil; and (iii) the form of actual field work done, it was possible to identify three social and economic classes in the Indian countryside. These were the maliks (landlords or proprietors), the kisan (cultivating peasants), and the mazdoors (landless labourers).[13]

Though these expressions are mostly used in north and north-western regions, it is not difficult to identify corresponding terms in other languages and regions of the subcontinent as well. These were also not simply abstract categories invented by social science observers. They have been in active usage as everyday social identities and structures of hierarchy, paralleling caste, and often carrying significant weight in rural social and political life.

Class relations among the bigger landowners and the landless, who worked for them, were often tied through debt and frequently resulted in their perpetual bondage to their employers. These relations of bondage survived for generations and were clearly exploitative and oppressive in nature. The locally popular categories of social class have also been in extensive usage in the state bureaucratic system and agriculture-related state policies. These categories are routinely used in the local level administration of land records.

A more popular usage of 'class' in the rural/agrarian context has been around the ownership and non-ownership of land. As discussed in detail in Chapters 6 and 7 of this book, most of the official data on agrarian economy is collected through acreage classification of rural households engaged in agriculture. The standard categories are: the landless/agricultural labourers; marginal farmers (holding size below 1 hectare); small farmers (holding size 1 to 2 hectares); middle-farmers (2 to 4 hectares); large farmers (more than 4 hectares). Most economists working on agriculture also work with the official data sets and the official classification.

The obvious limitation of such a classification is that it merely provides an idea of prevailing disparities in landownership patterns. It says little about the nature of relationships that different categories engaged in agriculture have with each other. Such a framing tends to also assume autonomy of agriculture as a sector of economy. In reality however, many among those who worked on land, as owner cultivators or as landless labourers, also worked elsewhere. Further, the produce of the farmers increasingly goes to market. Farmers also buy most of their inputs from the market. Thus the question of the relationship of agriculture with the wider market is also important, particularly in the context of the shrinking nature of the agrarian sector in the national economy. The changing relationship of agriculture and rural economy with the outside world also has implications for relations of caste, class, and gender within the village.

Changing Class and Caste

Beyond the question of language and categories of description, how do the relations of caste and class work on the ground? How have they been changing over time? I have invoked these questions in different ways in earlier chapters. It may be worthwhile to bring some of those points together here.

As mentioned earlier, scholars are nearly unanimous about the fact that, whatever might have been the sources or times of its origins, or its various forms and nomenclatures in different regional settings, the jajmani ties had weakened significantly, if not completely disappeared, all across the country by the late 1970s. Historians of modern India tell us that some of these changes had already been underway at least since the early decades of the twentieth century.[14] Independence of India and the process of development initiated by the Indian state through its various policies for economic growth accelerated the process significantly.

Different scholars have described these changes in different ways. Dutch social anthropologist, Jan Breman, who studied South Gujarat, called this a process of 'de-patronisation'. He attributed this to the introduction of new technology and its adoption by big farmers. With the growing use of machines for cultivation, the services of the artisanal castes were no longer required. The big landowners with whom they were tied through the local norms of the jajmani system gradually broke away from the relationship. Likewise, they also no longer needed the life-long services of the labouring poor and their families, who were not only paid a share of the farm yield by bigger landowners but were also provided a sense of security by their landed patrons.

The landowners took care of them and their families in times of crises and special needs.

However, in the changed scenario, the landed farmers preferred hiring them as daily wagers, with no obligation beyond payment of the mutually agreed wage, in cash or in kind. This process of de-patronisation, thereby, made the position of the landless poor in the village economy even more vulnerable.[15] Anthropologists working in the southern states of India also reported a similar process of growing formalization of class relations in the agrarian economy.[16]

Studying the north-western state of Haryana, economist Sheila Bhalla too found a similar process of change in the nature of class relations between rich cultivators and the labouring poor.[17] As was the case in south Gujarat, in rural Haryana too, the introduction of machines made many of the traditional artisans tied to the agricultural process redundant. Many of them had to move to full-time farm labour. The practice of keeping siris or sajhis, popular with big landowning cultivators, also began to decline. Traditionally, a landless sajhi/siri typically worked with his employer along with his entire family. In return, he was paid one-fourth to one-fifth share of the yield from the land they helped cultivate. Here too, the employer was the patron of the family in times of special needs.

By the early 1970s, the system changed to a formalized arrangement where the labourers began to be employed individually (without their family) for a fixed annual wage. The employing farmers and the landless labourers formally signed a contract, often affirmed by the local bigwigs as witnesses. The contract always mentioned the annual salary of the labourers, which often also included cooked meals to be provided by the employer farmer, the number of days of leave permitted during the year, and the cash amount to be paid by the employing farmer in advance. They also began to be called naukars (servants) instead of sanjhis (sharers). Quite like the sanjhis, the naukars remained tied to the employer because of the perpetual state of indebtedness; yet in the changed situation the farmers no longer had any obligation towards the well-being of the tied labourer beyond the payment of his wage.

The change, however, was not simply a matter of the landowning patrons abandoning their poor landless clients or imposing the shift from above. The landless too felt a kind of relief. My own fieldwork in Haryana[18] and Punjab[19] showed that the landless labourers did not look back at the older structures of patronage and jajmani relations with any kind of nostalgia. On the contrary they disliked all kinds of tied labour. Some of them did work on an annual contract with a specific farmer. But it was nearly always out of compulsion. Their compulsion stemmed from a need for credit, which they could raise from the employer farmer as advance annual wage, on which farmers did not charge any interest. Raising a loan from the local credit market meant paying a high interest, going up to 5 per cent for a month. For the landless poor in the village, with no assets to mortgage, obtaining such credit was also rather difficult.

However, once they entered such a relationship, despite its formal contractual nature, it was hard to come out of it. The money received as advance annual wage would often get spent for a special need, such as a wedding, house repair, or a major illness in the family, and the labourer would end up borrowing small amounts from the employer farmers to get through the rest of the year. When the contract year ended, he would have enough outstanding amounts to require him to commit to work for another year. In case he did not like working with the credit farmer, he had to find another farmer who was willing to clear his outstanding debt and to employ him on similar conditions.

Once a labourer accepted attachment, he had to invariably remain in the relationship, going up to ten or fifteen years. The growing dislike of attached and bonded labour among the labouring poor implied that such arrangements have been steadily declining across different regions of the country. Given that the average farm size has also been declining (see Chapter 7), demand for such labour has also reduced. The bigger farmers, who still have large holdings, resort to a greater use of machines, which reduces their dependence on farm labour.

In some regions, such as Punjab and Haryana, landowners have also resorted to hiring migrant labour from other states to meet the growing demand for agricultural labour, particularly during the early decades of the Green Revolution. The new technology enabled farmers to intensify their agricultural operations and significantly raised their stakes in farming. Increasing use of high yielding variety (HYV) seeds, chemical fertilizers, and pesticides made cultivation an expensive affair. Farmers also invested in farm machines, such as tractors, threshers, and a range of other equipment. Some of the new crops and modes of their cultivation, such as paddy, were also labour intensive.

With the fast weakening relations of patronage and loyalty, the labouring classes also began mobilizing for higher wages and better working conditions. Cases of conflict increased. Thus, the big farmers reached out to the poor in depressed regions of India, eastern Uttar Pradesh (UP) and Bihar, for example, to fulfil their need for labour. Beginning with the early 1970s, seasonal labour flows became an essential part of the agrarian operations in northwest Indian states and several other more affluent regions. Labourers initially came for peak seasons, such as during paddy transplantation and the harvesting of wheat and paddy. The migration flows have since continued, with many staying back through the year with bigger farmers.

These labour migration flows significantly helped the farmers of Green Revolution regions in availing relatively cheaper and assured supplies of labour. The availability of migrant labour obviously weakened the bargaining power of the local Dalit labourers. However, it also created space and opportunity for the local Dalits to explore options of employment outside agriculture, which, in many cases also implied going out of the village. They began to travel to neighbouring towns and cities for employment and found a sense of freedom in it. 'Casual' employment in a town, or on local construction sites did not carry the kinds of obligations and coercions that working with local farmers involved. However, such mobility did not make life easier for most of them. Employment available outside agriculture is mostly in the informal economy carrying with it a slew of vulnerabilities and exclusions.[20]

Something similar was happening to the rural poor migrating out of the less developed regions of Bihar, Jharkhand, and eastern UP to work in agriculturally developed regions. Besides providing them additional days of employment and income, working away from their native villages gave them a sense of autonomy. It helped them get out of the vicious cycle of dependence on the locally dominant landed elite. Reporting from their fieldwork in villages of Purnia district of Bihar, economists Gerry and Janine Rodgers write:

> In the 1970s and early 1980s, these villages were backward and stagnant, and poverty was intense. Wages barely sufficed to cover basic subsistence, and real incomes were if anything declining. Mortality was high and production relations 'semi- feudal', in the sense that debt bondage, tenancy and attached labour were widespread, served as mechanisms of labour control and exploitation, and were resistant to change. Communications were poor, facilities limited, education levels low. The government action was extremely weak.[21]

The pace of outmigration continued to grow over the years, and became a way of life for the poor in these regions. As the trend spread, they began migrating to urban areas as well. Reporting from her field site in the Madhubani district of Bihar,

Amrita Dutta shows that by 1980–81, nearly 24 per cent of the households had at least one migrant member in their family. By 1999, this had gone up to 54 per cent, and in 2011, Madhubani villages had as many as 78 per cent of households with at least one member of the family working outside. She reported that it had become a village norm with youth becoming its predominant stream. Nearly half of the male migrants were in the fifteen to thirty age group.[22]

Besides destinations, patterns of migration have changed over the years. These are no longer short-term migrations to rural northwest India for seasonal work in agriculture. Labouring poor from Bihar and other pockets of eastern India remain on the move through the year. A large majority of them work in urban centres, in industries, construction, private security, transport, and other odd jobs.

However, in most cases, these migrations do not conform to the classical model of demographic transition where, with the development process unfolding, a majority of the workforce moves its residence from village to city, leading to the larger process of urbanization. These migrants tend to go out for work, leaving their families behind in the village. They tend to come back, once or twice during their active work life and return back to the village for good when they find it hard to meet the demands of physical labour required of a migrant worker; generally when they are forty-five or fifty years of age. Thus, the pattern of their migration remains circular in nature, producing little demographic effect. For example, the villages in Madhubani district of Bihar, where nearly 78 per cent of the rural households have at least one person working outside, remains one of the least urbanized pockets of India. According to the Census of 2011, 94 per cent of its population was demographically rural.

However, the near absence of urbanization does not mean that migrations made no difference to rural life in these regions. Coupled with the fissures created by the introduction of democratic political processes, the opening up of the migration flows to the Green Revolution pockets of Punjab and Haryana worked as a 'trigger of change'. It began to undermine 'feudal relationships, creating new perspectives, generating additional income sources and pushing up local wages'.[23] It also produced some interesting political changes, locally in the village and at the regional levels, which will be discussed in the following chapter.

Caste, Persistence, and Change

During my field studies of villages in Punjab in 1999–2000 and 2006 and of villages in Haryana in 1987–88 and 2008, I found that the local caste relations had undergone a significant shift. Very few among the Dalit castes were involved with their traditional caste occupations. While some, such as the traditional blacksmiths, had to give up their traditional work because of growing redundancy, others gave up for the sake of dignity. For example, no one from the villages was willing to pick up dead cattle. The villagers in Punjab had to invite 'contractors' from nearby towns to get their dead cattle picked up. No one made or repaired shoes in the villages. Likewise, the barbers had their small shops and worked purely as service providers for a fixed price. Further, a good number of them were not even from the traditional caste of barbers. Even the scavengers preferred being paid formally, in cash, for their work. I call this a process of 'dissociation'.[24]

The landless Dalits had also been actively working towards distancing themselves from the local agrarian economy.[25] They disliked working as tied or attached labourers with farmers on annual contracts. Even those who worked as casual labouring hands preferred employment in the non-farm economy. Such distancing from the local farm economy gave them a sense of dignity since they were no longer dependent on the locally dominant castes for employment.

The local Dalits also worked towards gaining autonomy from the collective or 'community life' of the village, which was everywhere controlled by the locally dominant castes.[26] Wherever they could, they invested in building their autonomous institutions, such as gurdwaras/temples and community centres. This was done as a strategy to avoid any experience of communitarian interaction with those from the dominant castes and escape their caste-based prejudice.

Changing Gender Relations

The question of gender has emerged as an important and critical aspect of any discussion on social life. The early notion of biological determinism has been almost universally abandoned by social scientists. Differences between men and women are cultural realities and are produced by social and historical processes. They also undergo changes, structurally as well as culturally, as societies change. For sociologists the term 'sex' refers to the anatomical and physiological differences that define male and female bodies. Gender, by contrast, concerns the psychological, social, and cultural differences between males and females. Gender identities are always socially constructed, as are the notions of masculinity and femininity.[27]

Family and household are obviously important sites where gender is presumed to significantly matter. It is also in the families that gender differences are first taught to children. Male and female children are socialized very differently. The identities of being male and female that they acquire during their early socialization while growing up in their families are reinforced by the larger society, in schools, on the playground, on the streets, and at work.

Thus, the question of gender goes much beyond the sphere of family and household, or sexuality and reproduction. It also shapes economies and political life. For example, landownership patterns, the state policy of land reforms, modes of mechanizing agriculture, the structures and processes of marketing agricultural output, labour migrations, wage rates for labouring hands, all have a gender dimension. They tend to all exclude women, or include them on terms that are unfair to them.

Further, nearly all cultures have been patriarchal in nature and continue to be so even in contemporary times. However, their degrees and forms vary, across time and among social groups. Patriarchy is often stronger among agrarian communities. Landed farming communities tend to value masculinity more than others. This may be because of the contested nature of land rights in most places and the frequent occurrence of violent conflicts around them. It may also be because in most places the ruling regimes tend to recruit soldiers from amongst the farming communities. Even the British colonial rulers designated some such communities, such as Sikh Jatts and Rajputs as 'marshal' and preferentially recruited them in the colonial army.

Prevailing customs and marriage practices in the Indian context have also kept women at the margins of agrarian and rural social life. One of the most critical reflections of this is the near complete exclusion of women from ownership rights over agricultural lands across regions and communities of the subcontinent, except for a few notable exceptions such as among the Nairs of Kerala and the Khasis of Meghalaya. As social customs go, girls in Indian families are married off into other families and her parents give her dowry for setting up her own household with her husband. She is not expected to later make claims over the property of her native family, which customarily goes to the male children. This obviously also includes arable land.

Interestingly, the practice of excluding women from inheritance of landed property remains nearly unchanged even after the enactment of a new law, the 2005 Hindu Succession Act, which grants women the rights to an equal share in ancestral property, including agricultural land. A recent survey by the Asian Development Bank covering 8,000 households randomly selected from eastern Indian states found that only 3 per cent of the rural households had their lands registered in the names of women.[28] A majority of these are likely to be from households where there are no living adult males, which the demographers classify as 'female headed households'.

As the economist Bina Agarwal argues, ownership over arable land in rural India is not merely a matter of an economic endowment. It also has implications for women's position in the household, more than being employed. Even though we tend to assume households are internally homogenous, they too tend to discriminate against their women. In chronically poor households, for example, the woman and female children are more likely to stay hungry than their male kin. However, it is not only the family values that are biased against women, even the bureaucratic structure and the larger ideology works against granting equal rights and position to women.[29]

Given the prevailing patriarchal milieu, state-driven agrarian change too has mostly been exclusionary and biased against women. For example, the land reform legislations did not think of including the question of granting land rights to women. Land titles in most cases were granted exclusively to the men of the households. Likewise, the target group oriented programmes, such as the Integrated Rural Development Programme were initially gender-blind with the household being the unit of identification. By implication, the effective beneficiary, the head of the household, would invariably be the 'man' of the household.

The GR technology too had important 'gender effects'. Despite their patriarchal values, agrarian households tended to require active participation of women in farm labour who often worked collectively with other members of the family. The introduction of new technology and cultivation with the help of modern machines further marginalized the position of women in the agrarian economy. Machines tended to replace them more often than they did the men.

While on the one hand GR and increasing use of machines produced a process of what could be described as de-feminization of agriculture, some other regions of India experienced an opposite phenomenon, popularly known as feminization of agriculture. This mostly happened in the regions from where male labour began to migrate out of the village for work. As discussed above, when the migration outflows from the lesser developed rural regions began in the early 1970s, the men went out for seasonal work and returned later to take care of their own fields, mostly very small holdings that they cultivated. Some of them would work as wage labourers in their own village while there. However, as they began to stay away for longer durations, labouring on the farms increasingly became a woman's job.

Women in such situations were left not only to care for the tiny plots of land that their families owned, but also to take care of the young children and elderly parents of their husbands. In some cases, this could also be an empowering experience. They were forced to learn the ways of the world and negotiate with everyday realities of life. However, there are obvious limits to their 'empowerment' in the absence of economic resources.

Besides this, there were also social or status related anxieties that reduced women's participation in the agrarian economy. As a standard governing social norm, traditionally the high-status, high-caste families in rural India did not allow their women to work outside the four walls of their homes. The economic mobility that the GR ushered in among the landed middle castes was thus often accompanied by an increased 'housewife-ization' of women and their withdrawal from work outside the house, including from the agricultural fields.

The GR increased the productivity of land, and made even smaller holdings economically viable. This also encouraged joint households to split into nuclear households.[30] Nuclear households tend to be less patriarchal and allow more space for women's agency. This was perhaps also an indication of the growing middle-class aspirations within the household. A nuclear household could focus more on the education of children than would have been the case with joint households.

The richer farmers, aspiring to see their children join urban middle-class jobs, began to send them out for education. This also included their daughters. An educated girl had a greater chance of finding an educated groom employed in an urban area. However, this shifting aspiration also became a source of gender conflict. Educated women wished to assert their agency in matters of their marriages, a domain over which the patriarchs of their families earlier held total authority. A woman of a dominant caste marrying of her own choice is often seen as a loss of dignity for the family and the community she belongs to. Around the turn of the century, the state of Haryana, for example, frequently reported cases of murder of young women by members of their own family. Nearly all these cases were reported from the landed families of dominant caste farmers and were popularly described as 'honour killings'.

Making Sense of the Changes

As I have argued throughout this book, the popular view of social life in 'rural' and 'urban' settings as being binary opposites of each other is fundamentally flawed. Such a notion is not only empirically unsustainable, it also produces a hierarchy among the two: rural as being traditional and backward, and the urban as modern and evolved. The reality, however, is far more complex and is clearly reflected in the social science literature on the changing nature of rural social life in India. Patterns and processes of change in rural social life are very diverse even across regions of the Indian subcontinent. They do not follow a linear pattern of evolution, suggesting a change towards a presupposed 'urban way of life'.

While some of the development interventions in rural/ agrarian economy have produced predictable shifts on speculated lines, their social effects have been diverse, often contradictory. Growing use of machines and chemical inputs in cultivation and the increasing productivity of land in the GR regions significantly changed the attitudes of the cultivating farmers. Intensive agriculture required a greater engagement with land. Higher investments also implied higher stakes in agriculture. In parallel, the nature of labour input also changed. Farmers required much larger numbers of labourers at only certain times of the year, mostly during the peak seasons. This demand began to be met by migrant labour from outside which, in turn, allowed a greater distancing, dissociation, and autonomy for the traditional landless labouring castes in these villages, enabling them to seek wage employment outside agriculture and in the nearby town as well.

The process of growing autonomy of the ex-untouchable castes and increasing individualization of labouring employment has its gender implications. Women from these families too increasingly work as daily wage labourers, and not merely as appendages to their husbands. Some of them have also become mobile and go out of villages either with their husbands or alone. However, their employment and incomes have also become far more precarious. Besides altering the grammar of caste and class, the GR technology and associated changes in the agrarian economy also transformed relationships of gender within the village. With tractors and combine harvesters taking over, women workers tended to lose out and an increasing masculinization of agricultural processes came about. The social and economic mobility experienced by bigger landowners from the dominant upper castes also produced its gender effects within their families. They no longer liked that women from their families worked on the farms, turning them into housewives instead.

The regions that continue to be agriculturally poor have a diametrically opposite set of gender dynamics. A large proportion of adult male labourers tend to out-migrate for employment, leaving behind old parents and young women to look after their families and small land holdings. In the absence of able adult men, most agricultural work is increasingly carried out by women, as cultivators and as farm workers, resulting in a feminization of agriculture.

Thus, even as we speak, social life in the Indian village is undergoing change. However, the trajectories of these changes differ significantly across regions and, frequently, the processes in one region might influence and alter the dynamics in another in unexpected ways. Their effects are also felt differently by different categories of rural residents. Further, the categories of caste, class, and gender also intersect in a variety of different ways, depending upon the larger social, economic, and political contexts.

chapter 9

RURAL POWER
PANCHAYATS, DEMOCRACY, AND THE STATE

P ower is understood as the ability of an individual or a social group 'to significantly affect the lives of other people, even if the latter resist within normal institutional settings'.[1] Sociologists also make a distinction between 'authority' (legitimate power), and 'domination' (coercive power). Power is also distinguished from influence, or the effect that one group has over others in a society, which tends to be subtle and lasts as long as the other groups do not resist it. Power is held by institutions, such as the panchayats or the Parliament, as well as by individuals, the powerful elites. Elites are generally defined as 'those who have vastly disproportionate control over or access to resources' that are socially valued and scarce.[2] Their positions and profiles in a given society or social context matter much beyond the spheres of their personal lives.[3]

Who holds power and authority in rural India? Interestingly, this subject has invoked very diverse, often contradictory and extreme views. There are many who would virtually equate village life in 'pre-modern' India with 'crude power', its excessive and demonstrative use in everyday social relationships. Tyranny of village patriarchs and the coercive authority of the feudal lords are cited as obvious examples in such imaginaries of rural life. The presence of caste as a framing institution and ideology made it even worse, they would underline. It made violence a legitimate practice and a salient feature of everyday social life. They would argue that those at the receiving end of the traditional caste hierarchy tended to accept their subordinate position with a sense of duty, a consequence of their own karma. On the other hand, those in the superordinate position treated their power with a sense of entitlement, as if its exercise was a part of their religious duty.

Any violation of the prevailing order of hierarchy and disrespect to authority was mostly met with brutal force, they would argue. Examples of this could range from 'honour killings' of young women by their own families in case they dared to violate the social boundaries of caste and wished to exercise their will in choosing their life partners, to the popular stories of massacres of Dalit labourers fighting for their rights to dignity by the private armies of the landlords, the bhoomi senas. Such a view has been very widely held, and is often depicted in popular cinema and fiction. It also finds extensive references in popular journalistic accounts of rural life and occasionally also in social science writings on power and authority in rural India.

While such a framing of the traditional rural life has been quite popular, there have also been many in India who propose a different, almost opposite, view on the subject. While they may not deny the presence of violence as a reality of everyday rural life, they would attribute it to the loss of its 'essential' character because of outside influence. The 'original' design of the Indian village, in their view, had no place for violence or coercion. The traditional Indian village was a cohesive and harmonious community, characterized by a kind of 'innocence', where the idea of domination was simply absent. The village communities tended to live by their tradition, in a preordained pattern. The traditional values and norms were deeply inscribed in the minds of its residents.

With tradition being supreme, no individual could exercise any kind of arbitrary power. It would have never been required, would be the argument. The authority structure of the village was thus subsumed within the traditional order, which everyone accepted without exception. Even hierarchies of caste were viewed as cohesive values and cherished by all. The normative order of caste allocated roles and responsibilities to everyone. The calling of caste was a binding moral duty. By implication, the Indian village had also been a stable system, without any significant change over time. In the absence of conflict and contestation, there had hardly been a need for change. It continued to reproduce its social order, since time immemorial, presumably ever since it came into existence. Even though it sounds too romantic to be taken seriously, this view of the Indian village too has had its takers across a wide range of the political spectrum and for very different sets of reasons. Their names range from native nationalist thinkers, such as M. K. Gandhi and Rabindranath Tagore, to Western social scientists, such as Karl Marx and Sir Henry Maine. Their writings have played a role in constructing the popular beliefs that villages are peaceful places and villagers are simpletons, some which we have discussed in the previous chapters.

This chapter begins with a brief discussion of such a fallacious and mythical view of the Indian village being a 'power-free' collective. This is followed by a discussion of a wide variety of social science writings on the subject that have explored the nature of power and authority in rural India and how it has changed over the past decades. The chapter also provides a brief discussion of the Panchayati Raj system, along with a discussion of the emerging trends in the nature of rural power.

Village without Domination

As discussed above, proponents of this view of the Indian village tend to invoke its ancient past, and suggest that it only began to change during the British colonial period. Interestingly, it was during the British colonial period, and more precisely, in the writings of the British colonists, that such a view was first invoked. As we have discussed in the early chapters of this book, the British rulers not only colonized the region, they also propounded theories on the distinctive nature of social life in South Asia. Bernard Cohn (see Chapter 2) convincingly showed that the British rulers wilfully constructed the idea of an insulated village life, living as per ancient tradition, which had kept it unchanged for centuries and millennia. Even when they encountered evidence to the contrary, they persisted with such a view. They did so because such a conception of the Indian village was politically useful to them. It provided moral justification for their colonization of and continued presence in India to their own people in Britain.

As discussed earlier, even a critical scholar like Karl Marx bought into such an idea and thought that the British colonial rule would indeed serve India well and help break the stasis of communitarian agriculture, which had no notion of private property. Along with his co-author Friedrich Engels, he wrote that the British colonial onslaught would help India move on the path of progress. Most interestingly, even a section of Indian nationalist thinkers used such impressionistic accounts of village life to develop their own understanding on the subject. Gandhi was not the only one who built his theory of swaraj and a critique of Western modernity using such constructs. We can see reflections of this view even in the writings of Rabindranath Tagore who invokes ideas of femininity and a child-like innocence to describe the 'original' Indian village. As he writes in his well-known essay on 'City and Village':

> In their natural state—that is, when the community does not incline too much to one side—the village and the town have harmonious interactions. From the one flow food and health and fellow feeling. From the other return gifts of wealth, knowledge and energy.[4]

He goes on:

> Villages are like women. In their keeping is the cradle
> of the race. They are nearer to nature than towns, and
> in closer touch with the fountain of life. They possess a
> natural power of healing. It is the function of the village,
> like that of women, to provide people with their elemental
> needs, with food and joy, with the simple poetry of life
> and with those ceremonies of beauty which the village
> spontaneously produces and in which she finds delight.[5]

Perhaps the most interesting aspect of his essay is his treatment
of the prevailing social and economic inequalities. Even when
he recognizes the presence of class differences in the traditional
village communities, for him, they do not become a source of
conflict or domination. As he writes:

> Once upon a time the rich regarded it as an act of merit
> to provide water and education. Through their goodwill
> the villages were well off.[6]

Like Gandhi, he too locates the problem of social conflict and
a culture of exploitation as being a result of its exposure to the
Western modernity, which was responsible for disturbing its
balance:

> In the modern age the machine has not only multiplied
> working capacity but also the hunger for gain and the
> scale of profit. That is why there is disharmony between
> the interest of the individual and the community, leading
> ultimately to conflict. Greed severs the relations between
> town and village. The town has become a drain on the
> village because it has ceased to make its contribution to
> the village.[7]

Such writings also became a source for the idea of Panchayati
Raj that India institutionalized at the national level in order

to decentralize governance and empower local communities. As we have discussed at length in Chapter 3, it was this kind of an understanding of modernity that prompted Gandhi to argue for 'a recovery' of the self-governing village community, swaraj. This, he thought, could be done through a formal institutionalization of panchayats (the village councils). The panchayats, he envisaged, would not only save the village from its exploitation by the city, but would also help revive its presumed harmonious communitarian past, free of coercion and violence, which Western modernity had destroyed.

Resistance to the Romantic View

The idea of the Indian village without domination and conflict was one that did not find many takers among those who were given the task of framing the Indian Constitution, the members of the Constituent Assembly of India. Though the Gandhians wanted the village to be made the foundational unit of Indian democracy, they faced stiff resistance from several quarters. Even Jawaharlal Nehru, Gandhi's close comrade in the freedom struggle, showed little enthusiasm for the proposal. Dr B. R. Ambedkar, the chair of the drafting committee expressed his vehement opposition to the proposal that would have given autonomy to the village council over an individual's liberty and rights. Giving autonomy to the village council, he argued, would have implied accepting the status quo. As discussed in Chapter 3 of this book, Ambedkar's view of the Indian village had been different from that of Gandhi. He saw no merit in the so-called traditional social order of caste. For him, caste had always been a coercive practice, which had institutionalized inequality and exclusion. The spirit of democratic citizenship could not be instilled in a caste-divided collective.

However, the Gandhian view was not completely rejected after Independence. One of the early state initiatives for rural development, the Community Development Programme (CDP) introduced in 1952 was largely inspired by Gandhian philosophy (see Chapter 5). The programme had to be abandoned because of its flawed assumptions. As its critics pointed out, a non-recognition of internal differences of class, caste, and power resulted in its benefits being largely cornered by those who were already resourceful; the poor and the needy got close to nothing from the CDP. Therefore, when India decided to introduce Panchayati Raj, it was envisaged with a reserved quota for those from the marginalized social groups, the SCs and STs.

Realities of Rural Power

As indicated above, beyond these popular imaginations of village life, the nature and dynamics of rural power have also been extensively documented and conceptualized by social scientists. Instead of speculating using colonial and orientalist writings on the presumed 'essential' nature of Indian culture and its social life, or trying to comprehend the prevailing social practices and institutions based on their readings of some ancient Sanskrit texts, their mandate was to observe from the field, by being physically present. In other words, they were expected to look into questions of power and domination in rural India empirically, using the conceptual frames of their disciplines.

Social scientists have explored a wide range of questions in their field studies. Who holds power in the Indian village and how do they manage to hold on to it? Does it rest with a social group: a caste, class, community, or with certain individuals? How is it generally exercised? Is there a common pattern across regions of the subcontinent? Has the nature and content of rural power changed over the past seventy-five years? How have the processes of democratic politics and the processes of economic growth changed the internal dynamics of rural power? What have been the implications of the growing integration of rural life into the larger economy of the nation for the local politics? More recently, some have also been focusing on electoral processes and voting patterns across social groups and categories of rural voters. Do rural voters vote differently when compared to their urban counterparts?

Foremost among those who took up the task of empirically exploring the village life of India were social anthropologists and sociologists. They were joined by economists and political scientists in due course. While the early studies on rural power were mostly based on qualitative and ethnographic methods of research, more recently, such studies have also used large scale surveys and are carried out across regions of the country.

As discussed in the previous chapter, the early generation of social scientists who went to explore Indian village life carried with them the burden of the prevailing wisdom of their disciplines. For example, sociologists and social anthropologists worked with the framework of structural functionalism, which did not give centrality to questions of power and domination. They tended to look for the patterns of integration and interdependence in rural life. A good example of this is their approach to the system of caste hierarchies. Even though the most obvious fact about its practice is inequality, some looked at it as a system of reciprocal relationships across caste communities.

Such a framing of caste power is obviously flawed. Reciprocity would imply some kind of 'equality' among caste groups, which in the Indian context is simply unthinkable. Even though big landowners from an 'upper caste' depended on barbers or cobblers for their services, the latter could never be patrons (jajmans) of the former in any meaningful sense of the term. As discussed in Chapter 4 and 8, despite the persistent influence of functionalist theory, such a framing of rural realities of power relations had few takers.

The Dominant Caste

Caste was never about ritual hierarchy alone. Power too was its constitutive feature, always. Empirical studies of village life from across the country reported this extensively. Relations of power tended to overlap with ritual hierarchies. The mediating factor was control over agricultural land. The caste groups that tended to be in possession of land also held power. Notwithstanding significant regional differences, these tended to be all from upper or middling castes. Reporting from Tamil Nadu where traditionally Brahmins were the big landowners, sociologist André Béteille writes:

> Up to the 1940s, the Brahmins enjoyed a great measure of power in the village. Their power was based upon ownership of land, high social and ritual status, and superior education.... The panchayat president was a Brahmin, the panchayat room was in the *Agraharam* (the locality where Brahmin and other dominant groups in the village lived), and initiative in all important matters was in the hands of Brahmins.... Non-Brahmin members...had the position of second-class citizens.[8]

Likewise, reporting from Rajasthan, Anand Chakravarti found that until around the early 1950s, the Rajput jagirdars nearly completely dominated village life. Even though their numbers were not large in the local population, they owned as much as 84 per cent of the agricultural land. They were also locally seen as 'upholders of the traditional social order'.[9] The other caste communities lived in the village under their command.

However, the introduction of Land Reforms after Independence and the accompanying process of political democratization weakened the exclusionary power of the traditional upper castes, such as the landed Brahmins or Rajputs, in the village setting. In the Rajasthan village, for example, after the introduction of Land Reforms in 1954, the share of agricultural land owned by Rajputs came down from 84 per cent to 29 per cent. Likewise, the Brahmin lost their position to the non-Brahmin in Tamil Nadu because of the powerful mobilizations against them during the later decades of British colonial rule. The Brahmins of rural Tamil Nadu were among the first to move out of the villages to the emerging urban centres, such as Madras, or what is now known as Chennai.

The Land Reforms transferred land mostly to the middle castes of tenants and actual tillers of the land. As we have discussed in the sixth and seventh chapter, rarely did the Land Reforms transfer land titles to the Dalits, though many of them worked on the land as sharecroppers and labouring hands. Thus, the logic of rural power still revolved around caste. The middling castes emerged as main landowning groups. They also tended to be numerically larger groups within the rural demographics. In most regions of the country, therefore, they began to emerge as holders of rural power. Anthropologist M. N. Srinivas described them as the 'dominant castes'. Sources of their power were multiple. As Srinivas writes:

> A caste may be said to be 'dominant' when it preponderates numerically over the other castes, and when it also wields preponderant economic and political power. A large and powerful caste group can be more easily dominant if its position in the local caste hierarchy is not too low.[10]

Another variable that he found becoming increasingly significant was the number of educated persons in a caste community and the occupations they pursued outside the village. In other words, even in the rural setting, education and occupational diversification added to the power and influence of the communities they came from.[11] This would have also worked as a motivating factor for the rural families to educate their children, if they could afford it. For Srinivas, materiality had always been an important factor in caste relations. A socially and economically mobile caste could also make claims to a higher ritual status. He famously described such a process as 'sanskritization'.

....a caste which is numerically strong and wealthy will be able to move up in the ritual hierarchy if it Sanskritizes its ritual and way of life, and also loudly and persistently proclaims itself to be what it wants to be. It is hardly necessary to add that the more forms of dominance which a caste enjoys, the easier it is for it to acquire the rest.[12]

Beyond the ownership of agricultural land, power of the dominant caste was also realized through the institution of local panchayats. Contrary to the popular Gandhian notion, panchayats were not simply a communitarian institution. They tended to work to reinforce the power of the powerful patriarchs from the upper and dominant castes in the village. Despite their name, panchayats did not work with the notion of representation.

Though the idea and institution of panchayat functioned at different levels, one of their critical roles was juridical. Wherever they existed in the subcontinent, individual caste groups tended to have a panchayat of its elderly men, who resolved the internal disputes within the caste groups. However, the disputes involving members of different castes were in the domain of the village panchayat, which in effect tended to be the panchayat of the locally upper and dominant caste elderly men. Rarely would a Dalit or a woman sit in these panchayats. It was their ability to enforce their will over the larger village community, even when some did not agree, that made them 'upholders of the traditional social order'. In other words, as is the case with the dynamics of power everywhere, coercive violence was not alien to caste domination.

Furthermore, dominance of the dominant castes extended

beyond the village, to the region, which helped it reinforce its power locally, a subject we shall discuss in a later section of this chapter.

Landlords and Rich Peasants

While caste has indeed been an important axis for discussions on rural power in India, scholars have also pointed to the additional significance of 'class' and individual leadership in this context. Besides their social background, individual skills of leadership tended to be important. However, it would have been nearly impossible for a Dalit or a landless person or a woman to be a village leader.

Mostly using the language of Marxist political economy/ agrarian studies and drawing from Russian and Chinese history, the advocates of class framework tend to divide the rural residents into four or five categories: the big landlords; the rich peasants; the middle peasants; the small and marginal peasants; the landless labouring classes. As discussed in the last chapter, in effect, however, such a class model in the Indian countryside tended to overlap with the hierarchies of caste and also functioned within or through the logic of caste. The big landlords all tended to be from the so-called upper castes of their respective regions. The rich middle peasant tended to be all from the next level of hierarchy. The marginal cultivators and tenants tended to be from 'backward' castes. A large majority of the landless tended to be from the ex-Untouchable castes.

In the class model, rural power was held by the big landlords and the rich peasants. Given that these two categories owned or controlled most of the agricultural land, the primary source of rural livelihood, the poor labourers and the small/marginal landowners depended on them for employment and often also for credit. The marginal cultivators often leased land from the bigger landowners and worked as their tenants/sharecroppers. The landless often worked as tied-labourers. They all tended to borrow from their patron, cash and/or grain, particularly when there were some special needs, such as a wedding in the family, a major illness, or house repair, and remained perpetually indebted.

For the rich landowners of the village, lending was an opportunity to tie the labouring poor for labour. These dependency relations made the poor servile. Given their perpetual indebtedness, the tenants and sharecroppers were forced to sell the produce to the landlord moneylenders. This resulted in a hopeless situation where the poor worked like slaves, always unfree and dependent on their lords. Any resistance or disobedience was met with brutal violence. In some regions of the subcontinent, the big landowners also sexually exploited the women of the labouring classes. Reporting from South India during the early 1950s, M. N. Srinivas claimed that 'members of non-dominant castes may be abused, beaten, grossly underpaid, or their women required to gratify the sexual desires of the powerful men in the dominant caste'.[13]

While such 'semi-feudal' relations of production and social power had a long past, they became entrenched into the system during the British colonial period. However, the agrarian policies of the British varied across regions of the subcontinent. The power of 'semi-feudal' interests was most visibly present in the regions, such as Bengal, Bihar, and Rajasthan, where the British had introduced land revenue systems that were clearly pro-landlords, the zamindars and jagirdars, i. e. the Permanent Settlement. This is not to suggest that they were absent elsewhere. Under such a regime, the landlords emerged as an important support base for colonial rule. Even after Independence, they remained a conservative lot and tended to be averse to any initiatives that would empower the rural poor. They invariably lobbied against the introduction of developmental projects, initiated by the independent Indian state. They preferred keeping the local agrarian economy in a state of 'backwardness' often marked by low productivity of land and relationships of bondage and servitude.[14] They feared that economic development would usher in changes that would weaken their hold and power over the rural society.

Changing Patterns of Rural Power

Even though patterns of change have been very diverse across regions, independence from colonial rule, the introduction of Land Reform legislation, state policies of rural development and agrarian change and the institutionalization of democratic politics together brought about many shifts in the social and economic life of the rural residents. They unleashed forces that, over a period of time, also changed the nature of power relations, locally in the village as well as in wider society.

As we have discussed above and in the previous chapters, even though the independent Indian state did not pursue policies of radical land reforms and the process of their implementation was marred with many compromises, their limited success dented the power of the intermediary classes, the traditional zamindars and jagirdars, who invariably also belonged to the upper stratum of caste hierarchy, such as the Rajputs and Brahmins. Land moved to the middling caste groups, who had traditionally been the actual tillers of land. A much larger proportion of rural households came to have their own land for cultivation. Though disparities persisted, land reforms helped in democratizing the rural economy.

The following decades saw the extension of the irrigation network and the introduction of a wide range of programmes of rural development (see Chapters 5 and 6). The union government heavily invested in building dams and laying canals across different regions of the country. The Green Revolution technology and setting up of marketing networks, though confined to some pockets, transformed the nature of the agrarian economy. The growing intensity and commercialization of agriculture helped the middling castes gain in economic strength. It also enhanced the integration of the agrarian economy with the larger national economy. Even those who could not afford to buy tractors used GR technology and began to produce for profit. The political sociologists Llyod and Susan Rudolph famously described them as 'bullock capitalists'.[15] In due course, many of them disposed of their bullocks and moved to smaller size tractors, or simply to hiring tractors and other machines from their richer counterparts.

Their growing economic position also gave them political confidence. Using their social base within the 'dominant caste' clusters, the bigger landowners among them began to aspire for space in the regional politics. They mobilized around their caste identities and articulated their political aspirations by invoking a populist language of ruralism and agrarianism. Thus, the idiom of caste began to increasingly emerge as the dominant mode of doing democratic politics at the local (village) and regional (state) levels. They challenged the hegemonic dominance of the erstwhile urban elite and articulated 'rural' interests using the platform provided by the democratic political process. Perhaps the most prominent political voice in this context was that of Chaudhary Charan Singh from western Uttar Pradesh, who rose to be the prime minister of India for a brief while in July–August 1979.

Such a process helped the rural landowning castes consolidate their position in the local as well as the regional power structure across regions of India, though there were some notable exceptions, such as Bengal, Bihar, Odisha, and some other pockets. Perhaps the reason for this lay in the ways landownership patterns evolved in these regions during the British colonial period and the weak position of middling caste groups. Even when land reforms legislations effectively transferred land from the big landlords to the tillers, their ability to consolidate politically was rather limited because the effective size of their holdings in these regions remained small or marginal.

The rise of the dominant caste in the regional political economy also marginalized the local moneylending castes, such as the Banias in northwest India. Their debtors began to default and they could do little to force them to pay back what they owed. The prosperity brought about by Green Revolution technology also meant that many of the cultivating farmers no longer needed credit from the moneylenders which often carried a high rate of interest. The farmers also sold their farm yields in the local mandis, to state agencies like the Food Corporation of India (FCI) through the arhatiyas, who also offered them loans for crop cultivation. The farmers could also raise crop loans from commercial banks at nominal interest rates. Realizing their fading function and influence, the moneylending castes too began to move to the local towns and cities. By the 1980s, a large majority of them had moved out of the villages.[16]

Further Changes in Rural Power

The abolition of intermediary rights through the Land Reform legislations and state policies of rural development after Independence significantly expanded the social base of rural power. While they helped the landowning agrarian castes consolidate their power in local politics and beyond, the Indian village did not experience a significant process of democratization as a result of these policy measures. As indicated above, the local 'upper' and dominant castes continued to use coercive methods of enforcing their power. Their growing influence outside the village further helped strengthen their position in the village. It was from among them that regional/state-level politicians began to be chosen. Even those who were chosen/selected for the police force and local bureaucracy tended to belong to the locally dominant castes.

However, by the 1980s, Indian rural life entered a different phase which, together with the social and political forces unleashed during the earlier decades, produced profound changes in the rural power structure. The state-initiated development programmes brought prosperity and also altered relational structures of caste and class, making them more instrumental. The increasing integration of rural settlements into the national life through expanding road and communication networks enabled labour migrations across regions. The growing aspirations of the rural rich for mobility began to take them out of the village.

Even more, perhaps, was the growing sense of autonomy among the rural poor with an increased appreciation for democratic life and citizenship, some of which was also made possible by their repeated and increased participation in electoral processes. They no longer felt the need or the compulsion to show reverence to the rural rich. Besides the changing political milieu of the village, the shifts taking place in its economy further reinforced this process.

Scholars working on the social dynamics of technological usage in the agrarian economy and its increasing commercial orientation during the post-Independence period have also observed significant changes in the rural social relations. The older forms of attached labour where the labouring families worked for a share in the total produce no longer made sense to the landowners. They preferred hiring them on a daily wage, and paying mostly in cash. These new arrangements were purely instrumental in nature. The older ties of patronage and loyalty between the landed and landless began to weaken. With instrumentalities of wage and work replacing the older system of patronage and loyalty, tensions began to mount between the two groups, producing mistrust and conflict. Labourers often demanded higher wages and time-bound work. The farmers, used to old habits of unquestioned domination, found it hard to negotiate and adjust to changed realities. The older ties of caste, and the jajmani-type relationship, also began to crumble.

Even though the new economic arrangements initially produced a sense of anxiety and uncertainty for those from the poorer servicing castes, they also found them liberating. They liked the sense of autonomy and freedom that the formalized wage work offered them. As is evident from the previous chapter, these changes were not limited to the GR pockets that experienced a shift towards capitalist agriculture. The labour outmigration from Bihar and eastern Uttar Pradesh also brought about profound social and political changes in those regions. The rise of backward-caste politics and the decline of 'semi-feudal' landlord power in Bihar and some other regions during the 1980s and 1990s was partly made possible by such processes of outmigration. The labouring poor were no longer dependent exclusively on the local 'lords' for employment and credit. Their exposure to the world outside would have also given them a sense of self and their rights as citizens.

The traditional power of the feudal patriarch began to decline. They now wished to move out of the village, for education and from there to jobs in the urban economy, never to return to the village. In such a fast changing political, social, and economic scenario, many of the landlords simply sold their lands to the upwardly mobile from 'forward-backward' caste groups. Others moved to towns, while leasing out their lands to small farmers. Still others began to cultivate on their own.[17]

Even those who still have large holdings within the village no longer command power and authority like their counterparts did a couple of decades ago. During my fieldwork in the Madhubani district of Bihar in 2015, one such person, whose family reportedly still owns more than 100 acres of land in and around Satghara village of Bihar, described this situation with poetic vividity: 'Pahale ek ko bulate thhe to sao dodde aate thhe. Aab sao ko bulate hain to ek mushkil se aata hai.' (Previously if we called for one, a hundred came running. Now we call a hundred and one turns up with difficulty.)

Numbers matter in democratic political process. The first to assert themselves in these regions from the backward castes were the OBCs. Besides their populations being much larger than the erstwhile dominant upper castes, such the Bhoomihar and Rajputs in Bihar, they were also not completely landless. Once they acquired some degree of economic autonomy, they began to mobilize around their caste identities and make claims over political power. The political sociologist Christophe Jaffrelot described their rise as 'India's silent revolution'.[18] By the late 1980s, most north Indian states saw the regional political power shifting from the traditional upper castes to the middling castes and the OBCs, such as Jats, Yadavs, and Kurmis. A similar trend also unfolded in several other states, such as in Rajasthan, Gujarat, Maharashtra, Karnataka, and Andhra Pradesh. As mentioned above, some of the southern states had begun to see the rise of such a politics even earlier, during the later decades of colonial rule.

The rise of the OBCs to power also brought 'caste' to the centre stage of Indian politics. However, this narrative of caste was not a celebration of India's traditional hierarchies. The OBCs's position was just the opposite. They framed their politics through the language of justice and argued that their marginality was not limited to the village. They also lacked representation in modern institutions, such as the bureaucracy and the centres of higher education. They demanded an expansion of India's affirmative action programme and quotas for the OBCs, which had hitherto been confined to the SCs and STs. Adoption of the Mandal Commission Report, which had made recommendations for such quotas, by the Government of India in 1990, was clearly a result of these politics.

The opening up of political space with the rise of OBCs also made it easier for the emergence of an autonomous

Dalit politics in northern India with the Bahujan Samaj Party emerging as an important contender for political power in UP, India's most populous state. However, unlike the OBCs who had nearly all come from rural and agrarian families, Dalit politicians were mostly from the first generation of educated office-goers in urban settlements. They were the beneficiaries of India's reservation system. However, despite having moved out of their rural habitus of hierarchy to middle-class urban–secular occupations, they could not rid themselves of their caste identity and the accompanying social prejudices. They needed to acquire political power, advocated their new leaders. In order to achieve this, the beneficiaries of the quota system were called upon to provide selfless leadership, 'paying back' to their communities of origin.

These changes in the rural power dynamics were also enabled by a steady dissolution and exit of the landed elite. Their dissolution itself was mostly a consequence of the generational subdivision of land holdings among brothers that stemmed from the prosperity ushered in by the GR. The growing use of machines and increasing productivity of land had been useful incentives for families to get divided. The aspirations of nuclear families also began to change. They began to focus more on educating their children to enable mobility into urban occupations. Growing commercial orientation and instrumentalization of the agrarian economy also worked towards alienating them from the labouring castes and everyday life of the village. They could no longer command authority in the village. Even in the developed GR pockets, the growing prosperity of the dominant caste capitalist farmer thus set in motion a process of their moving out of the village for greener pastures beyond agriculture.

The Local and the Regional

Changes in social and political relations at the village level clearly were reflected in the emerging regional politics, particularly during the 1970s and 1980s. The rise of backward castes to political power and the growing mobilization of ex-untouchable communities around a pan-Indian Dalit identity during the following decades also had implications for village politics. While sections of the rich among the dominant and upper castes found roots in urban life, the relatively poorer with smaller holdings, along with a larger proportion of OBCs and Dalits, continued to live in the villages.

However, with the weakening of ties of caste and kin-based hierarchies, the village experienced a process of democratization. The villagers across castes and communities began to vote on their own, without feeling any pressure from the traditional rural patriarchs. Even women began to increasingly vote, exercising their individual choice. Over the years, they have also been voting in larger numbers in comparison to their male counterparts. As is well-known, unlike the Western democracies, electoral participation of the poor and those from social margins in India tends to be higher than of those in socially privileged positions.

This growing autonomy of political agency among the traditionally marginalized implied that nobody could take anybody's vote for granted. Even political leaders from the 'upper' and 'dominant' castes, or those from national-level political parties, had to rework their relationship with different categories of rural societies. They had to actively cultivate their ties with them by keeping in mind their specific demands and aspirations while framing their political programmes and party manifestos. Given the size and social diversities of electoral constituencies, it is virtually impossible for an individual leader to do this on their own. The task is normally done by local level cadres of the political parties. However, as institutions, they are not strong everywhere in India and many of them come up only during the elections.

This gap is filled by a new generation of actors, the intermediaries. They are 'political entrepreneurs' who help the villagers connect with the urban bureaucracy and the political elite. They aspire to be full-time politicians, are willing to 'serve' members of their primary constituency, and in the process become a medium for the political elite to connect with the local voters. This has also been described by scholars as 'clientele politics', which goes on to strengthen the power of the political patriarchs (most being men) sitting above, in the state assemblies and national parliament.

How does it work? As suggested above, and discussed in the previous chapters, with richer farmers moving out, a good proportion of those who stay back in the village tend to be relatively poor. To put it differently, a larger proportion of the Indian poor live in rural settlements. While many of them are able to make their living by working on land and in non-farm occupations, a good number of them also depend on state-sponsored development schemes to supplement their incomes.

With growing integration of the village in the national economy and ever-expanding development schemes, the presence of the state has been steadily growing in the everyday life of villagers. According to one estimate, the last decade of the twentieth century saw a fourteen-fold increase in government expenditure in rural areas.[19] However, accessing development schemes always requires going through a bureaucratic process. Beyond the bureaucratic system of certifications and applications, such development schemes are made possible by political actors. These politicians also play a crucial role in getting funds allocated for their constituencies and actively influence local bureaucracy in the selection of beneficiaries.

It is in this context that this new generation of political actors have emerged in the Indian villages. In order to be effective these political entrepreneurs have to also enjoy a degree of influence outside the village. Besides helping the rural poor with negotiating bureaucratic processes, they also mobilize the goodwill of some important politicians, like members of the legislative assembly (MLAs), who could help in getting a preferred scheme approved.

In a study of changing politics in rural Andhra Pradesh, political scientists G. Ram Reddy and G. Haragopal were the first to report the emergence of these political actors, whom they described as 'the fixers' in rural politics.[20] Political sociologist and long-time observer of Indian politics, James Manor too found such a new breed of intermediaries whom he described as 'small time freelance political fixers'.[21] Speaking about his field observations from Karnataka, he writes:

> These people are middlemen...who serve as crucial political intermediaries between the localities and powerful figures (bureaucrats and, especially, politicians) at higher levels... they have their uses for local groups.... They also provide critically important assistance to politicians, especially but not only at election time.[22]

Beyond connecting the poor with the state bureaucracy, they have also emerged as new leaders in the village. They are not leaders in the classical sense of the term, nor do they carry the stature of traditional rural patriarchs. But they have come to occupy positions of authority in formal institutions, such as the local panchayats. In 2008–2009, when I revisited the Haryana villages that I had first studied during the late 1980s, such a change was clearly visible.

During the 1980s, political power in these villages was almost exclusively held by the 'big men' from dominant or upper castes and with large landholdings, often more than 50 acres. They were locally known as the Chaudharies. They even controlled the village Panchayat through forming vertical alliances. It was with their support that an SC candidate could function in the Panchayat office. Though villages were politically divided across factions, their leaders were all from the dominant and upper castes with large landholdings.

They were no longer visible during my revisit twenty years later. Their absence was not merely demographic. They had also moved out of the mindscape of the village. 'Chaudhar is a thing of the past', was a statement I heard repeatedly from a cross-section of respondents. A respondent from a landless 'backward' caste put this very sharply: 'No one cares for anyone simply because he thinks he is a Chaudhary. Chaudharies, if they are, they must be in the four walls of their homes. We do not care.'

There was a clear decline in the power of individual patriarchs and their families in the everyday life of the village. Power and authority had become much more fluid and were no longer shaped by caste and land. These villages no longer had the 'big men', the landed patriarchs who were feared and respected. Around the same time, Price, a Norwegian anthropologist, observed a similar change in a South Indian village. 'The families who had ruled the village in the 1970s and 1980s had lost much of their authority and influence' because they were no longer the primary source of employment and credit for the rural poor. Most people 'wanted to make their own decisions and they did not want to be told what to do by somebody outside their family'.[23]

However, such a decline of the traditional authority structure did not necessarily imply a complete democratization of village life or empowerment of the rural poor. While the decline of traditional hierarchies had indeed given the rural poor a sense of citizenship and they had become very aware of their political rights, their economies remained precarious. When I asked a villager from a backward caste as to why no one from his community ever becomes a village sarpanch even when they are the largest group in the village, his response was very candid:

We are poor people. We know our votes are more than any other caste community of the village. However, we are also aware of our limits (aukat). I want to live in this village. If I were to take your words seriously, I may even have to leave the village.

The new leaders in the emerging system needed access to all kinds of resources. Besides being able 'to do something for the village as a whole' and network with leaders in the state capital and local bureaucracy to get things done, they were also expected have the capacity to help supporters, sometimes also financially.[24]

Panchayats, Patriarchs, and the State

In a landmark move in 1993, the Indian Parliament amended the Constitution, popularly known as the 73rd Amendment, making it mandatory for every state to institutionalize the Panchayati Raj system. As discussed above, it was Gandhi, and latter-day Gandhians, who had been passionately advocating for the need to give power to rural communities to govern themselves. The argument in favour of the new Act was also made using the language of democratic decentralization.

As the previous sections indicate, forms of the Panchayati Raj system had already been functioning in different states of the country, but it neither had a common format, nor was it an essential component of the Indian governance system, such as the state legislative assemblies or the Indian Parliament. Post the 73rd Amendment, every state had to follow a common format, which included mandatory elections after every five years. Besides reserving seats for SCs and STs in proportion to their population in a given state, the new Act also mandated one-third of the seats to be reserved for women, at all levels. The quota for women has now been increased to 50 per cent in most states of the country. The system of 'reservations' for specific categories was to ensure that the panchayats not only function as local democratic institutions but also help inculcate values of representation, inclusion, and diversity.

How has it worked? The Panchayati Raj system certainly does not function as it was initially imagined by Gandhi, or his followers. It has also not been a major source of social change and political democratization. Interestingly, the timing of the 73rd Amendment coincided with the loosening of caste power and a steady process of the fading out of the traditional rural patriarchs. During the early years after Independence, it would have perhaps been much harder, if not unimaginable, to think of a Dalit woman as an elected leader of the village in most parts of the subcontinent. Until around the turn of the century, even Dalit men could contest panchayat elections only on reserved seats and that too only when they were supported by a leader and a faction of the local dominant caste.

However, the quotas introduced by the 73rd Amendment, have certainly made a difference to rural women. While in most cases, the de facto position of official power stays with a male member of the family, often the elected woman's husband or father-in-law, her being in the position of authority does make a difference to her self-image and somewhat changes her position within the family. Some younger women, particularly those from marginalized social categories, have begun to act as leaders in their villages. Their being in a position of authority invariably improves local governance and service delivery for the larger community.

Have the panchayats been effective in decentralization, a source of empowering local communities to govern themselves? Answering this question also requires us to go back to our discussion on the increasing integration of the rural settlements into the larger national economy. If juridical power was evidence of their authority, for the panchayat it no longer exists, legally or customarily. The emerging patterns of rural power, involving patronage flowing into the village from above and outside, tends to make their so-called traditional functions redundant. Thus, instead of working as autonomous systems of political self-governance, they effectively function as institutions through which the state operates in the everyday life of the rural people.

The panchayats hardly ever generate their own resources. Their funds almost entirely come from the state. There has also been a deep-seated sense of mistrust in the local leadership among the urban elite and the administrative functionaries of the state. Funds allocated to the village panchayats are all governed by the national and the state-level bureaucratic system. Even when they work effectively, the village panchayats end up functioning as a primary institution of state delivery, perhaps completely opposite of what they were visualized to do. This is not an accident. As Kuldeep Mathur argues, the push for the 73rd Amendment also came from international development agencies that were advising countries of the Global South to prioritize good governance over politics of social transformation.[25] The panchayats were visualized as local level institutions of civil society that could help the emerging neoliberal vision of 'development delivery' become easier and more effective.

They, along with the new leaders of the village, the fixers, thus become a medium through which state power flows into the village along with the 'red tape' that almost always accompanies money flowing from above. Instead of weakening, the process works to enhance the power of the central authority. Thus, over the past decades, the relationship of villages with regional politics has seen a near complete reversal. Until around the 1970s, the flow of power was from the village to the region as villages produced powerful elites that emerged as political functionaries at the regional level, and occasionally also the national level.

The process of democratization has been an important source

of change in rural life. Given the diverse regional histories and multiple trajectories of economic change, institutionalization of democratic politics has also been varied. However, its effects are present everywhere. While the village has receded as a site of priority for the 'neoliberal' ruling elite of India, given its demographic weight, it is hard for them to entirely ignore the village. It is in this context that we need to understand the continued political support for the rural development programmes. The expanding reach of the developmental state has also played a critical role in altering the village level politics, as has its integration into the national framework of democratic politics through institutions such as the Panchayati Raj system.

However, despite its growing integration into the national economy and political process, regional differences remain. The processes of caste, class, and the nature of elite formation invariably shape the local and regional level political processes.[26] This chapter has been an attempt at capturing some of these processes and how they translate as processes that shape rural power.

Writing the conclusion to this book, I return once again to the story that I began this book with, my chance encounter with a retired bureaucrat at the India International Centre in New Delhi. I can still vividly recall the conversation and the manner in which he kept emphasizing, 'The village is not what it used to be'. His words conveyed a sense of despair and cynicism mixed with a touch of personal loss. He had also spoken with authority and a sense of finality, as though what he had said was too obvious to be refuted. The source of his confidence also lay in the fact that he had been a witness to the changes occurring in the Indian villages over the past fifty years or so. He was one of those who hailed from a village and whose parents had moved out to the city in the early years of nation-building even while a part of his extended family still lived there. Over the years he also continued to return to the village and watch it transform, in a very personal sense. But in a professional sense too, as a senior administrator working for the Government of India and administering governmental schemes for rural development, he had been well aware of the changes happening on the ground.

He is certainly not the only one to voice such a point of view, nor is his angst unique. Over the past several years I have heard similar statements made, with the same sense of nostalgia and loss, by people from many different walks of life, including from some academics. As I have discussed at length in this book, the villages of India have indeed seen many changes over the past century. A good number of rural settlements have grown to become towns. Many have been subsumed by the ever-expanding cities. Even where they retain their identity of being 'villages' of some kind, they look more like congested urban slums where poor migrant workers find relatively cheap accommodation.

The changes in village life are not limited to those located in the urban peripheries or close to big cities. Even those located far away from cities have seen many changes. Their economy, their social arrangements, the dynamics of their political life, their patterns of self-identification as groups and individuals, even their religious lives and ways of worshipping have undergone many changes. The pace of these changes has perhaps been faster over the past fifty or sixty years than in earlier times. They have also been much talked about, not only by social science researchers, but also by journalists reporting for popular media and by fiction writers. They have also been frequently portrayed in documentaries, cinema, and television serials.

The changes are also not confined to the so-called developed pockets of the country. Even the 'backward interiors' of India have undergone many shifts and in some cases, they are more radical than those experienced in the prosperous pockets. The Madhubani district of Bihar is a good example of this. It is among the least urbanized districts of India, with more than 90 per cent of its residents still living in rural settlements. However, over the past fifty years or so its villages have completely changed thanks to the increasing number of its young adults going out of their village to work. By the early years of the twenty-first century, nearly two-thirds of its households had between one to four of its members working away from the village. Even though a large majority of them tend to eventually return to their villages, these migrations have completely altered the social and economic life of the villages. As reported by economist Amrita Datta, only a little over 10 per cent of households in these villages earned their livelihood exclusively from agriculture.[1] In fact, remittances received from the migrants have become the primary source of livelihood, followed by the income generated in the local non-farm economy.

Migrating out of the village is not a completely new phenomenon. However, with the arrival of new communication technologies, the experience and culture of migrations have also changed. For example, remittances coming from the men working away from home previously came as money orders through the local post office. The local postman, dakia, was not merely a low-grade official. He was also the most critical confidant of the poorer families with no formal education. It was through him that such families connected with the outside world. Besides delivering the cash received through money orders, he also read out their letters and penned their replies. In most rural hinterlands, he has largely been replaced by Automated Teller Machines (ATMs). The dakia is also no longer called upon to read and write letters. The increasing use of mobile phones has made them nearly redundant for personal communications almost everywhere.

These patterns of change in rural life have obviously been very different in regions such as Kerala, Punjab, or Tamil Nadu. The nature of outmigration and its implications for the local communities have been very different. Most of the migrations out of Kerala, for example, are to the countries of the Gulf. Quite like the Bihari labour, Malayalis who migrate to the Gulf for work too tend to eventually return back to their villages, though the quality of their work abroad and the received remittances are of very different natures. Rural Punjabis, mostly the Sikhs, tend to migrate to the developed countries of Europe, North America, and Australia but they tend to eventually also move their families out to the countries where they work. However, they too send remittances to their kin in their native villages. Some of them also come back to help in the 'development' of the villages they left for good. The more industrialized belt of western states, such as Maharashtra and Gujarat, or the hill regions of the north, such as Himachal Pradesh, Uttarakhand, Sikkim, Nagaland, or Manipur, too see rural outmigrations, but the patterns vary significantly, sometimes even within a state, across its different sub-regions, and even among different communities and caste groups. What is true of migration flows and their regionally varied consequences for everyday social life in the villages of the subcontinent also applies to other processes of change, such as patterns of economic growth, rural politics, social conflicts, gender relations, or availability of quality healthcare and education.

While the trajectories of change vary significantly, there are also some emergent similarities in rural settlements across regions, which have mostly been produced as a result of them being part of the democratic nation state since Independence. State policies, its common bureaucratic structures, and electoral politics, have unleashed some common processes, the most important of which is the growing aspiration for mobility through education and a longing for citizenship entitlements, often articulated through the language of development.

An equally important claim that I have tried to make in this book is the reiteration of an obvious fact about the Indian village: its internally differentiated nature. Unlike the peasant villages of Europe and some other regions of the world, Indian villages have always been divided. Nearly half of the rural households did not own or were not entitled to cultivate land, mostly because of caste-related customary norms and restraints. Even when they worked for the landowning cultivating households, they did not enjoy the status of being peasants or kisans. Their primary identities tended to be the identities of their caste occupations. Someone who belonged to a scavenging caste or those who were associated with leatherwork tended to be identified as such in everyday life even when they worked as full-time tied labourers with a big landowner.

Landowning households too were divided across caste and

class lines. The bigger landowners mostly belonged to upper and dominant castes while smaller landowners and tenants often belonged to lower castes, above the line of pollution (most of whom are currently classified as OBCs, the other backward classes). Villages tended to also have other caste groups who had little to do with agriculture.

These differences also imply that the experience of rural social change has been felt very differently by diverse segments of the rural residents. The bigger landowners from the locally dominant caste groups and communities were among the first to benefit from the state induced development programmes. It was from amongst them that a new 'provincial propertied class' emerged. The bigger farmers were also the first to invest in the education of their wards and diversify into urban occupations. They were quick to enter electoral politics and emerge as the regional political elite. Many of them also used their new-found political clout to accumulate big wealth by expanding into businesses and real estate.

Economic diversification and outmigration flows of poorer households follow very different trajectories. Over the years, rural non-farm economy has emerged as an important source of employment and income for the local residents. With increasing disposable income and spreading consumer culture, the number of petty shops has been steadily growing in rural settlements. Construction is another sector, which employs a good number of rural workers. As discussed above and in Chapter 7, migrations of the relatively poor tend to be circular in nature. After working elsewhere for their active adult life, most of them return back to their villages. In regions where viable employment is available in neighbouring towns, many prefer to commute from the village for work.

The changing economies and shifting grammars of local politics have also had some interesting implications for those living on the margins of village society. The growing use of new technology also changed caste relations. Increasing formalization of labour employment practices and the growing presence of electoral politics created a new space for Dalit political agency. Even though these processes did not greatly change their position in the emerging social hierarchies, they did experience a certain sense of freedom. Some of them were able to use the channel of 'reservation policy' to get into regular urban jobs. Their quest for education has also been growing. However, there are obvious limitations to their mobility and a large majority of them, listed as the SCs and STs, continue to be counted among the poorest of the poor in twenty-first century India.

The experience of change for those in the middle of these two extremes is also internally very diverse. Not being a Dalit and not being landless still makes a difference in one's prospects of social and economic mobility in rural India. For example, those who own even small plots of agricultural land are far less likely to experience abject poverty than those who are landless or nearly landless. Caste status also matters. Someone from a dominant or 'upper' caste with a couple of acres of agricultural land will have a much greater chance of diversifying into a non-farm occupation in the neighbouring town than a landless Dalit. With their caste status, non-Dalits have a much better chance of mobilizing the required social network for setting up a business in town. With even two acres of agricultural land, they may also find it much easier to raise a bank loan required for the business. Neither of these are likely possibilities for a landless Dalit household from a village, anywhere in the subcontinent.

Gender too continues to be an extremely relevant category, across regions, and across caste and class categories. However, here too the implications and experience of change vary. Even when gender bias continues to be a stark reality, those from the well-to-do dominant castes are increasingly sending their daughters to good schools and colleges to study. Some are even willing to send them to far off places to pursue higher education. There are growing merits to investing in a daughter's education. It might be easier for an educated daughter to find an urban employed groom. In some regions, such as in parts of Punjab, families encourage their daughters to continue with their education as they are considered more likely to remain focused on their studies and finally find good jobs in the West, in Canada or the United Kingdom. They could then become channels for their entire families to move abroad. However, in some cases, women's education also becomes a source of intra-household conflict, particularly when a woman attempts to exercise her own agency in matters of marriage.

Rural outmigrations too are gendered and have differential gender effects. Generally, in the case of 'circular migrations' of the poor, men go out for work, leaving their wives, young children, and old parents behind in the village. This is mostly the case even with international migrations to the countries of the Gulf from Kerala and other states. Men going out to work for longer periods could also be an empowering experience for women staying behind. In the absence of the men, they are forced to learn the ways of the world and to deal with it on their own terms.

Besides the above-mentioned changes, different chapters of this book have also listed and analysed many other processes that have quite significantly altered village life. As mentioned above, shifts in rural settlements have taken place across the board, notwithstanding the diversity of their trajectories. Furthermore, it is not only the rural in India that has seen changes. India's urban settlements too have undergone many significant alterations over the past century, as have villages and cities elsewhere in the world. The emerging patterns of spatial configuration are, in a sense, reflections of the larger changes taking place in the national and global economy. They also manifest in the lives of individuals and communities, social classes and ethnic groups, ideas, ideologies, and political regimes, and across regions of the contemporary world.

What is then so special or distinctive about 'the village not being what it used to be?' Why does it sound like a statement of despair, as if everything else changing would be fine but not 'village life' in India? What kind of loss is being articulated while framing this issue in the manner in which it is being done?

I suggest that the source of this despair lies in the popular imagination of the Indian village, which came to view as one of the foundational signifiers of India's distinctive cultural identity and its past tradition. Along with caste, the village came to be imagined as an institution that had been a source of its continuity as a civilization since ancient times. As a cradle of the presumed 'Indian culture', it was imagined as a peaceful place, characterized by values of reciprocity and social harmony. Even when organized hierarchically into segmentally divided caste groupings, it had presumably remained free of conflict.

As I have repeatedly argued, such a static view of Indian village life was, in fact, a colonial and orientalist construct, produced to project India as being a land of hopelessness, which desperately needed colonial intervention for its own 'progress', for it to move onto the path of modernity. Indian nationalist leaders and thinkers, such as Gandhi and Tagore, found such a framing of village life politically useful as well as morally tempting. They invoked such an imaginary to argue for its civilizational unity and to make their case for an independent nation. Gandhi, for example, saw in such a notion a possible alternative way of organizing a good society. The 'real' Indian village for him was a 'superior' alternative to the materialist and consumption driven cultures and economies of the modern West. Indeed, the view that the 'village' was a cradle of Indian civilization found many takers and continues to tempt a section of the civil society activists, environmentalists, and policy advocates of sustainable economic growth and decentralized governance even today. To put it differently, such a view of the Indian village came to imbibe a considerable amount of moral weight. Its influence has also been felt far and wide.

The social anthropologists who carried out long drawn ethnographic studies of Indian village life during the 1950s and 1960s also bought into this discourse and began to see in the village a microcosm of Indian tradition and larger patterns of its social, economic, and political life. The Indian sociologist André Béteille summarizes this well when he writes, 'the village was not merely a place where people lived; it had a design in which reflected the basic values of Indian civilisation'.[2] Though their empirical studies soon revealed that the ground realities of rural life were far more diverse and fluid than suggested by the popular construct or stereotype, they continued to approach the village as an appropriate methodological entry point to the study of Indian society.

While some long for the lost village, there are also many who found nothing worth celebrating in Indian rural life. As discussed in Chapter 3, Dr B. R. Ambedkar was among its most vehement critics. His obvious reason for its denunciation was the preoccupation that the villagers of India had with the caste system. Rigid social hierarchies, which could be best practised in the rural setting, made it impossible for his fellow Dalits to lead a life of dignity. They were not even allowed to be part of the village settlement and constantly encountered the violence of untouchability while interacting with the 'caste Hindus'.

Another source of its negative image has been the twentieth century social science theories of development and change that came to be accepted as common wisdom by emerging elites in developing countries after their decolonization. Mostly founded on the Eurocentric and evolutionist visions of human futures, the theories of modernization and development tended to view the village as a 'relic' of the pre-modern past. Its end was taken for granted. Villages were to eventually disappear, either through outmigration of its residents to urban centres, or through their demographic expansion and occupational/economic differentiation. Since this had presumably happened in the West, it was bound to happen elsewhere with the unfolding of the process of development.

Despite their fallacious and empirically unsustainable assumptions, such a view prevails. It even entered the textbooks of economics, sociology, and political science. The ruling elites of the newly independent 'developing countries' were encouraged by the global experts to provide a push in this direction. Urbanization thus emerged as a core indicator of a country's modernization. Social scientists working in rural settings thus began to look for evidence that would indicate such an imminent decline of the village. Writing in 2005 in the popular social science journal, the *Economic and Political Weekly*, sociologist Dipankar Gupta seemed to suggest the arrival of such a moment:

> The village in India, where life was once portrayed as 'unchanging' and 'idyllic', has in recent decades seen profound changes. The twin shackles that once decided matters for India's villagers, caste and agriculture, no longer exercise their vigorous hold. While a break in caste rigidities has fostered greater fluidity in occupational choices, agricultural stagnation has ensured the constant march, in increasing numbers, of employable people in the villages towards urban areas....[3]

He goes on to virtually pronounce the death of the Indian village:

> The villager is as bloodless as the rural economy is lifeless. From rich to poor, the trend is to leave the village....[4]

Such a framing of change also made sense in the emerging realities of post-1990s India. Policies of economic liberalization had helped the urban economy grow at a much faster pace. Along with it grew a new middle class, mostly employed in the corporate service economy. An expanding urban economy and the growing centrality of the consuming middle classes also began to change the popular self-image of the country. A 'new' India was on the anvil, a nation on the way to becoming a global power. The rising cities of Bengaluru, Gurgaon, Hyderabad, and many others, increasingly came to be seen as the sites of India's self-realization in the emerging world.

The fast-paced growth of the 'new economy' and its service sector soon changed the class balance in the country. Newly acquired urban prosperity marginalized the status and share of agriculture in the national economy, as also the value of village life. Being part of the urban middle class soon emerged as the hegemonic norm, a site of mobility, a statement of status. Educated rural youth from farming families too aspired to move out of the village and into urban occupations, to join the ranks of the middle classes.

The Village Lives on

The patterns of village life have changed significantly in most parts of the country and the globe. The tendency of villagers to migrate out for economic and social mobility has also been an obvious reality for quite some time, even though its nature and forms have been significantly diverse. Agriculture has indeed declined. Caste relations have also altered significantly even when hierarchies and inequalities persist. However, the village lives on, demographically and otherwise. This is very clearly shown by the data presented in Chapter 1 (Table 1.1). While the share of the urban population has been growing at a pace faster than that of the rural population, in absolute numbers India has nearly three times more residents living in its rural settlements in the early decades of the twenty-first century than it had in the middle of the twentieth century, or at the time of its Independence. As per the decadal census data, the absolute number of its rural settlements has also been growing over the decades.

More importantly, the village has not given up on itself. Despite it receding from the national self-imagination, rural India keeps coming back to the front pages of national dailies and the chat rooms of television channels. I would like to mention three important stories of the 'rural resurgence' that acquired prominent reportage during the period that I was writing this book.

The Village Is Where Home Is

India has more than 600 to 700 million workers. A good proportion of them are temporary migrants, who tend to return to their homes in the villages where their families reside. Most of them are engaged in precarious work, employed casually through a private contractor or an agency. They work on construction sites, as security guards or in other sectors providing low-grade services to urban residents. On 24 March 2020, the Prime Minister of India suddenly announced a countrywide indefinite lockdown in order to stop the spread of the looming Covid-19 pandemic.[5] Besides being anxious about families and their own health, for many of them, the nationwide lockdown also resulted in loss of work. As part of the lockdown, the Indian railways were also directed to cancel train services. The same applied to buses and other sources of road transport.

The migrants were left in the lurch. Not knowing what was going to be their fate, many of them decided to walk back to their 'homes', located hundreds of kilometres away from the places where they worked. Their numbers were not in the hundreds or thousands but in the millions. India's roads were suddenly flooded with groups of migrants, walking for weeks and months to reach their home. Like everyone else, they too wanted to be in a place where they could feel safe, within the boundaries of their homes, located in their villages, even if it meant walking for a thousand kilometres or more. There were many who were accompanied by their young children, carrying all the belongings they had accumulated while working in the city.

The Cosmopolitan Kisan

The second case of the rural resurgence in twenty-first century India is the massive year-long sit-in by farmers on the borders of the national capital during 2020–21.

Encouraged by the official data showing an overall decline of the working population fully employed in agriculture and the rural youth aspiring for urban jobs, the union government decided to introduce a new set of three laws governing agriculture and the marketing of agricultural produce. The new laws were designed to make it easier for private corporate capital to enter and manage agriculture. If implemented, they had the potential to rework the entire ecosystem of India's agrarian economy, enabling the corporate capital to purchase, store, and even decide what crops a farmer should produce, albeit, through contract farming.

In the Indian legal system, issues concerning agriculture are a part of the 'state list' where the provincial governments have the jurisdiction to frame laws. However, the new laws were enacted by the Union Government using the 'ordinance' route at a time when the country was under a complete lockdown and at the height of the first wave of Covid-19 infections. Further, they were enacted without any meaningful consultations with all the different stakeholders.

Alarmed by the possible implications of the new laws, the farmers from the agriculturally better-off regions began protesting with all their might. Beginning with the north-western state of Punjab, sometime in July 2020, the protests gradually spread to other regions of the country. The most spectacular of these protests was when they arrived in large numbers at the borders of the national capital on 26 November 2020. Estimates of their size and strength at this point vary, but they were certainly in excess of 50,000, and their numbers swelled to around 300,000 in about a week. By 26 January 2021, at the height of the sit-in, nearly a million more had arrived from across the country for a bigger protest, driving their tractors on the belt roads of the capital city.[6]

The farmers sat on the roads for a whole year, surrounding Delhi from all four sides, and occupying the major highways connecting the national capital to different parts of the country. Their sit-ins were so large that they looked like distinct townships covering an area of 10 to 15 kilometres at each site. They slept in the trolleys, which they had brought along with them tied to their tractors. They also put up huge pandals for their protest speeches and mobilized support from a wide spectrum of Indian civil society members and those living abroad.

Their resilience was remarkable. They sat through the harsh winter, when night temperatures in Delhi dropped to as low as 1–2 °C and continued through the hot summer months when temperatures touched 45–46 °C. In their 'battle' to save the kisani (autonomous farming as an occupation), nearly 700 protesting farmers died,[7] mostly at the protest sites around Delhi, due to the hardships of weather and living conditions. It was a hard price to pay, but as the farm union leaders put it:

> ...if we let the new laws prevail our lands will be lost forever. Our children will have no lands to cultivate. This is a battle for saving *kisani*, our livelihood and our dignity.[8]

Nearly a year after they arrived on the borders of Delhi, on 19 November 2021, the Prime Minister of India announced, in a national telecast, that his government had decided to withdraw the three farm laws.

Agriculture, a 'Sponge'?

The third point is a revisit to the popular narrative on the decline of agriculture. As I have discussed in an earlier chapter of the book, available data on the Indian economy clearly suggest a steady decline of agriculture in terms of its contribution to the national income. It has also been declining as a preferred economic activity, or an occupation. The share of agriculture in the national economy has come down to less than one-third of what it was during the early decades after Independence. Even within the rural economy, a larger proportion of incomes is now earned from non-farm sources. The share of those who depend exclusively on farming for their livelihood has also been shrinking, though at a slower pace. Many of those who report themselves as cultivating farmers in surveys are increasingly engaged in pluriactivity.

However, a purely economic lens, often presented in aggregate statistics or data sets, could produce a wrong judgement. The worth of agriculture is much larger than its quantifiable value addition to gross national income. As economist Barbara Harriss-White puts it, 'Agriculture is growing in a mediocre way...it is rapidly dwindling as a proportion of GDP, vanishing from macroeconomic policy, but remains a massive and vital sponge for absorbing surplus labour.'[9] It functions as critical support for the livelihood and sustenance of a very large number of people. Even when they move out of agriculture, as the above discussion on migrant workers suggests, the security that a retreat to it provides is much greater. Thus, despite the uncertainty that the craft of agriculture entails in a country like India, it continues to provide a source of social and cultural security. In times of crisis, it also remains a source of economic refuge. As Harish Damodaran and Mekhala Krishnamurthy have pointed out, during the 2020–21 financial year, when the pandemic hit the Indian economy badly and its overall growth declined to minus 6.2 per cent, Indian agriculture grew by 3.6 per cent.[10]

In summary, 'rural' and 'urban' are not sui-generis categories, as if representing two stages in the life of a biological organism. Nor is 'agriculture' a static activity, or a quintessentially peasant way of life. As was clearly evident from their political acumen and strategies of struggle, the farmers sitting on the borders of Delhi were not simple-minded 'rustic peasants', as their stereotypes generally popular among the urban middle classes tend to suggest. They were as cosmopolitan as other globally mobile netizens of twenty-first century India. 'Rural' and 'urban' are also not simply demographic or economic processes. They are human realities—fluid, inherently diverse, and ever changing. As relational structures, they also need to be seen through the prisms of history, culture, and power. An economic or demographic reductionism only serves to blind us to their obvious realities.

ACKNOWLEDGEMENTS

I have been working on aspects of rural India and agrarian change for three and half decades. Over the years I have published half a dozen books and more than two dozen research papers dealing with different facets of the subject. Some ideas and arguments in this book draw from these research writings.

Over the years, I have also worked with a good number of scholars from whom I have learnt a great deal. They include Adarsh Kumar, Alagh Sharma, Alpa Shah, Andre Betielle, Aninhalli R. Vasavi, Anirudh Krishna, Aparna Rayaprol, Aparna Vaidik, Aseem Prakash, Ashutosh Varshney, Barbara Harriss-White, Carol Upadhya, David Gellner, Dipankar Gupta, Divya Vaid, Edward Simpson, Gurpreet Mahajan, Himanshu, Indrajit Roy, James Manor, Jerry Rogers, John Harriss, Judith Heyer, Jules Naudet, Kalpana Kannabiran, Maitrayee Chaudhuri, Maitreyi Das, Mekhala Krishnamurthy, Mukulika Banerjee, Nandini Gooptu, Nicolas Martin, Nilkantha Rath, Praveen Jha, Rajeshwari Raina, Rammanohar Reddy, Ratheesh Kumar, Ravi Srivastava, Ravinder Kaur, Richa Kumar, Sanjay Palshikar, Sanjay Srivastava, Satendra Kumar, Satish Deshpande, Sudha Pai, Sukhadeo Thorat, Tanweer Fazal, Vamsicharan Vakulabharanam, and Vinod Pavarala.

Some of my students read chapters of the book and provided valuable comments. I am particularly grateful to Kriti Sharma, Mallika Chaudhuri, Shivam Mogha, Taniya Chakrabarti, and Vikash Sharan. As with all my writings, Sneha Sudha Komath read the entire manuscript and provided valuable suggestions. I would also like to thank the Aleph editors Aienla Ozukum, Kanika Praharaj, and (formerly) Pallavi Goswami for persuading me to work on the book.

Surinder S. Jodhka
26 June 2023

NOTES

Introduction

1. Hannah Ritchie and Max Roser, 'Urbanization', *Our World in Data*, available at ourworldindata.org/urbanization, accessed 9 March 2022.

Chapter 1: 'Village': The Lost Home?

1. Prashant Kidambi, 'South Asia', Peter Clark (ed.), *The Oxford Handbook of Cities in World History*, Oxford: Oxford University Press, 2013, p. 562.
2. B. S. Cohn, *Colonialism and its Forms of Knowledge: The British in India*, Princeton: Princeton University Press, 2000, pp. 142–43.
3. IDFC, *India Rural Development Report 2012/13*, Hyderabad: Orient Blackswan, 2013, pp. 142–43.
4. Leo Lucassen, 'Population and Migration', Peter Clark (ed.), *The Oxford Handbook of Cities in World History*, Oxford: Oxford University Press, 2013, p. 675.
5. Available at censusindia.gov.in/census.website.
6. See www.statista.com/statistics/616121/urban-population-by-state-and-union-territory-india, accessed 19 January 2022.

Chapter 2: How the Village Comes to Be Seen as a Site of Deficit

1. Louis Wirth, 'Urbanism as a Way of Life', *American Journal of Sociology*, Vol. 44, 1938, pp. 1–24.
2. *Peasants and Peasant Societies*, T. Shanin (ed.), London: Blackwell, 1987, p. 468.
3. H. Newby, 'Trend Report: Rural Sociology', *Current Sociology*, Vol. 28 (Spring), 1980, p. 10.
4. H. K. Schwarzweller (ed.), *Research in Rural Sociology and Development*, Vol. 1, Greenwich: Jai Press, 1984, p. xi.
5. L. Nelson, *Rural Sociology: Its Origins and Growth in the United States*, Minneapolis: University of Minnesota Press, 1948, p. 14.
6. A. R. Desai, *Rural Sociology in India*, Bombay: Popular Prakashan, 1969.
7. A. Bonnano, *Sociology of Agriculture*, New Delhi: Concept Publishing House, 1989, p. ix.

8. D. R. Gadgil, *Industrial Evolution of India in Recent Times*, London: Oxford University Press, 1933.
9. M. N. Srinivas, 'The Indian Village: Myth and Reality', Vandana Madan (ed.) *The Indian Village*, Delhi: Oxford University Press, 1987/2002, p. 52.
10. C. T. Metcalfe, 'Minutes', *Report from the Select Committee*, Revenue III, Parliament Papers XI, 1931–32, pp. 331–32.
11. Ibid.
12. Karl Marx, *Capital: A Critique of Political Economy*, New York: Cosimo, 2007 (1867), p. 393.
13. B. S. Cohn, *An Anthropologist among the Historians and Other Essays*, Delhi: Oxford University Press, 1987, p. 212.

Chapter 3: The Village as the Nation: Making of the Indian Common Sense

1. Ronald Inden, 'Orientalist Constructions of India', *Modern Asian Studies*, Vol. 20 (3), 1986, pp. 401–46.
2. Gurminder K. Bhambra, *Rethinking Modernity: Postcolonialism and the Sociological Imaginations*, New York: Palgrave, 2007.
3. Quoted in Surinder S. Jodhka, 'Nation and Village: Images of Rural India in Gandhi, Nehru and Ambedkar', *Economic and Political Weekly*, Vol. 37, No. 32, August, 2002, p. 3343.
4. Srinivas, 'The Indian Village: Myth and Reality', p. 57.
5. M. K. Gandhi, *The Collected Works of Mahatma Gandhi*, Volume I. Delhi: Government of India, 1958, p. 14.
6. Ibid., pp. 94–95.
7. J. A. Parel (ed.), *Hind Swaraj and Other Writings*, Cambridge: Cambridge University Press, 1997, p. xlii.
8. M. K. Gandhi, *The Collected Works of Mahatma Gandhi*, Volume XI, Delhi: Government of India, 1963, p. 509.
9. M. K. Gandhi, *The Collected Works of Mahatma Gandhi*, Volume XXI, Delhi: Government of India, 1966, pp. 288–89.
10. M. K. Gandhi, *The Collected Works of Mahatma Gandhi*, Volume LXXXVI, Delhi: Government of India, 1982, p. 232.
11. M. K. Gandhi, *The Collected Works of Mahatma Gandhi*, Volume LXVIII, Delhi: Government of India, 1977, p. 369.
12. M. K. Gandhi, *The Collected Works of Mahatma Gandhi*, Volume XXXIII, Delhi: Government of India, 1969, p. 151.
13. A. T. Embree, *Imagining India: Essays on Indian History*, Delhi: Oxford University Press, 1989, p. 165.
14. S. Khilnani, *The Idea of India*, New York: Farrar Straus Giroux, 1998, p. 125.

15. M. K. Gandhi, *The Collected Works of Mahatma Gandhi*, Volume LXXI, Delhi: Government of India, 1978, p. 4.
16. M. K. Gandhi, *The Collected Works of Mahatma Gandhi*, Volume LIX, Delhi: Government of India, 1974, p. 409.
17. M. K. Gandhi, *The Collected Works of Mahatma Gandhi*, Volume LXIV, Delhi: Government of India, 1976, pp. 116–17.
18. Ibid., pp. 409–10.
19. M. K. Gandhi, *The Collected Works of Mahatma Gandhi*, Volume LI, Delhi: Government of India, 1972, p. 406.
20. Ibid.
21. M. K. Gandhi, *The Collected Works of Mahatma Gandhi*, Volume XLI, Delhi: Government of India, 1970, p. 445.
22. M. K. Gandhi, *The Collected Works of Mahatma Gandhi*, Volume XXXIII, Delhi: Government of India, 1969, p. 76.
23. M. K. Gandhi, *The Collected Works of Mahatma Gandhi*, Volume LXXVII, Delhi: Government of India, 1979, p. 228.
24. M. K. Gandhi, *The Collected Works of Mahatma Gandhi*, Volume LXXVI, Delhi: Government of India, 1979, pp. 308–309.
25. M. K. Gandhi, *The Collected Works of Mahatma Gandhi*, Volume LXII, Delhi: Government of India, 1975, pp. 319–20.
26. Jawaharlal Nehru, *An Autobiography*, Delhi: Oxford University Press, 1980 (first published 1936), p. 49.
27. Ibid., p. 52.
28. Jawaharlal Nehru, *The Discovery of India*, New York: The John Day Company, 1946, p. 244.
29. Ibid., p. 248.
30. Ibid., p. 246.
31. Ibid.
32. Ibid., p. 252.
33. Nehru, *The Discovery of India*, p. 254.
34. Nehru, *An Autobiography*, p. 52.
35. S. Gopal, *Selected Works of Jawaharlal Nehru*, Vol. 5 (Old Series), Hyderabad: Orient Longman, 1973, p. 82.
36. Nehru, *An Autobiography*, p. 52.
37. Nehru, *The Discovery of India*, p. 246.
38. S. Gopal, *Selected Works of Jawaharlal Nehru*, Vol. 3 (Old Series), Hyderabad: Orient Longman, 1972, p. 365.
39. Nehru, *An Autobiography*, p. 306.
40. Gopal, *Selected Works of Jawaharlal Nehru*, p. 82.
41. Jawaharlal Nehru, *Jawaharlal Nehru's Speeches*, Vol. II, Publications Division, Ministry of Information and Broadcasting, New Delhi: Government of India, 1954, p. 94.
42. S. Gopal (ed.), *Selected Works of Jawaharlal Nehru*, Vol. 4 (New Series), Delhi: Oxford University Press, 1986, p. 566.

43. Nehru, *Jawaharlal Nehru's Speeches*, p. 84.
44. Nehru, *The Discovery of India*, pp. 534–35.
45. E. Zelliot, 'The Meanings of Ambedkar', Ghanshyam Shah (ed.), *Dalit Identity and Politics*, New Delhi: Sage Publications, 2001, p. 1.
46. B. R. Ambedkar, 'Untouchables or the Children of India's Ghetto', *Dr Babasaheb Ambedkar Writings and Speeches,* Vasant Moon (ed.), Volume 5, Bombay: Government of Maharashtra, 1989, p. 19.
47. B. R. Ambedkar, *Dr Babasaheb Ambedkar Writings and Speeches*, Volume 7, Vasant Moon (ed.), Bombay: Government of Maharashtra, 1979, p. 266.
48. B. R. Ambedkar, *Dr Babasaheb Ambedkar Writings and Speeches*, Volume 7, Vasant Moon (ed.), Bombay: Government of Maharashtra, 1979, p. 198.
49. B. R. Ambedkar, 'Draft Constitution – Discussion', *Dr Babasaheb Ambedkar Writings and Speeches*, Vasant Moon (ed.), Volume 13, Bombay: Government of Maharashtra, 1994, p. 62.
50. Ambedkar, 'Untouchables or the Children of India's Ghetto', p. 19.
51. Ibid., p. 19.
52. Ibid., p. 22.
53. Ibid., p. 23.
54. Ibid., p. 24.
55. Ibid., pp. 25–26.
56. Ibid., p. 104.
57. Ibid., p. 193.

Chapter 4: The Actually Existing Villages: History and Ethnography

1. See C. A. Bayly, *Indian Society and the Making of the British Empire*, Cambridge: Cambridge University Press, 1987; David Washbrook, 'Economic Depression and the Making of "Traditional" Society in Colonial India 1820–1855', *Transactions of the Royal Historical Society*, Vol. 3, 1993, pp. 237–63; David E. Ludden, *The New Cambridge History of India, Volume 4, Part 4: An Agrarian History of South Asia*, Cambridge: Cambridge University Press, 1999.
2. Irfan Habib, 'Agrarian Relations and Land Revenue: North India', T. Raychaudhury and Irfan Habib (eds.), *The Cambridge Economic History of India*, Vol. 1, Delhi: Orient Longman, pp. 235–48, 1982.
3. Sumita Chatterjee and Ashok Rudra, 'Relations of Production in Pre-colonial India', *Economic and Political Weekly*, Vol. 24 (21), 1989, p. 1172.
4. Dharma Kumar, *Land and Caste in South India*, New Delhi: Manohar, 1992.
5. Irfan Habib, *Agrarian Systems of Mughal India*, Bombay: Asia Publishers,

1963; B. Moore Jr., *Social Origins of Dictatorship and Democracy*, Middlesex: Penguin, 1966, p. 332.

6. Ludden, *The New Cambridge History of India, Volume 4, Part 4*, p. 113.
7. Ibid., p. 117.
8. Ibid., pp. 117–18.
9. Ludden, *The New Cambridge History of India, Volume 4, Part 4*, pp. 147–48.
10. Moore, *Social Origins of Dictatorship and Democracy*, p. 345
11. A. R. Desai, *Social Background of Indian Nationalism*, Bombay: Popular Prakashan, 1948, p. 39.
12. J. Scott, *The Moral Economy of the Peasantry: Rebellion and Subsistence in Southeast Asia*, New Haven: Yale University Press, 1976.
13. Moore, *Social Origins of Dictatorship and Democracy*, p. 346.
14. E. Stokes, *The Peasants and the Raj*, New Delhi: Vikas Publishing House, 1978.
15. Habib, 'Agrarian Relations and Land Revenue: North India', pp. 235–48.
16. A. Satyanarayana, 'Commercialization, Money Capital and the Peasantry in Colonial Andhra 1900–1940', S. Bhattacharya et al. (eds.), *The South Indian Economy: Agrarian Change, Industrial Structure and State Policy 1914–1947*, Delhi: Oxford University Press, 1991, p. 57.
17. G. Blyn, *Agricultural Trends in India 1891–1947*, Philadelphia: University of Philadelphia Press, 1966.
18. A. Sen, 'Famines as Failures of Exchange Entitlements', *Economic and Political Weekly*. Vol. 11 (31–33), 1976, pp. 1273–80.
19. Richa Kumar, 'India's Green Revolution and Beyond: Visioning Agrarian Futures on Selective Reading of Agrarian Pasts', *Economic and Political Weekly*, Vol. 54 (34), 2019, p. 42.
20. Ibid.
21. Washbrook, 'Economic Depression and the Making of "Traditional" Society in Colonial India 1820–1855', pp. 237–63.
22. See David Clingingsmith and Jeffrey G. Williamson, 'Mughal Decline, Climate Change, and Britain's Industrial Ascent: An Integrated Perspective on India's 18th and 19th Century Deindustrialization' (working paper), 2005, available at scholar.harvard.edu/files/jwilliamson/files/w11730.pdf, accessed 28 June 2021.
23. Ranajit Guha, *Elementary Aspects of Peasant Insurgency in Colonial India*, Delhi: Oxford University Press, 1983, p. 8.
24. Ludden, *The New Cambridge History of India, Volume 4, Part 4*, p. 158.
25. Ibid.
26. M. N. Srinivas, 'The Social System of a Mysore Village', McKim Marriott (ed.) *Village India*, Chicago: Chicago University Press, 1955, pp. 1–35
27. Ibid., pp. 92–94.
28. Andre Béteille, *Caste, Class and Power: Changing Patterns of Stratification in a Tanjore Village*, New Delhi: Oxford University Press, 1996, pp. 136–37.

29. S. C. Dube, 'A Deccan village', M. N. Srinivas (ed.), *India's Village*, London: Asia Publishing House, 1960 (first published in 1955), p. 202.

30. W. H. Wiser, *The Hindu Jajmani System*, Lucknow: The Lucknow Publishing House, 1969/1936, p. 10.

31. P. G. Hiebert, *Konduru: Structure and Integration in a South Indian Village*, Minneapolis: University of Minnesota Press, 1971, p. 13.

32. Béteille, *Caste, Class and Power*, 1996, p. 39.

33. O. Lewis, *Village Life in Northern India: Studies in a Delhi Village*, Urbana: University of Illinois Press, 1958, p. 314.

34. Ibid., p. 94.

35. F. G. Bailey, *Tribe, Caste and Nation*, Bombay: Oxford University Press, 1960, p. 258.

36. Srinivas, 'The Social System of a Mysore Village', p. 176.

37. Ibid., pp. 175–76.

38. Dube, 'A Deccan village', p. 161.

39. A. M. Shah, 'Changes in the Indian Family: An Examination of Some Assumptions', *Economic and Political Weekly*, Annual Number: 127–34, 1968, p. 162.

40. Ibid., p. 129.

Chapter 5: Rural Development: State Policies and the Village Life

1. 'P530: Rural Development', prepared by Mike Stockbridge with Andrew Dorward, and updated for 2015, SOAS, University of London, p. 9.

2. A. G. Frank, 'The Development of Underdevelopment', *The Monthly Review*, Vol. 18 (4), 1966, pp. 16–31

3. Ibid., p. 24.

4. John Harriss, *Rural Development: Theories of Peasant Economy and Agrarian Change*, London: Century Hutchinson Ltd., 1982, p. 15.

5. Subir Sinha, 'Lineages of the Developmentalist State: Transnationality and Village India, 1900–1965', *Comparative Studies in Society and History*, Vol. 50 (1), 2008, p. 61.

6. Harriss, *Rural Development*, p. 62.

7. Sinha, *Lineages of the Developmentalist State: Transnationality and Village India*, p. 63.

8. Ibid., pp. 63–4.

9. F. Tönnies, *Community and Society—the Basic Concepts of Pure Sociology*, Jose Harris (ed.), Cambridge: Cambridge University Press, 1887/2001.

10. E. Durkheim, *The Division of Labour in Society*, tr. Qu J. D., Beijing: SDX Joint Publishing Company, 1893/2000.

11. Moore, *Social Origins of Dictatorship and Democracy*, p. 392.

12. Ibid., p. 401.

13. S. C. Dube, *India's Changing Villages: Human Factors in Community Development*, New Delhi: Allied Publishers, 1958.
14. David Graeber, *Debt: The First 5,000 Years*, New Delhi: Penguin, 2014.
15. See www.co-op-society.com/history.html, accessed September 07 2021.
16. Ibid.
17. R. J. Herring, 'Land Tenure and Credit-Capital Tenure in Contemporary India', R. E. Frynkenberg (ed.), *Land Tenure and Peasants in South Asia*, New Delhi: Manohar, 1977, pp. 121–32.
18. S. S. Jodhka, 'Bureaucratisation, Corruption and Depoliticisation: Changing Profile of Credit Co-operatives in Rural Haryana', *Economic and Political Weekly*, Vol. 30 (1), 1995, pp. 53–56.
19. Nilakantha Rath, '"Garibi Hatao": Can IRDP Do It?', *Economic and Political Weekly*, 20 (6), 1985, p. 238.
20. Quoted in N. J. Kurien, 'IRDP: How Relevant is it', *Economic and Political Weekly*, Vol. 22 (52), 1987, p. A161.
21. James Manor, *When Local Government Strikes It Rich*, Malmo: Swedish International Centre for Local Democracy, Research Report 1, 2013, p. 2.
22. Ibid., p. 1.
23. Sonalde Desai, Prem Vashishtha, and Omkar Joshi, *Mahatma Gandhi National Rural Employment Guarantee Act: A Catalyst for Rural Transformation*, New Delhi: National Council of Applied Economic Research, 2015.
24. Manor, *When Local Government Strikes It Rich*.
25. Ibid., p. 11.
26. John West, 'Amartya Sen on Development as Freedom', *Asian Century Institute*, 28 March 2014, available at www.asiancenturyinstitute.com/development/333-amartya-sen-on-developmentas-freedom, accessed 10 August 2021.
27. Ibid.
28. Ibid.
29. Ibid.
30. Ibid
31. 'P530: Rural Development', pp. 13–14.

Chapter 6: Rural Livelihoods: Agriculture and Non-farm Economy

1. Cohn, *An Anthropologist among the Historians*, p. 212.
2. Kumar, 'India's Green Revolution and Beyond', p. 141.
3. Moore, *Social Origins of Dictatorship and Democracy*, p. 358.
4. D. Thorner, *The Agrarian Prospects of India*, Delhi: University Press, 1956, p. 12.

5. P. C. Joshi, *Land Reforms in India: Trends and Perspectives*, New Delhi: Allied Publishers, 1976.

6. P. Radhakrishanan, *Peasant Struggles, Land Reforms and Social Change: Malabar 1836–1982*, New Delhi: Sage, 1989.

7. C. Bell, 'Ideology and Economic Interests in Indian Land Reform', D. Lehmann (ed.), *Agrarian Reform and Agrarian Reformism: Studies of Peru, Chile, China, and India*, London: Faber and Faber, 1974, p. 196.

8. T. J. Byres, 'Land Reforms, Industrialization and Marketed Surplus in India: An Essay on the Power of Rural Bais', D. Lehmann (ed.) *Agrarian Reform and Agrarian Reformism: Studies of Peru, Chile, China, and India*, London: Faber and Faber, 1974, pp. 221–61.

9. A. Chakravarti, *Contradiction and Change: Emerging Patterns of Authority in a Rajasthan Village*, Delhi: Oxford University Press, 1975, pp. 97–98.

10. Rajeshwari S. Raina, 'Agriculture and the Development Burden', Knut A. Jacobsen (ed.), *Routledge Handbook of Contemporary India*, London: Routledge, 2016, p. 101.

11. Ibid.

12. Kumar, 'India's Green Revolution and Beyond', p. 44.

13. Raina, 'Agriculture and the Development Burden'; Kumar, 'India's Green Revolution and Beyond'.

14. Some scholars have also questioned the claims about the Green Revolution technology having significantly increased productivity of land. The pace of growth of Indian agriculture, they argue, had already started growing with the end of colonial rule. The pace of growth of Punjab's agriculture had already grown 4.6 per cent during 1950 to 1964 with food grain yields rising by as much as 45 per cent during the same period. India's food availability per capita also went up from 144.1 kilograms per person per annum in 1951 to 171.1 kilograms per person per annum in 1961 (Kumar, 'India's Green Revolution and Beyond', p. 43; also see F. Landy, *Feeding India: The Spatial Parameters of Food Grain Policy*, New Delhi: Manohar Publishers, 2009).

15. *Pocket Book Of Agricultural Statistics*, New Delhi: Government of India, 2017, p. 26.

16. Ibid., p. 26.

17. Ibid., p. 19.

18. Mihar Shah, P. S. Vijayshankar, and Francesca Harris, 'Water and Agricultural Transformation in India: A Symbiotic Relationship', *Economic and Political Weekly*, Vol. 56 (29), 2021, pp. 43–55.

19. M. N. Srinivas, 'The Dominant Caste in Rampura', *American Anthropologist*, Vol. 61 (1), 1959, pp. 1–16.

20. M. Rutten, *Capitalist Entrepreneurs and Economic Diversification: Social Profile of Large Farmers and Rural Industrialists in Central Gujarat, India*,

Rotterdam: Academisch proefschrift, 1991; C. B. Upadhya, 'The Farmer-Capitalists of Coastal Andhra Pradesh', *Economic and Political Weekly*, Vol. 23 (27–28), 1988, pp. 1376–82.

21. B. Harriss-White, *A Political Economy of Agricultural Markets in South India: Masters of the Countryside*, New Delhi: Sage, 1996.
22. K. Balagopal, 'An Ideology of the Provincial Propertied Class', *Economic and Political Weekly*, Vol. 21 (36–37), 1987, p. 1545.
23. Kumar, 'India's Green Revolution and Beyond', p. 42.
24. Ramesh Chand, S. K. Srivastava, and Jaspal Singh, 'Changing Structure of Rural Economy of India Implications for Employment and Growth', Discussion Paper, New Delhi: NITI Aayog, 2017, p. 4.
25. Ibid.
26. D. N. Reddy, A. A. Reddy, N. Nagaraj N., and C. Bantilan, 'Rural Non-Farm Employment and Rural Transformation in India', *Working Paper No. 57*, Hyderabad: ICRSAT, 2014, p. 10.
27. Himanshu, 'Rural Non-farm Employment in India: Trends, Patterns and Regional Dimensions', *India Rural Development Report*, Hyderabad: Orient Blackswan, 2015, p. 90.

Chapter 7: Rural Transformations: Declining Agriculture and the Crises of Village Life

1. Alice Thorner, 'Semi-Feudalism or Capitalism? Contemporary Debate on Classes and Modes of Production in India', S. S. Jodhka (ed.), *Agrarian Change in India*, Hyderabad: Orient Blackswan, 2021 (1982), pp. 195–218.
2. See www.worldbank.org/en/topic/agriculture/overview#1, accessed 7 May 2022.
3. Ritchie and Roser, 'Urbanization', accessed May 07 2022.
4. Ibid.
5. S. S. Jodhka and Aseem Prakash, *The Indian Middle Class*, New Delhi: Oxford University Press, 2016.
6. Dipanjana Roy, 'Farmer Suicides in India, 1997–2013: Taking Stock of Data, Arguments and Evidence', *Economic and Political Weekly*, Vol. 56 (15), 2021, p. 50.
7. 'Rising number of farmer suicides in rural India', UCLA International Institute, available at www.international.ucla.edu/institute/article/145702.
8. 'Agriculture Census 2015–16 (Phase 1)', New Delhi: Government of India, 2019, pp. 1–2.
9. Sheila Bhalla, 'New Relations of Production in Haryana Agriculture', *Economic and Political Weekly*, Vol. 11 (13), 1976, pp. A23–30.
10. T. J. Byres, 'The Dialectics of India's Green Revolution', *South Asian Review*, Vol. 5 (2), 1972, p. 100.

11. 'Farmer Suicides Trends in India', available at https://thewire.in/wp-content/uploads/2017/04/Annex-1-%E2%80%93-Farmer-suicides-2016-and-2017.pdf, accessed 18 May 2022.

12. J. Hardikar, *Ramrao: The Story of India's Farm Crisis*, Delhi: Harper and Collins, 2021 (Kindle edition).

13. S. S. Jodhka, 'Beyond "Crises": Rethinking Contemporary Punjab Agriculture', *Economic and Political Weekly*, Vol. XLI (16), 2006, pp. 1530–37; Roy, 'Farmer Suicides in India, 1997–2013'.

14. Hardikar, *Ramrao*.

15. Roy, 'Farmer Suicides in India, 1997–2013', p. 54.

16. Ibid., p. 53.

17. See K. C. Suri, 'Political Economy of Agrarian Distress', *Economic and Political Weekly*, Vol. 41 (26), 2006, pp. 1523–29; Srijit Mishra, 'Farmers' Suicides in Maharashtra', *Economic and Political Weekly*, Vol. 41 (16), 2006, pp. 1538–1545; Anita Gill and Lakhwinder Singh, 'Farmers' Suicides and Response of Public Policy: Evidence, Diagnosis and Alternatives from Punjab', *Economic and Political Weekly*, Vol. 41 (26), pp. 2762–68; Bhupinder Kaur, 'Indebtedness among Farmers in Punjab', *Economic and Political Weekly* Vol. 56 (26 and 27), 2021, pp. 14–21.

18. Jodhka, 'Beyond 'Crises': Rethinking Contemporary Punjab Agriculture', pp. 1530–7.

19. Steffan Lindberg, 'Whom and What to Fight? Notes and Queries on Indian Farmers Collective Action under Liberalisation and Globalisation', unpublished seminar paper, Patiala: Punjab University, 2005, p. 11.

20. S. S. Jodhka, 'The Decline of Agriculture', S. K. Bhaumik (ed.), *Reforming Indian Agriculture: Towards Employment Generation and Poverty Reduction*, New Delhi: Sage Publications, 2008.

21. Anthony Giddens, *Modernity and Self–Identity*, Cambridge: Polity Press, 1991.

22. Satendra Kumar, 'Agrarian Transformation and New Sociality in Western Uttar Pradesh', *Economic and Political Weekly*, Vol. 53 (26–27), 2018, p. 45.

Chapter 8: Caste, Class, and Gender: Changing Social Life

1. See S. S. Jodhka, *Caste* (Oxford India Short Introductions), New Delhi: Oxford University Press, 2012; S. S. Jodhka, *Caste in Contemporary India*, 2nd edn, London and New Delhi: Routledge, 2015.

2. P. Tandon, 'Punjabi Century' (first published 1961), *Punjabi Saga* (1857–1987), New Delhi: Viking, Penguin Books, 1988, p. 79.

3. Ibid., p. 76.

4. Wiser, *The Hindu Jajmani System*, p. xxi.

5. T. O. Beidelman, A Comparative Analysis of the *Jajmani* System, In

Monographs of the Association of Asian Studies, Locust Valley, NY: J. J. Augustin Inc. for the Association for Asian Studies, 1959, p. 6; G. Djurfeldt and S. Lindberg, *Behind Poverty: The Social Formation of a Tamil Village*, New Delhi: Oxford and IBH, 1976, p. 42.

6. Béteille, *Caste, Class and Power*, 1996, p. 168.

7. Sumit Guha, 'Civilisations, Markets and Services: Village Servants in India from the Seventeenth to the Twentieth Centuries', *Indian Economic Social History Review*, Vol. 41 (1), 2004, pp. 79– 101.

8. Peter Mayer, 'Inventing Village Tradition—The Late-19th-Century Origins of the North Indian "Jajmani System"', *Modern Asian Studies*, Vol. 27, 1993, pp. 357– 395.

9. See Jodhka, *Caste*; Jodhka, *Caste in Contemporary India*.

10. G. Shah et al., *Untouchability in Rural India*, New Delhi: Sage Publication, 2006.

11. J. Manor, 'Accommodation and Conflict', *Seminar*, Vol. 633, pp. 14–18, May 2012; M. N. Srinivas, 'An Obituary on Caste as a System', *Economic and Political Weekly*, Vol. 38 (5), pp. 455–59, 2003.

12. M. N. Srinivas, 'The Social System of a Mysore Village', McKim Marriott (ed.), *Village India*, Chicago: Chicago University Press, 1955, pp. 1–35.

13. Thorner, *The Agrarian Prospects of India*.

14. N. Bhattacharya, 'Agricultural Labour and Production: Central and South–East Punjab', K. N. Raj (ed.), *Essays on the Commercialization of Indian Agriculture*, Delhi: Oxford University Press, 1985, pp. 105–62.

15. J. Breman, *Patronage and Exploitation: Changing Agrarian Relations in South Gujarat India*, Berkley: University of California Press, 1974.

16. Kathleen Gough, 'The Hindu Jajmani System', *Economic Development and Cultural Change*, IX (1, Part 1), 1960, pp. 83–91; Andre Béteille, *Caste, Class and Power: Changing Patterns of Stratification in Tanjore Village*, Berkeley: University of California Press, 1971; J. P. Mencher, *Agriculture and Social Structure in Tamil Nadu: Past Origins, Present Transformations and Future Prospects*, New Delhi: Allied Publishers, 1978.

17. Bhalla, 'New Relations of Production in Haryana Agriculture'.

18. S. S. Jodhka, 'Agrarian Changes and Attached Labour: Emerging Patterns in Haryana Agriculture', *Economic and Political Weekly*, 2004, Vol. 29 (39), pp. A102–106; S. S. Jodhka, 'Agrarian Changes in the Times of (Neo-liberal) "Crises": Revisiting Attached Labour in Haryana Agriculture', *Economic and Political Weekly*, Vol. XLVII, No. 48 (26–27), 2012, pp. 5–13.

19. Jodhka, 'Beyond "Crises": Rethinking Contemporary Punjab Agriculture'.

20. See J. Breman, *Of Peasant, Migrants and Paupers: Rural Labour Circulation and Capitalist Production in West India*, Delhi: Oxford University Press, 1985.

21. G. Rodgers and J. Rodgers, 'Inclusive Development? Migration, Governance and Social Change in Rural Bihar', *Economic and Political*

Weekly, Vol. 46 (23), 2011, p. 43.

22. Amrita Datta, 'Strangers in the City? Rural Bihari Migrants in Delhi', unpublished paper, 2014, p. 4.

23. Rodgers and Rodgers, 'Inclusive Development? Migration, Governance and Social Change in Rural Bihar', p. 44.

24. S. S. Jodhka, 'Caste and Untouchability in Rural Punjab', *Economic and Political Weekly*, Vol. 37 (19), 2002, pp. 1813–23.

25. Ibid.

26. Ibid.

27. Anthony Giddens, *Sociology*, 5th edn, Cambridge: Polity Press, 2006, pp. 432–78.

28. Harold Glenn A. Valera, Takashi Yamano, Ranjitha Puskur, et al., 'Women's Land Title Ownership and Empowerment: Evidence from India', ADB Economics Working Paper Series, No. 559, September 2018, available at www.adb.org/sites/default/files/publication/453696/ewp-559-women-land-title-ownership-empowerment.pdf, accessed 5 January 2023.

29. B. Agarwal, *A Field of One's Own: Gender and Land Rights in South Asia*, Cambridge: Cambridge University Press, 1994.

30. Bhalla, 'New Relations of Production in Haryana Agriculture'.

Chapter 9: Rural Power: Panchayats, Democracy, and the State

1. J. MacDougall, 'Dominant castes or rich peasants?', *Economic and Political Weekly*, Vol. 14 (12–13), 1979, p. 625.

2. Shamus Rahman Khan, 'The Sociology of Elites', *Annual Review of Sociology*, Vol. 38, 2012, p. 1.

3. See S. S. Jodhka and Jules Naudet (eds.), *Mapping the Elite: Power, Privilege and Inequality*, Delhi: Oxford University Press, 2019, p. 1.

4. Rabindranath Tagore, 'City and Village' (*Palli-prakriti*), *Towards Universal Man*, London: Asia Publishing House, 1924/1961, pp. 302–22, available at http://tagoreanworld.co.uk/?page_id=68.

5. Ibid.

6. Ibid.

7. Ibid.

8. Béteille, *Caste, Class and Power*, p. 152.

9. A. Chakravarti, *Contradiction and Change: Emerging Patterns of Authority in a Rajasthan Village*, Delhi: Oxford University Press, 1975, p. 58.

10. Srinivas, 'The Dominant Caste in Rampura', p. 1.

11. Ibid., p. 1.

12. Ibid., p. 3.

13. Srinivas, 'The Social System of a Mysore Village', p. 15.

14. A. Bhaduri, *The Economic Structure of Backward Agriculture*, Delhi:

Macmillan, 1984; Pradhan Prasad, 'Towards a Theory of Transformation of Semi-feudal Agriculture', *Economic and Political Weekly*, Vol. 22 (31), 1987, pp. 1287–90.

15. Lloyd I. Rudolph and Susanne H. Rudolph, *In Pursuit of Lakshmi: The Political Economy of the Indian State*, Chicago: Chicago University Press, 1987.

16. See Jodhka, 'Bureaucratisation, Corruption and Depoliticisation'.

17. Arvind N. Das, *Changel: The Biography of a Village*, New Delhi: Penguin Books, 1996, pp. 14–15.

18. See Christophe Jaffrelot, *India's Silent Revolution: The Rise of the Lower Castes in North India*, Delhi: Permanent Black, 2003.

19. A. Krishna, *Active Social Capital: Tracing the Roots of Development and Democracy*, New York: Columbia University Press, pp. 43–45.

20. Ram G. Reddy and G. Haragopal, 'The Pyraveekar: The Fixer in Rural India', *Asian Studies* Vol. 25 (11), 1985, pp. 1148–82.

21. James Manor, 'Small-Time Political Fixers in India's States: "Towel over the Armpit"', *Asian Survey*, Vol. 40 (5), 2000, p. 817.

22. Ibid.

23. Pamella Price, 'Changing Meanings of Authority in Contemporary Rural India', *Qual Sociol*, Vol. 29, 2006, p. 304.

24. Ibid., p. 313.

25. Kuldeep Mathur, *Panchayati Raj*, Delhi: Oxford University Press, 2013.

26. See, for example, Purendra Prasad, 'Agrarian Class and Caste Relations in "United" Andhra Pradesh, 1956–2014', *Economic and Political Weekly*, Vol. 50 (16), 2015, pp. 77–83.

Conclusion: Revisioning the Futures of Village Life

1. Amrita Datta, 'Migration, Remittances and Changing Sources of Income in Rural Bihar (1999–2011) Some Findings from a Longitudinal Study', *Economic and Political Weekly*, 2016, Vol. 51 (31), pp. 85–93.

2. André Béteille, 'The Indian Village: Past and Present', E. J. Hobsbawm et al. (eds.), *Peasants in History: Essays in Honour of Daniel Thorner*, Calcutta: Oxford University Press, 1980, p. 108.

3. D. Gupta, 'Whither the Indian Village: Culture and Agriculture in "Rural" India', *Economic and Political Weekly*, Vol. 40 (8), 2005, p. 751.

4. Ibid., p. 757.

5. Soutik Biswas, 'Coronavirus: India's pandemic lockdown turns into a human tragedy', *BBC*, 30 March 2020, available at www.bbc.com/news/world-asia-india-52086274.

6. Surinder S. Jodhka, 'Re-looking the rural', *Seminar*, 2021, available at www.india-seminar.com/2021/748/748-SURINDER%20S.%20JODHKA.htm.

7. '2020: Farmers take the country by storm', *Frontline*, 15 August 2022,

available at frontline.thehindu.com/the-nation/agriculture/india-at-75-epochal-moments-2020-farmers-protests-take-the-country-by-storm/article65722271.ece.

8. Jodhka, 'Re-looking the rural'.
9. Barbara Harriss-White, 'The India Cable: Many Kinds of Farm Protest Evolving, Vaccine Rollout Amidst Questions', *India Cable*, 15 January 2021, available at www.theindiacable.com/p/the-india-cable-many-kinds-of-farm, accessed 25 June 2021.
10. Harish Damodaran and Mekhala Krishnamurthy, 'Explained: Rural India played the economy's "saviour" in 2020–21. Can it do so again?', *The Indian Express*, 2 June 2021.

BIBLIOGRAPHY

Agarwal, B., *A Field of One's Own: Gender and Land Rights in South Asia*, Cambridge: Cambridge University Press, 1994.

Ambedkar, B. R., 'Draft Constitution – Discussion', *Dr Babasaheb Ambedkar Writings and Speeches*, Vasant Moon (ed.), Vol. 13, Bombay: Government of Maharashtra, 1994.

———'Untouchables or the Children of India's Ghetto', *Dr Babasaheb Ambedkar Writings and Speeches*, Vasant Moon (ed.), Vol. 5, Bombay: Government of Maharashtra, 1989.

———*Dr Babasaheb Ambedkar Writings and Speeches*, Vol. 5, Vasant Moon (ed.), Bombay: Government of Maharashtra, 1979.

Bailey, F. G., *Caste and the Economic Frontier: A Village in Highland Orissa*, Bombay: Oxford University Press, 1958.

———*Tribe, Caste and Nation*, Bombay: Oxford University Press, 1960.

Balagopal, K., 'An Ideology of the Provincial Propertied Class', *Economic and Political Weekly*, Vol. 21 (36–37), 1987, pp. 2177–78.

Bayly, C. A., *Indian Society and the Making of the British Empire*, Cambridge: Cambridge University Press, 1987.

Beidelman, T. O., 'A Comparative Analysis of the *Jajmani* System', *Monographs of the Association of Asian Studies*, Locust Valley, NY: J. J. Augustin Inc. for the Association for Asian Studies, 1959.

Bell, C., 'Ideology and Economic Interests in Indian Land Reform', D. Lehmann (ed.), *Agrarian Reform and Agrarian Reformism: Studies of Peru, Chile, China, and India*, London: Faber and Faber, 1974, pp. 190–220.

Béteille, André, *Caste, Class and Power: Changing Patterns of Stratification in a Tanjore Village*, Berkeley: University of California Press, 1971.

———*Caste, Class and Power: Changing Patterns of Stratification in a Tanjore Village*, New Delhi: Oxford University Press, 1996.

Bhaduri, A., *The Economic Structure of Backward Agriculture*, Delhi: Macmillan, 1984.

Bhalla, Sheila, 'New Relations of Production in Haryana Agriculture', *Economic and Political Weekly*, 1976, Vol. 11 (13), pp. A23–30.

Bhambra, Gurminder K., *Rethinking Modernity: Postcolonialism and the Sociological Imaginations*, New York: Palgrave, 2007.

Bhattacharya, N., 'Agricultural Labour and Production: Central and SouthEast Punjab', K. N. Raj (ed.), *Essays on the Commercialization of Indian Agriculture*, Delhi: Oxford University Press, 1985, pp. 105–162.

Blyn, G., *Agricultural Trends in India 1891–1947*, Philadelphia: University of

Philadelphia Press, 1966.

Bonnano, A., *Sociology of Agriculture*, New Delhi: Concept Publishing House, 1989.

Breman, J., *Of Peasant, Migrants and Paupers: Rural Labour Circulation and Capitalist Production in West India*, Delhi: Oxford University Press.

——*Patronage and Exploitation: Changing Agrarian Relations in South Gujarat India*, Berkley: University of California Press, 1974.

Byres, T. J., 'Land Reforms, Industrialization and Marketed Surplus in India: An Essay on the Power of Rural Bais', D. Lehmann (ed.), *Agrarian Reform and Agrarian Reformism: Studies of Peru, Chile, China, and India*, London: Faber and Faber, 1974, pp. 221–61.

——'The Dialectics of India's Green Revolution', *South Asian Review*, Vol. 5 (2), 1972, pp. 99–106.

Chakravarti, A., *Contradiction and Change: Emerging Patterns of Authority in a Rajasthan Village*, Delhi: Oxford University Press, 1975.

Chand, Ramesh, Srivastava, S. K., and Singh, Jaspal, 'Changing Structure of Rural Economy of India Implications for Employment and Growth', Discussion Paper, New Delhi: NITI Aayog, 2017.

Chatterjee, Sumita and Rudra, Ashok, 'Relations of Production in Pre-colonial India', *Economic and Political Weekly*, Vol. 24 (21), 1989, pp. 1171–75.

Cohn B. S., *Colonialism and its Forms of Knowledge: The British in India*, Princeton: Princeton University Press, 2000 (1996).

——*An Anthropologist among the Historians and Other Essays*, Delhi: Oxford University Press, 1987.

Damodaran, Harish and Krishnamurthy, Mekhala, 'Explained: Rural India played the economy's 'saviour' in 2020–21. Can it do so again?', *The Indian Express*, 2 June 2021.

Das, Arvind N., *Changel: The Biography of a Village*, New Delhi: Penguin Books, 1996.

Datta, Amrita, 'Migration, Remittances and Changing Sources of Income in Rural Bihar (1999–2011) Some Findings from a Longitudinal Study', *Economic and Political Weekly*, Vol. 51 (31), 2016, pp. 85–93.

——'Strangers in the City? Rural Bihari Migrants in Delhi', unpublished paper, 2014.

Desai, A. R., *Rural Sociology in India*, Bombay: Popular Prakashan, 1969.

——*Social Background of Indian Nationalism*, Bombay: Popular Prakashan, 1948.

Desai, Sonalde, Vashishtha, Prem, and Joshi, Omkar, *Mahatma Gandhi National Rural Employment Guarantee Act: A Catalyst for Rural Transformation*, New Delhi: National Council of Applied Economic Research, 2015.

Djurfeldt, G. and Lindberg, S., *Behind Poverty: The Social Formation of a Tamil Village*, New Delhi: Oxford and IBH, 1976.

Dube, S. C., 'A Deccan village', M. N. Srinivas (ed.) *India's Village*, London: Asia Publishing House, 1960 (first published in 1955).

Dube, S. C., *India's Changing Villages: Human Factors in Community Development*, New Delhi: Allied Publishers, 1958.

——*Indian Village*, London: Routledge and Kegan Paul, 1955.

Durkheim, E., *The Division of Labour in Society*, tr. Qu J. D., Beijing: SDX Joint Publishing Company, 1893/2000.

Embree, A. T., *Imagining India: Essays on Indian History*, Delhi: Oxford University Press, 1989.

Frank, A. G., 'The Development of Underdevelopment', *The Monthly Review*, Vol. 18 (4), pp. 16–31, 1966.

Gadgil, D. R., *Industrial Evolution of India in Recent Times,* London: Oxford University Press, 1933.

Gandhi, M. K., *The Collected Works of Mahatma Gandhi*, Volume I, Delhi: Government of India, 1958.

——*The Collected Works of Mahatma Gandhi*, Volume LI, Delhi: Government of India, 1972.

——*The Collected Works of Mahatma Gandhi*, Volume LIX, Delhi: Government of India, 1974.

——*The Collected Works of Mahatma Gandhi*, Volume LXII, Delhi: Government of India, 1975.

——*The Collected Works of Mahatma Gandhi*, Volume LXIV, Delhi: Government of India, 1976.

——*The Collected Works of Mahatma Gandhi*, Volume LXIX, Delhi: Government of India, 1977.

——*The Collected Works of Mahatma Gandhi*, Volume LXVIII, Delhi: Government of India, 1977.

——*The Collected Works of Mahatma Gandhi*, Volume LXXI, Delhi: Government of India, 1978.

——*The Collected Works of Mahatma Gandhi*, Volume LXXVI, Delhi: Government of India, 1979.

——*The Collected Works of Mahatma Gandhi*, Volume LXXVII, Delhi: Government of India, 1979.

——*The Collected Works of Mahatma Gandhi*, Volume LXXXVI, Delhi: Government of India, 1982.

——*The Collected Works of Mahatma Gandhi*, Volume LXXX, Delhi: Government of India, 1980.

——*The Collected Works of Mahatma Gandhi*, Volume XI, Delhi: Government of India, 1963.

——*The Collected Works of Mahatma Gandhi*, Volume XLI, Delhi: Government of India, 1970.

——*The Collected Works of Mahatma Gandhi*, Volume XXI, Delhi: Government of India, 1966.

——*The Collected Works of Mahatma Gandhi*, Volume XXXIII, Delhi: Government of India, 1969.

Giddens, Anthony, *Modernity and Self–Identity*, Cambridge: Polity Press, 1991.

————*Sociology*, 5th edn, Cambridge: Polity Press, 2006.

Gill, Anita and Singh, Lakhwinder, 'Farmers' Suicides and Response of Public Policy: Evidence, Diagnosis and Alternatives from Punjab', *Economic and Political Weekly*, Vol. 41 (26), 2006, pp. 2762–68.

Gopal, S. (ed.), *Selected Works of Jawaharlal Nehru*, Vol. 4, (New Series), Delhi: Oxford University Press, 1986.

————*Selected Works of Jawaharlal Nehru*, Vol. 20 (New Series), Delhi: Oxford University Press, 1997.

————*Selected Works of Jawaharlal Nehru*, Vol. 3 (Old Series), Hyderabad: Orient Longman, 1972.

————*Selected Works of Jawaharlal Nehru*, Vol. 5 (Old Series), Hyderabad: Orient Longman, 1973.

Gough, Kathleen, 'The Hindu Jajmani System', *Economic Development and Cultural Change*, IX (1, Part 1), 1960, pp. 83–91.

Graeber, David, *Debt: The First 5,000 Years*, New Delhi: Penguin, 2014.

Guha, Ranajit, *Elementary Aspects of Peasant Insurgency in Colonial India*, Delhi: Oxford University Press, 1983.

Guha, Sumit, 'Civilisations, Markets and Services: Village Servants in India from the Seventeenth to the Twentieth Centuries', *Indian Economic Social History Review*, Vol. 41 (1), 2004, pp. 79–101.

————*Beyond Caste: Identity and Power in South Asia*, Leiden: Brill, 2013.

Gupta, D., 'Whither the Indian Village: Culture and Agriculture in "Rural" India', *Economic and Political Weekly*, Vol. 40 (8), 2005, pp. 751–58.

Habib, I., *Agrarian Systems of Mughal India,* Bombay: Asia Publishers, 1963.

————'Agrarian Relations and Land Revenue: North India', T. Raychaudhury and Irfan Habib (ed.), *The Cambridge Economic History of India*, Vol. 1, Delhi: Orient Longman, 1982, pp. 235–48.

Hardikar, J., *Ramrao: The Story of India's Farm Crisis*, Delhi: Harper Collins, 2021.

Harriss, John, *Rural Development: Theories of Peasant Economy and Agrarian Change*, London: Century Hutchinson Ltd, 1982.

Harriss-White, Barbara, 'The India Cable: Many Kinds of Farm Protest Evolving, Vaccine Rollout Amidst Questions', *India Cable*, 15 January 2021, available at www.theindiacable.com/p/the-india-cable-many-kinds-of-farm, accessed 25 June 2021.

————*A Political Economy of Agricultural Markets in South India: Masters of the Countryside*, New Delhi: Sage, 1996.

Herring, R. J., 'Land Tenure and Credit–Capital Tenure in Contemporary India', R. E. Frynkenberg (ed.), *Land Tenure and Peasants in South Asia*, New Delhi: Manohar, 1977, pp. 120–58.

Hiebert, P. G., *Konduru: Structure and Integration in a South Indian Village*, Minneapolis: University of Minnesota Press, 1971.

Himanshu, 'Rural Non–farm Employment in India: Trends, Patterns and Regional Dimensions', *India Rural Development Report*, Hyderabad: Orient

Blackswan, 2015, pp. 81–106.

Inden, Ronald, 'Orientalist Constructions of India', *Modern Asian Studies*, Vol. 20 (3), 1986, pp. 401–46.

India Rural Development Report 2012/13, IDFC, Hyderabad: Orient Blackswan, 2013.

Jaffrelot, Christophe, *India's Silent Revolution: The Rise of the Lower Castes in North India*, Delhi: Permanent Black, 2003.

Jodhka, S. S. and Kumar, Adarsh, 'Social Dynamics and Exclusionary Rural Transformations: Non-farm Economy in Madhubani, Bihar', *Economic and Political Weekly*, Vol. 52 (25 and 26), 2017, pp. 14–24.

Jodhka, S. S. and Naudet, Jules (eds.), *Mapping the Elite: Power, Privilege and Inequality*, Delhi: Oxford University Press, 2019.

Jodhka, S. S. and Prakash, Aseem, *The Indian Middle Class*, New Delhi: Oxford University Press, 2016.

Jodhka, S. S., 'Agrarian Changes and Attached Labour: Emerging Patterns in Haryana Agriculture', *Economic and Political Weekly*, Vol. 29 (39), 1994, pp. A102–106.

———'Agrarian Changes in the Times of (Neo–liberal) "Crises": Revisiting Attached Labour in Haryana Agriculture', *Economic and Political Weekly*, Vol. XLVII, No. 48 (26–27), 2012, pp. 5–13.

———'Agrarian Structures and their Transformations', Veena Das (ed.), *Oxford India Companion to Sociology and Social Anthropology*, Volume II, New Delhi: Oxford University Press, 2003, pp. 1213–42.

———'Beyond "Crises": Rethinking Contemporary Punjab Agriculture', *Economic and Political Weekly*, Vol. XLI (16), 2006, pp. 1530–7.

———'Bureaucratisation, Corruption and Depoliticisation: Changing Profile of Credit Co-operatives in Rural Haryana', *Economic and Political Weekly*, Vol. 30 (1), 1995, pp. 53–56.

———'Caste and Untouchability in Rural Punjab', *Economic and Political Weekly*, Vol. 37 (19), 2002, pp. 1813–23.

———'Emergent Ruralities: Revisiting Village Life and Agrarian Change in Haryana', *Economic and Political Weekly*, Vol. XlIX, No. 26 and 27, 2014, pp. 5–17.

———'The Decline of Agriculture', S. K. Bhaumik (ed.), *Reforming Indian Agriculture: Towards Employment Generation and Poverty Reduction*, New Delhi: Sage Publications, 2008.

———*Caste* (Oxford India Short Introductions), New Delhi: Oxford University Press, 2012.

———*Caste in Contemporary India*, 2nd edn, London and New Delhi: Routledge, 2015.

Joshi, P. C., *Land Reforms in India: Trends and Perspectives*, New Delhi: Allied Publishers, 1976.

Kaur, Bhupinder, 'Indebtedness among Farmers in Punjab', *Economic and Political Weekly* Vol. 56 (26 and 27), 2021, pp. 14–21.

Khan, Shamus Rahman, 'The Sociology of Elites', *Annual Review of Sociology*, Vol. 38, 2012, pp. 361–77.

Khilnani, S., *The Idea of India*, New York: Farrar Straus Giroux, 1998.

Kidambi, Prashant, 'South Asia', Peter Clark (ed.), *The Oxford Handbook of Cities in World History*, Oxford: Oxford University Press, 2013, pp. 561–80.

Krishna, A., *Active Social Capital: Tracing the Roots of Development and Democracy*, New York: Columbia University Press, 2002.

Kumar, Dharma, *Land and Caste in South India*, New Delhi: Manohar, 1992.

Kumar, Richa, 'India's Green Revolution and Beyond: Visioning Agrarian Futures on Selective Reading of Agrarian Pasts', *Economic and Political Weekly*, Vol. 54 (34), 2019, pp. 41–47.

Kumar, Satendra, 'Agrarian Transformation and New Sociality in Western Uttar Pradesh', *Economic and Political Weekly*, Vol. 53 (26–27), 2018, pp. 39–47.

Kurien, N. J., 'IRDP: How Relevant is it', *Economic and Political Weekly*, Vol. 22 (52), 1987, pp. A161–76.

Landy, F., *Feeding India: The Spatial Parameters of Food Grain Policy*, New Delhi: Manohar Publishers, 2009.

Lenin, V. I., *The Development of Capitalism in Russia*, Moscow: Progress Publishers, 1899.

Lewis, O., *Village Life in Northern India: Studies in a Delhi Village*, Urbana: University of Illinois Press, 1958.

Lindberg, Steffan, 'Whom and What to Fight? Notes and Queries on Indian Farmers Collective Action under Liberalisation and Globalisation', unpublished seminar paper, Patiala: Punjab University, 2005.

Lucassen, Leo, 'Population and Migration', Peter Clark (ed.), *The Oxford Handbook of Cities in World History*, Oxford: Oxford University Press, 2013, pp. 664–82.

Ludden, David E., *The New Cambridge History of India, Volume 4, Part 4: An Agrarian History of South Asia*, Cambridge: Cambridge University Press, 1999.

MacDougall, J., 'Dominant castes or rich peasants?', *Economic and Political Weekly*, Vol. 14 (12–13), 1979, pp. 625–34.

————'Two Models of Power in Contemporary Rural India', *Contributions to Indian Sociology*, Vol. 14 (1), 1980, pp. 77–94.

Manor, James, 'Accommodation and Conflict', *Seminar*, No. 633, May 2012, pp. 14–18.

————'Small–Time Political Fixers in India's States: "Towel over the Armpit"', *Asian Survey*, Vol. 40 (5), 2000, pp. 816–35.

————*When Local Government Strikes It Rich*, Research Report 1, Malmo: Swedish International Centre for Local Democracy, 2013.

Marx, Karl, *Capital: A Critique of Political Economy*, New York: Cosimo, 2007 (1867).

Mathur, Kuldeep, *Panchayati Raj*, Delhi: Oxford University Press, 2013.

Mayer, Peter, 'Inventing Village Tradition—The Late-19th-Century Origins of the North Indian "Jajmani System"', *Modern Asian Studies*, Vol. 27, 1993, pp. 357–395.

Mencher, J. P., *Agriculture and Social Structure in Tamil Nadu: Past Origins, Present Transformations and Future Prospects*, New Delhi: Allied Publishers, 1978.

Metcalfe. C. T., 'Minutes', *Report from the Select Committee*, Revenue III, Parliament Papers XI, 1931–32, pp. 331–2.

Mishra, Srijit, 'Farmers' Suicides in Maharashtra', *Economic and Political Weekly*, Vol. 41 (16), 2006, pp. 1538–45.

Moore, B. Jr., *Social Origins of Dictatorship and Democracy*, Middlesex: Penguin, 1966.

Nehru, Jawaharlal, *An Autobiography*, Delhi: Oxford University Press, 1980 (first published 1936).

——*Jawaharlal Nehru's Speeches*, Vol. II, Publications Division, Ministry of Information and Broadcasting, New Delhi: Government of India, 1954.

——*The Discovery of India*, New York: The John Day Company, 1946.

Nelson, L., *Rural Sociology: Its Origins and Growth in the United States*, Minneapolis: University of Minnesota Press, 1948.

Newby, H., 'Trend Report: Rural Sociology', *Current Sociology*, Vol. 28 (Spring), 1980, pp. 1–141.

Parel, J. A. (ed.), *Hind Swaraj and Other Writings*, Cambridge: Cambridge University Press, 1997.

Prasad, Pradhan, 'Towards a Theory of Transformation of Semi-feudal Agriculture', *Economic and Political Weekly*, Vol. 22 (31), 1987, pp. 1287–90.

Prasad, Purendra, 'Agrarian Class and Caste Relations in "United" Andhra Pradesh, 1956–2014', *Economic and Political Weekly*, Vol. 50 (16), 2015, pp. 77–83.

Price, Pamella, 'Changing Meanings of Authority in Contemporary Rural India', *Qual Sociol*, Vol. 29, 2006, pp. 301–16.

Radhakrishanan, P., *Peasant Struggles, Land Reforms and Social Change: Malabar 1836–1982*, New Delhi: Sage, 1989.

Raina, Rajeshwari S., 'Agriculture and the Development Burden', Knut A. Jacobsen (ed.), *Routledge Handbook of Contemporary India*, London: Routledge, 2016.

Rath, Nilakantha, '"Garibi Hatao": Can IRDP Do It?', *Economic and Political Weekly*, Vol. 20 (6), 1985, pp. 238–46.

Reddy, D. N., Reddy, A. A., Nagaraj, N., and Bantilan, C., 'Rural Non–Farm Employment and Rural Transformation in India', *Working Paper No. 57*, 2014, Hyderabad: ICRSAT.

Reddy, Ram G. and Haragopal, G., 'The Pyraveekar: The Fixer in Rural India,' *Asian Studies* Vol. 25 (11), 1985, pp. 1148–82.

Redfield, R., 'The Folk Society', *American Journal of Sociology*, Vol. 52 (1), 1947, pp. 292–308.

——*Peasant Society and Culture*, Chicago: University of Chicago Press, 1965.

Rodgers, G. and Rodgers, J., 'Inclusive Development? Migration, Governance and Social Change in Rural Bihar', *Economic and Political Weekly*, Vol. 46 (23), 2011, pp. 43–50.

Roy, Dipanjana, 'Farmer Suicides in India, 1997–2013: Taking Stock of Data, Arguments and Evidence', *Economic and Political Weekly*, Vol. 56 (15), 2021, pp. 50–56.

Rudolph, Lloyd I. and Rudolph, Susanne H., *In Pursuit of Lakshmi: The Political Economy of the Indian State*, Chicago: Chicago University Press, 1987.

Rutten, M., *Capitalist Entrepreneurs and Economic Diversification: Social Profile of Large Farmers and Rural Industrialists in Central Gujarat, India*, Rotterdam: Academisch Proefschrift, 1991.

Satyanarayana, A., 'Commercialization, Money Capital and the Peasantry in Colonial Andhra 1900–1940', S. Bhattacharya et al. (eds.), *The South Indian Economy: Agrarian Change, Industrial Structure and State Policy 1914–1947*, Delhi: Oxford University Press, 1991, pp. 51–77.

Schwarzweller, H. K. (ed.), *Research in Rural Sociology and Development*, Vol. 1, Greenwich: Jai Press, 1984.

Scott, J., *The Moral Economy of the Peasantry: Rebellion and Subsistence in Southeast Asia*, New Haven: Yale University Press, 1976.

Sen, A., 'Famines as Failures of Exchange Entitlements', *Economic and Political Weekly*, Vol. 11 (31–33), 1976, pp. 1273–80.

Shah, A. M., 'Changes in the Indian Family: An Examination of Some Assumptions', *Economic and Political Weekly*, Annual Number: 127–34, 1968.

Shah, G., Mander, H., Thorat, S., et al., *Untouchability in Rural India*, New Delhi: Sage Publication, 2006.

Shah, Mihar, Vijayshankar, P. S., and Harris, Francesca, 'Water and Agricultural Transformation in India: A Symbiotic Relationship', *Economic and Political Weekly*, Vol. 56 (29), 2021, pp. 43–55.

Shanin, T. (ed.), *Peasants and Peasant Societies*, London: Blackwell, 1987.

Sinha, Subir, Lineages of the Developmentalist State: Transnationality and Village India, 1900–1965, *Comparative Studies in Society and History*, Vol. 50 (1), No. 57–90, 2008.

Srinivas, M. N., 'The Indian Village: Myth and Reality', Vandana Madan (ed.), *The Indian Village*, Delhi: Oxford University Press, 1987/2002, pp. 51–70.

———*The Remembered Village*, New Delhi: Oxford University Press, 1976.

———'An Obituary on Caste as a System', *Economic and Political Weekly*, Vol. 38 (5), 2003, pp. 455–59.

———'The Dominant Caste in Rampura', *American Anthropologist*, Vol. 61 (1), pp. 1–16, 1959.

———'The Social System of a Mysore Village', McKim Marriott (ed.), *Village India*, Chicago: Chicago University Press, 1955, pp. 1–35.

Stokes, E., *The Peasants and the Raj*, New Delhi: Vikas Publishing House, 1978.

Suri, K. C., 'Political Economy of Agrarian Distress', *Economic and Political*

Weekly, Vol. 41 (26), 2006, pp. 1523–29.

Tagore, Rabindranath, 'City and Village' (Palli–prakriti), *Towards Universal Man*, London: Asia Publishing House, 1924/1961, pp. 302–22.

Tandon, P., 'Punjabi Century', *Punjabi Saga* (1857–1987), New Delhi: Viking/ Penguin Books, (first published 1961) 1988.

Thapar, Romila, 'Imagined Religious Communities? Ancient History and the Modern Search for a Hindu Identity', *Modern Asian Studies*, Vol. 23 (2), 1989, pp. 209–231.

Thorner, Alice, 'Semi–Feudalism or Capitalism? Contemporary Debate on Classes and Modes of Production in India', S. S. Jodhka (ed.) *Agrarian Change in India*, Hyderabad: Orient Blackswan, 2021 (1982), pp. 195–218.

Thorner, D., *Agricultural Co–operatives in India*, Bombay: Asia Publishers, 1964.

———*The Agrarian Prospects of India*, Delhi: University Press, 1956.

Tönnies, F., *Community and Society—the Basic Concepts of Pure Sociology*, Jose Harris (ed.), Cambridge: Cambridge University Press, 1887/2001.

Upadhya, C. B., 'The Farmer–Capitalists of Coastal Andhra Pradesh', *Economic and Political Weekly*, Vol. 23 (27–28), 1988, pp. 1376–82.

Valera, Harold Glenn A., Yamano, Takashi, Puskur, Ranjitha, et al., 'Women's Land Title Ownership and Empowerment: Evidence from India', Asian Development Bank (ADB), 2018, available at www.adb.org/sites/default/ files/publication/453696/ewp–559–women–land–title–ownership– empowerment.pdf.

Washbrook, David, 'Economic Depression and the Making of "Traditional" Society in Colonial India 1820–1855', *Transactions of the Royal Historical Society*, Vol. 3, 1993, pp. 237–63.

Wirth, Louis, 'Urbanism as a Way of Life', *American Journal of Sociology*, Vol. 44 (2), 1938, pp. 1–24.

Wiser, W. H., *The Hindu Jajmani System*, Lucknow: The Lucknow Publishing House, 1969/1936.

Witsoe, Jeffrey, *Democracy Against Development: Lower-Caste Politics and Political Modernity in Postcolonial India*, Chicago: The University of Chicago Press, 2013.

Zelliot, E., 'The Meanings of Ambedkar', Ghanshyam Shah (ed.), *Dalit Identity and Politics*, New Delhi: Sage Publications, 2001.

INDEX